THE AGE OF CHANGE

THE AGE OF CHANGE

How Urban Youth Are Transforming African Politics

MICHELLE D. GAVIN

A Council on Foreign Relations Book

BLOOMSBURY ACADEMIC
NEW YORK • LONDON • OXFORD • NEW DELHI • SYDNEY

BLOOMSBURY ACADEMIC

Bloomsbury Publishing Inc, 1359 Broadway, New York, NY 10018, USA
Bloomsbury Publishing Plc, 50 Bedford Square, London, WC1B 3DP, UK
Bloomsbury Publishing Ireland, 29 Earlsfort Terrace, Dublin 2, D02 AY28, Ireland

BLOOMSBURY, BLOOMSBURY ACADEMIC and the Diana logo are trademarks of Bloomsbury Publishing Plc

First published in the United States of America 2025

Copyright © Michelle Gavin, 2025

Cover design: Sally Rinehart
Cover image © iStock.com/bgblue

All rights reserved. No part of this publication may be: i) reproduced or transmitted in any form, electronic or mechanical, including photocopying, recording or by means of any information storage or retrieval system without prior permission in writing from the publishers; or ii) used or reproduced in any way for the training, development or operation of artificial intelligence (AI) technologies, including generative AI technologies. The rights holders expressly reserve this publication from the text and data mining exception as per Article 4(3) of the Digital Single Market Directive (EU) 2019/790.

Bloomsbury Publishing Inc does not have any control over, or responsibility for, any third-party websites referred to or in this book. All Internet addresses given in this book were correct at the time of going to press. The author and publisher regret any inconvenience caused if addresses have changed or sites have ceased to exist, but can accept no responsibility for any such changes.

Library of Congress Cataloging-in-Publication Data

A catalog record for this book is available from the Library of Congress.

ISBN: HB: 978-1-5381-9458-4
       ePDF: 979-8-7651-5241-6
       eBook: 978-1-5381-9459-1

The mission of the Council on Foreign Relations is to inform U.S. engagement with the world. Founded in 1921, CFR is a nonpartisan, independent national membership organization, think tank, educator, and publisher, including of *Foreign Affairs*. It generates policy-relevant ideas and analysis, convenes experts and policymakers, and promotes informed public discussion—all to have impact on the most consequential issues facing the United States and the world. The Council on Foreign Relations takes no institutional positions on policy issues and has no affiliation with the U.S. government. All views expressed in its publications and on its website are the sole responsibility of the author or authors.

Typeset by Integra Software Services Pvt. Ltd.
Printed and bound in the United States of America

For product safety related questions contact productsafety@bloomsbury.com.

To find out more about our authors and books visit www.bloomsbury.com and sign up for our newsletters.

CONTENTS

List of Illustrations vi
Acknowledgments vii

Introduction 1

1 Familiar Faces 7

2 Young, Urban, and Connected 25

3 Tired Old Stories 45

4 Camouflage Comes Back in Style 63

5 Impatient Politics 81

6 The Status Quo Strikes Back 105

7 The Outsiders 123

Postscript 142
Bibliography 144
Index 172
About the Author 181

ILLUSTRATIONS

Figures

2.1 Africa is Growing Much Faster than Other Regions 26
2.2 By 2050, Africa Will Have a Majority-Urban Population 29
2.3 An Increasing Share of Africans Use the Internet Daily 33
2.4 Most Young Africans Get News from the Internet and Social Media 33
3.1 Cartoon Laying Out ZANU-PF's "Work" 48

Maps

0.1 Map of Africa viii
2.1 Which African Countries Have the Youngest Populations? 28
6.1 Most African Countries Have Imposed Internet Shutdowns 114

ACKNOWLEDGMENTS

I am enormously grateful to all of the politically engaged Africans who have shared their ambitions, frustrations, and observations with me over many years in response to my ceaseless questions. I would never claim to speak for any of them, but I am grateful to have learned from so many thoughtful people and to be able to quote some of their voices directly in these pages.

I'm also grateful to the Council on Foreign Relations for supporting this project. A rotating team of stellar CFR interns helped comb through social media for years to find the most viral, politically salient, and often hilarious nuggets of online discourse: Aimée Ihirwe, Victoria Kipngetich, Celia Ngompe Mbiegue, Grace Kurtz-Nelson, Elizabeth Linsenmayer, Kosi Ogbuli, Maela Ngantcha-Ouandja, and Tima Dasouki. I am grateful to them all and look forward to following their careers. Their work was orchestrated and augmented by Alexandra Dent, my research associate. In addition to being a brilliant researcher, Alex has been a thoughtful sounding board, careful editor, organizational guru, motivational coach, and gentle guide to Gen Z memes and slang throughout this project. There would be no book without Alex, and I marvel at my good fortune in having had the opportunity to work with and learn from her.

Ebenezer Obadare has been a wonderful colleague and thought partner, listening to my ideas and concerns on a weekly basis and sharing his deep experience as an accomplished author. Reina Patel, Ebenezer's former research associate and another rising star, contributed to the social media research as well. If the character and intellect of Alex and Reina are any guide, the future looks quite bright.

President of the Council on Foreign Relations, Michael Froman, and Shannon O'Neil, Director of Studies and the Maurice R. Greenberg Chair at the Council, provided sage advice and excellent suggestions. Trish Dorff, CFR's publications guru, has been a steady voice of encouragement and guidance. Will Merrow provided extraordinarily helpful data visualization assistance. Michael Kerns at Bloomsbury has been an insightful and patient editor.

My wonderful husband, David Bonfili, and my children Clara and Max supported me through too many episodes of will-I-ever-finish anxiety to count. I cannot thank them enough for putting up with me.

All errors and oversights are mine alone.

Map 0.1 Map of Africa
Africa is made up of fifty-four countries, with a total population of 1.5 billion. *Credit: Will Merrow, Council on Foreign Relations.*

INTRODUCTION

When I traveled to Cameroon as a college undergraduate in 1994, I was hoping to improve my French and deepen my understanding of African politics. I spent months doing both by listening to Cameroonians talk about their president, Paul Biya, whose ubiquitous photograph gazed down upon me at nearly every office, hotel, or restaurant I visited. At that point, Biya had been in office for a dozen years, and his person already seemed inseparable from the state itself. Since then, I went on to graduate school, had a fulfilling career in government that included running the Africa Directorate at the National Security Council and serving as the United States Ambassador in Botswana, started a family, and am now the middle-aged parent of a teenager and a tween. Cameroon went from being a peaceful country of about thirteen million people to a state of over twenty-nine million mired in civil conflict. But as I write, in 2024, Paul Biya is still the president of Cameroon. Just days after marking Youth Day with a presidential speech that warned young Cameroonians about "moral decay, irresponsible and deviant behaviour," as well as the abuse of social media,[1] Biya's government organized nationwide parties to celebrate his ninety-first birthday.

I wrote this book because I don't think Biya's feat of longevity, or that of other very long-serving leaders, is likely to be repeated in the decades ahead. As many African populations grow ever younger, ever more urban, and ever-more digitally connected, their requirements and desires will be increasingly difficult for political authorities to meet, or to ignore. An era of dissatisfaction and experimentation is dawning in the region, and it will require new thinking for those in non-African capitals who wish to engage productively with a region that will soon represent one-quarter of the global population.

I know this because I worked on Africa policy in Washington, DC for many years. I saw how senior policymakers prized "stability" and often conflated it with political consistency. I noticed how I was often the youngest person in the room at meetings our embassies abroad organized to help me get a better sense of the local zeitgeist, even though the median age in these societies was typically far younger than mine. A gnawing sense that we were missing something important prompted me, and others, to devote significant effort to calling attention to the realities of Africa's staggering youthful demographics. The

US government has gotten better at cultivating younger contacts. But I'm not convinced that Washington, or other capitals, are really prepared for the political demands, frustration, and volatility that is coming.

This is not because of some obliviousness to African realities. In foreign policy circles, citing Africa's youth-heavy population profiles seems to have become an unspoken requirement when discussing the region. Initially, Africa's ever-growing population of young people were cast in the role of latent threat—Robert Kaplan's "loose molecules in a very unstable social fluid" that would usher in a "coming anarchy."[2] In this school of thought, young, urban populations—especially young men—are associated with violence and insecurity.[3] After the terrorist attacks on the United States in September 2001, efforts to understand radicalization and countering violent extremism sometimes reinforced this idea, describing vast, frustrated youth populations as ideal recruiting grounds for terrorist organizations.[4] Lessons drawn from the Arab Spring added new momentum to the notion of youth as fundamentally destabilizing, with the phrase "ticking time bomb" regularly employed by government officials, international organization representatives, and journalists to describe young Africans.[5]

A related discourse, unsurprisingly more common in Europe than elsewhere, focuses on the potential for Africa's population boom to drive a massive wave of migration to the north. Stephen Smith's book, *The Scramble for Europe: Young Africa on its Way to the Old Continent*[6] argues that "a large-scale 'migratory encounter' is set to occur in the near future between Africa and Europe," and considers the potential consequences, both positive and negative, for each region. Seeing opportunity, several observers have mused that Africa's excess labor could be matched with the needs of aging European and even Asian societies. Others see peril in African migration to Europe, which far-right leaders like Italy's Prime Minister Giorgia Meloni and French politician Marine Le Pen have made a centerpiece of their agendas, again casting African youth as potential problems requiring drastic policy solutions.

Yet another perspective, sometimes associated with the "Africa rising" narrative that gained currency between roughly 2005 and 2015, cast urban youth as an upwardly mobile engine of growth, prone to entrepreneurism and, if not yet members of the middle class, clearly on their way. In this discourse, the region's vast reserves of human capital would drive the economic progress that its natural resources failed to deliver. Burgeoning young populations were a development opportunity to be seized, even if it was never entirely clear how sufficient jobs would be created to accommodate them.

Whether centered on security threats, disruptive waves of migration, saviors of aging societies or engines of development, there is no shortage of analysis and discourse around Africa's youth. A recent contribution, Edward Paice's excellent *Youthquake: Why African Demography Should Matter to the World* provides a

INTRODUCTION

helpful history of African demography, with a focus on shifting trends regarding family planning polices and the different ways African demographic trends have been centered or ignored in donor states' development approaches over the past sixty years.

This book concerns itself with what Africa's unique demographics might mean for politics on the continent. I believe that the demands of young, urban, digitally connected Africans will continue to find increasingly powerful political expression, and that these demands will be very difficult for governments to meet. Demographic and technological changes are converging with an inflection point in national narratives to create a surging demand for change. The mismatch between aspirations and delivery is likely to lead to less consistency in the region's political landscape, and more experimentation. Some of those experiments will work, and some will not. All will be shaped by individual countries' unique political histories. But the common thread will be volatility, and a churning search for governing systems, leaders, and narratives that can meet the moment. I am not arguing that youth-driven politics will be fundamentally dangerous, rather that what is coming will be dramatically different from the period of political consistency (and, in many cases, stagnation) that has characterized the past two decades in the region.

Not only are African labor forces expanding rapidly with each year, but so too are African electorates (in the vast majority of African states, citizens are eligible to vote at eighteen years of age). While the integrity of the region's nominal democracies varies widely, very few African states have political systems that maintain themselves without any regard to popular will. Even authoritarian democracies have to create an appearance of legitimacy in the face of demand signals coming from increasingly young, increasingly urban populations.

This book accounts for the dramatic change in digital connectivity in urban African settings, which enables new forms of political organizing and greater awareness of alternative models and experiences. While social media can be easily caricatured as frivolous, the way young Africans engage in political discourse online is profoundly important, and this book takes that engagement seriously. Over a decade ago, Alcinda Honwana wrote powerfully about the struggle of marginalized young Africans, noting that despite their exclusion from formal employment and even social recognition as adults, they were forming their own spaces to express themselves and mitigate problems—spaces Honwana called "youthscapes."[7] Since then, the digital realm has become a natural home to these youthscapes, and a space in which they can confront and challenge the status quo. As Nanjala Nyabola wrote in *Digital Democracy, Analogue Politics*, "people in the partly free world fight for digital access for the rights to be seen and heard in nationals that will not hear or see them any other way."[8]

I'm wary of the dangers that come with trying to make this argument. Of course, there is never one African story. A continent of fifty-four countries, many of them spectacularly diverse, is never trending entirely in one direction or another. Particularly when it comes to the age structure of the population, North Africa looks completely different from the rest of the continent, having seen fertility rates decline substantially since the 1970s, with Namibia, Botswana, and South Africa also now trending in the same direction of lower fertility rates that stabilize the population size and age distribution. Because I'm interested in how disproportionately large youth populations might affect political trajectories, this book focuses on what has been called sub-Saharan Africa, a distinction that scholars have increasingly, and fairly, interrogated (see the map of Africa in the front of this book). But in this instance the demographic differences are real and meaningful.

These states comprise most of the continent and share demographic characteristics, but the youthful energy and desire for change in any given place is shaped by the political history and prevailing political narratives of that specific society. Some countries have well-established histories of democratic transfers of power; others have none. Some have persistent experience with military coups. Some have powerful diaspora communities that remain deeply engaged in the political discourse of their homelands. Experimentation and volatility will take on a wide range of context-specific forms, and politically engaged populations across the continent will be drawing lessons from their observations of one another.

It's also important to acknowledge that these African trends are occurring amid a wider global context of surging populism and authoritarianism, and skepticism about the global economic order that produces and perpetuates vast inequalities. Social scientists have found that young adults are becoming more dissatisfied with democracy around the world.[9] Africans are not unique in being frustrated with their political leaders and economic opportunities. But they are unique in meeting this moment while their societies are dominated— to a staggering degree—by youth and by new urban majorities, persistently increasing the pressure on governments that are already underperforming. Moreover, in Africa, demographic trends are converging with the expiration of old political narratives in a profoundly powerful call for change.

For external powers that wish to build effective relationships with African states, political volatility will require serious changes to how they approach building bilateral relationships. Grappling with the massive job-creation and urban infrastructure challenges must be a part of the "partnerships" policymakers are so fond of discussing. Focusing on the needs of those in power today makes less sense when leaders have a short shelf life. Instead, Africa's suitors will need to develop greater expertise and broader networks, and to focus on enduring shared interests with an entire society rather than a narrow political elite. Global

INTRODUCTION

powers offering authoritarian solutions will find eager takers as the powerful seek to maintain their positions in the face of popular demands for change, but their assistance may not buy lasting influence. Despite all the hand-wringing about a new "scramble for Africa,"[10] the demands and concerns of young Africans will ultimately be the most important driver of policy choices in African capitals, not the competition among distant powers.

Notes

1. "Head of State's Message to the Youth on the 58th Edition of the National Youth Day," Republic of Cameroon—Presidency of the Republic, February 10, 2024, https://www.prc.cm/en/news/speeches-of-the-president/7047-head-of-state-s-message-to-the-youth-on-the-58th-edition-of-the-youth-day.
2. Robert D. Kaplan, "The Coming Anarchy," *The Atlantic*, February 1994, https://www.theatlantic.com/magazine/archive/1994/02/the-coming-anarchy/304670/.
3. Richard Cincotta, "Demographic Security Comes of Age," *Environmental Change and Security Program Report* 10 (Wilson Center, 2004), https://www.wilsoncenter.org/publication/demographic-security-comes-age?collection=14103.
4. See, for example, United Nations Development Programme, *Journeys to Extremism in Africa: Pathways to Recruitment and Disengagement* (UNDP, 2023), https://www.undp.org/africa/publications/journey-extremism-africa-pathways-recruitment-and-disengagement#:~:text=February%207%2C%202023,and%20what%20makes%20them%20leave.
5. See, for example, Martina Schwikowski, "Africa's Youth: A Ticking Time Bomb," *DW*, December 4, 2017, https://www.dw.com/en/africas-youth-a-ticking-time-bomb/a-41605664; from the African Development Bank Governors, "Africa's Population Explosion is a Ticking Time Bomb—African Development Bank Governors," African Development Bank, March 7, 2018, https://www.afdb.org/en/news-and-events/africas-population-explosion-is-a-ticking-time-bomb-african-development-bank-governors-17900; or President Nana Akufo-Addo of Ghana, "President Launches National Youth Policy for Next Decade," *Business Ghana*, August 15, 2022, http://www.businessghana.com/site/news/General/268623/President-launches-National-Youth-Policy-for-next-decade.
6. Stephen Smith, *The Scramble for Europe: Young Africa on its Way to the Old Continent* (Cambridge: Polity Books, 2019).
7. See Alcinda M. Honwana, *The Time of Youth: Work, Social Change, and Politics in Africa* (Boulder, CO: Kumarian Press, 2012).
8. Nanjala Nyabola, *Digital Democracy, Analogue Politics: How the Internet Era Is Transforming Politics in Kenya* (London: Bloomsbury Publishing, 2018), 77.
9. R. S. Foa, A. Klassen, D. Wenger, A. Rand, and M. Slade, *Youth and Satisfaction with Democracy: Reversing the Democratic Disconnect?* (Cambridge: Centre for the Future of Democracy, October 2020), https://www.bennettinstitute.cam.ac.uk/wp-content/uploads/2022/06/Youth_and_Satisfaction_with_Democracy-lite.pdf.

10 See, for example, "The New Scramble for Africa," *The Economist*, March 7, 2019, https://www.economist.com/leaders/2019/03/07/the-new-scramble-for-africa; or in a follow-up to his *Atlantic* article above, Robert D. Kaplan, "Anarchy Unbound: The New Scramble for Africa," *New Statesman*, August 16, 2023, https://www.newstatesman.com/long-reads/2023/08/anarchy-unbound-scramble-africa-niger-robert-kaplan.

1
FAMILIAR FACES

Look what you're doing to this nation
What are you teaching the future generation?
See our leaders become misleaders
And see our mentors become tormentors
Freedom fighters become dictators
They look pon the youth and say we're destructors.
  —*LYRICS TO "FREEDOM" BY BOBI WINE, UGANDAN*
  MUSICIAN AND OPPOSITION POLITICIAN[1]

I've been working on US–Africa policy for most of my adult life. My career has given me frequent opportunities to travel to the continent, and over the years, I've noticed that when new acquaintances learn about my work, they often ask about safety issues, and assume that my travels take me to unstable, tumultuous places in some kind of constant state of upheaval. Without much direct exposure to the continent, they are probably relying on the media narratives they have absorbed. Several analysts have noted that mainstream news coverage of Africa (and, to be fair, many other parts of the world) tends to focus on "crisis, failed governance and states, conflict and humanitarian emergencies."[2]

But for a region that is too often associated with turmoil in the Western popular imagination, Africa has been the site of a great deal of political stasis in recent decades. Political consistency, of course, is not the same as stability, nor does it guarantee an absence of major crises. Nonetheless, it's a somewhat surprising feature of the African political landscape. The wave of democratization that swept over the continent in the 1990s was met with a powerful set of adaptive strategies by those elites unwilling to leave decisions about political power in the hands of an electorate.[3] Some countries genuinely democratized, and in others leaders merely adopted multiparty elections while maintaining tight control over political space and speech and continuing to operate a highly politicized judiciary.[4] Those strategies have enabled long-serving individual leaders to increasingly personalize the politics of their countries, building leadership dynasties to keep power within a specific family, and dominant party systems to ensure control is never transferred away from the existing power structure. These political leaders have dug in, largely through electoral authoritarian systems that retain the window dressing of regular elections and multipartyism, but in which dominant political powers use the state apparatus to constrain political competition and limit democratic accountability.

This book is about how young, urban populations will inform more frequent political change going forward. But to understand why that will be such a sea change, it is necessary to understand just how much political consistency has characterized the region in recent decades, even across differing regime types. The fading status quo does not dictate the contours of political imagination in an age of connectivity, but it does give form to what young Africans are rejecting.

The Forever Presidents

Cameroon's President Paul Biya, in power for four decades, turned ninety in 2023. The occasion was celebrated at state-sponsored events countrywide, including a bash sponsored by the National Youth Council,[5] where young Cameroonians were reportedly paid to turn out and have a slice of cake. While his allies in Cameroon's elite political class tried to spin the milestone positively—one former minister claimed "the more you add up the age, the wiser you become—the more experienced, tolerant, logical you become,"[6] Biya himself made no public appearances, in keeping with his reclusive habits in recent years (reportedly he spends most of his time at the Intercontinental Hotel in Switzerland).[7] This may have been for the best. When Biya participated in the US African Leaders Summit in 2022, he became the subject of a viral video in which he appeared utterly unaware of his location or purpose, despite being onstage, wearing a microphone, with scheduled remarks in hand, and repeatedly urged by his aides to begin his presentation.[8] Social media may have found the video comical, but the questions around Cameroon's future leadership are serious. Biya has maintained power for so many years by keeping rivals off balance; anxiety pervades discussions around who might be his successor, and whether the constitution would be honored or, more likely, ignored should he pass away while still in office. As of this writing, Biya intended to stand for reelection to an eighth term in 2025.

But Biya is not even Africa's longest-serving leader. Equatorial Guinea's president, Teodoro Obiang Nguema Mbasogo, seized power in 1979 and has never let go, making him the longest-serving head of state in the world. The vast majority of Equatorial Guinea's population, which has a median age of twenty-two, has no memory of another leader, or any experience with real political competition.[9] Since 1989, the country has periodically held elections characterized by fraud, coercion, and extreme political violence. Obiang regularly wins by cynicism-inducing margins of well over 90 percent of the vote.

In contrast, there is no pretense of holding elections in Eritrea. Since the country achieved independence from Ethiopia in 1991 and formal recognition as an independent state in 1993, President Isaias Afwerki has been Eritrea's ultimate authority. He declined to adopt the constitution that was drafted and approved in 1997; Eritrea simply operates without one. It is among the most isolated and repressive states in the world, forcing its citizens into military service for indefinite periods, denying them access to independent sources of information,[10] and requiring that Eritreans obtain a visa in order to exit their own country (such visas are not available to Eritreans between the ages of eighteen and fifty). The only consequential political changes in the country for the last thirty years have been driven by one man's change of tactics or new ideas. When reporters had a rare opportunity to ask him questions during his 2023 visit to Kenya, he declined to respond to questions about his succession plans.[11]

Uganda's Yoweri Museveni has been the president of his country since 1986. In 2005, when he finally relented to multiparty politics in the country, he also ensured that presidential term limits would be removed from the constitution. His long tenure was accommodated by another constitutional change in 2017,[12] which removed age limits for the office of the president. Rather than mellowing with age, Museveni's tolerance for opposition seems to diminish by the year. His political opponents are regularly harassed, assaulted, and jailed. Museveni likes to frame his leadership as that of a wise and benevolent teacher guiding sometimes wayward students; in 2021 he told a reporter that he couldn't leave office because the population would not follow the right path without his leadership:

> When the social direction of a society is already set, anybody can run it. The problem is, in our case, the direction is not set, so it's very risky, very risky. Actually, it showed the lack of seriousness of those who talk the way you're talking, that you just go. Just go (laughter). People don't know whether to go north or south. And you say you just go. Yes, if people are already clear that the direction is the north and everybody is no longer—there's no more argument about that, then anybody can lead. I can say now you know the way. Let me go.[13]

Though Uganda's population has more than tripled since Museveni came to power, resulting in one of the youngest-skewing populations in the world, the head of state is prone to using youth as justification for dismissing opinions he does not like. Whether it's derisively calling the latest leader of the opposition,

Robert Kyagulanyi Ssentamu (Bobi Wine), a "young boy"[14] or decrying a general lack of knowledge and seriousness among young people,[15] Uganda's president, who often address his citizens as grandchildren (*Bazzukulu*), wants the three-quarters of the population that are under the age of thirty to know their place.

In neighboring Rwanda, Paul Kagame has held the title of president since 2000, but has clearly been in charge of his country since the defeat of the regime that perpetrated the Rwandan genocide in 1994. In 2015, a reported 98 percent of Rwandan voters approved an amendment to the 2003 constitution that moved the country from a system with a maximum of two seven-year presidential terms to one allowing Kagame a third seven-year term—then resetting the clock by permitting two five-year terms after that.[16] Given political space in Rwanda is tightly restricted, and that Kagame won his last election with nearly 99 percent of the vote,[17] the upshot was to ensure that President Kagame can remain in office until 2034.

As of this writing, Cote d'Ivoire's president, Alassane Ouattara, was considering a 2025 run for a constitutionally dubious fourth term in the presidency, despite being eighty-two years old.[18] Ouattara has insisted that he would step down if his longtime political opponents also agree not to seek office. This condition suggests that leadership of the country of over thirty million people, with a median age of 18.2, is hostage to the rivalries of the past, and that to avoid a return to the kind of civil conflict that broke out when Ouattara was first elected in 2010, Ivorians must simply wait the old men out.

When eighty-one-year-old US President Joe Biden acknowledged widespread concerns about his age that made his reelection a very tenuous prospect, bowing out of the 2024 race, many Africans on social media noted his example. Drawing contrasts with their own aging leaders, they made jokes about African presidents "leaving the Zoom call,"[19] or being puzzled by why such a "young man" would voluntarily step down.[20]

The Dynasties

When these long-serving heads of state are self-aware enough to recognize that they are not immortal, they often take pains to keep power in the family. The African political landscape includes several long-serving families, and even more rumors of planned dynastic succession.

In both Kenya and Botswana, sons of founding presidents have ascended to the same office, but in neither case did they directly follow their fathers, nor did their fathers orchestrate their ascent.[21] But in numerous other cases, the story is quite different.

In the Democratic Republic of Congo, lifelong rebel fighter Laurent Desiré Kabila finally seized the mantle of national leadership in May 1997, chasing out his predecessor, Mobutu Sese Seko, who had been in charge for over thirty years. Kabila's tenure was short; after falling out with his Rwandan backers, he was assassinated in January 2001. But he had found time to make his son Joseph the head of the army, and in the wake of his father's murder, Joseph Kabila was chosen to be the next president, likely because he had no political base of his own and therefore represented no threat to Congo's fractious political elites.[22] The younger Kabila would go on to surprise most observers, consolidating power and staying in office until 2019, giving the Kabilas over twenty years at the top. Constitutional term limits and international pressure eventually convinced Joseph Kabila to step down from formal leadership, though he sought to maintain power behind the scenes and even suggested he might make another run for the presidency in 2023.[23] Ultimately, his plans to retain influence were unsuccessful.

But in several other states dynasties persist. Gnassingbé Eyadema was the president of the West African country of Togo from the success of his coup d'etat in 1967 until 2005. When he died of a heart attack that year, the circle of elites who benefited from his long and largely dictatorial tenure wanted nothing left to chance. Despite the constitution indicating that the president of the National Assembly should have succeeded the deceased president, it was the Minister of Equipment, Mines, Posts, and Telecommunications—who also happened to be Eyadema's son, Faure Gnassingbé, who was sworn in as acting president within hours, having bested his many siblings in a scramble for power. Togo's power brokers sought to assuage regional and international concerns about respect for the constitution with a flurry of frantic political maneuvers to justify their choice. In the hours and days following Eyadema's death, the National Assembly president was impeached, Faure was installed in his role, and the term of the new "acting" president was extended. But the Economic Community of West African States (ECOWAS) and the African Union were not satisfied, and Faure stepped down about two weeks into his acting presidency.[24] The setback was only temporary. Thanks to a constitutional amendment championed by his late father which excluded the main opposition leader from participating in elections, Faure was able to secure victory a few months later in flawed polls[25] that the International Federation for Human Rights called "an electoral masquerade."[26] Faure has been in power ever since, having encouraged the compliant National Assembly to pass a constitutional amendment in 2019 that would permit him to stay in office until 2030.[27] But even that was not enough. In 2024, Faure orchestrated yet another constitutional overhaul that would reduce the presidency to a ceremonial post and create a powerful new President of the

Council of Ministers—essentially a prime minister—to be selected by the majority party in the parliament. This new configuration allows Faure to retain power even after reaching his term limits.

Dynastic succession in the region got easier after Togo forged the way ahead. Like Gnassingbé Eyadema, Omar Bongo of Gabon also came to power in 1967. He had been serving as vice president of the country when Leon M'ba, the country's first postindependence leader, died late that year. Once Bongo was in charge, he did not let go, establishing Gabon as a one-party state in 1968, comfortably retaining power through the introduction of multiparty elections in the early 1990s, and serving until his death in 2009. When Bongo passed away, Gabon's power brokers were under pressure to adhere to the constitution, and the President of the Senate became the country's interim leader until elections could be organized. Roughly three months later, Ali Bongo Ondimba, son of the former president, who was the defense minister when his father died, was declared the electoral victor and new president.[28]

Ali Bongo remained in office until August of 2023, despite suffering a serious stroke in 2018 that kept him entirely out of the public eye for months and clearly left him debilitated. He relied on the same system of compromised institutions that ensured support for his father. Having weathered a controversial and significantly flawed 2016 election in which his main rival was his sister Pascaline's former partner,[29] he contested again for a third term in 2023. But Bongo's physical weakness, popular frustration with economic inequality and unemployment, and consternation around changed election rules and a compressed electoral timetable designed to limit the efficacy of political organizing among the opposition provided an opportunity for rivals. General Brice Oligui Nguema seized power in a military coup d'etat just after Bongo's victory was announced. Nguema was not an outsider; he was a distant cousin of the man he deposed, had been close to Omar Bongo, had led security for Ali Bongo, and is reported to be very close to Ali's sister Pascaline, who had been in competition with her brother for power when their father died. The Gabonese ruling junta has indicated it intends to prosecute Ali Bongo's son, Noureddin Bongo-Valentin, who had gained influence after his father's stroke and was being groomed as a potential successor.[30]

Rather than a rejection of the Bongo dynasty, this may represent a soap opera–like power struggle within it. As Gabonese opposition politician Albert Ondo Ossa told reporters, "the Bongos have decided to put Ali Bongo aside and continue their system by putting in place a Bongo CEO system. And they have put forward Oligui Nguema . . . the Bongo clan continues being in power."[31] Altogether, Gabon, like Togo, was led by a single family for more than fifty years, and even after the coup, it appears that a significant faction of the Bongo clan and their inner circle remain extremely influential. Whether or not the extended clan's political grip can be retained remains to be seen.

FAMILIAR FACES   **13**

The latest dynastic passing of the torch occurred in the Sahelian country of Chad. In 2021 Idriss Déby, who had been president for thirty-one years, died on the battlefield in his native Chad, just days after securing an utterly unsurprising sixth term in farcical elections.[32] Chad's constitution called for the president of the National Assembly to assume the powers of the head of state on a provisional basis. Instead, Déby's son Mahamat was hastily elevated to the presidency by his military colleagues, ensuring that power and access to resources among Chadian elites would remain relatively stable—and that the security partnerships upon which France and the United States had come to rely would remain intact, leading to a muted international reaction. Predictably, in October 2022, the eighteen-month transition period that the military assured Chadians and the international community would lead to fresh elections was extended by an additional two years. By April 2024, Mahamat Déby's main political opponents had been murdered or co-opted, and he coasted to electoral victory.

It's highly likely that Africa will see more of these orchestrated efforts to safeguard power within a ruling family; whether they will succeed is another question. Most of the region's aging, long-serving leaders appear to be keeping the dynastic option open, although the next generation leadership may prove even more likely to provoke popular discontent. Equatorial Guinea's President Obiang has elevated his son, Teodoro Nguema Obiang Mangue, known as Teodorin, to the vice presidency, and observers of the country agree that the younger man is being groomed for the presidency. Teodorin appears to have won out over siblings also eager to lead the family business, despite his track record of legal entanglements in the United States, the United Kingdom, Switzerland, and France relating to lavish spending on exclusive cars, palatial estates, and even Michael Jackson memorabilia with corruptly obtained riches.[33] Most recently, South African authorities seized a yacht and luxury homes belonging to Teodorin after a South African businessman won a lawsuit for damages.[34]

In Uganda, President Yoweri Museveni's son and likely successor, Muhoozi Kainerugaba, is almost equally colorful. Much of Ugandan society must take care not to anger the powerful with online criticism; Freedom House reports that "journalists, activists, and ordinary users who criticized the president and his family online remained subject to arrests, detentions, and physical violence."[35] But Muhoozi appears to operate under a far less restrictive set of rules. Although he serves as a senior military officer in his country and was elevated to the post of Chief of Defense Forces in 2024, his freewheeling social media presence includes wild deviations from official Ugandan policy. These include boasts about how quickly he and his military colleagues could seize control of Nairobi, the capital of neighboring Kenya, as well as expressions of solidarity and even support for the M23 rebel group operating in another neighboring country, the Democratic Republic of Congo. They also speak directly to his presidential ambitions, as in his March 15, 2023, missive:

The Prime Minister of UK is 42 years old, the Prime Minister of Finland is 37 years. Some of us are hitting 50 years old. We are tired of waiting forever. We will take a stand! Fidel Castro, my HERO, became President at 32 years. I'm about to hit 49 years old. It's really not right. The Presidency of the nation is meant for young men. How many agree with me that our time has come? Enough of the old people ruling us. Dominating us. It's time for our generation to shine.[36]

Despite his son's obvious impatience, President Museveni continues to elevate and protect him. Although technically prohibited from participating in politics due to his military responsibilities, Muhoozi holds rallies around the country, having converted his "MK movement" from one explicitly devoted to celebrating him to one ostensibly promoting patriotism in general—although substantively that brand of patriotism includes verbal attacks on Museveni's son-in-law, a potential rival.[37]

More opaque politics make it difficult to assess the validity of speculation around Eritrean President Isaias's son Abraham, who appears to have taken on more official duties in recent years,[38] or Rwandan President Kagame's daughter Ange, a "presidential advisor"[39] and son Ian, who reportedly recently joined his country's presidential guard.[40] The Republic of Congo's President Denis Sassou-Nguesso, in office since 1997 (after a previous stint as president from 1979 to 1992), may also be grooming his son, Denis-Christel, to succeed him.[41]

The Permanent Ruling Parties

Beyond the political consistency provided by individual leaders or ruling families, many African countries are governed by extremely strong ruling parties that have dominated state offices since independence. The US National Intelligence Council noted in its 2018 Global Trends report that, "since 1990, fewer than one out of six African elections produced a change in the ruling party, in large part because of incumbents' access to state resources, electoral manipulation, and often high public approval ratings."[42] This phenomenon is especially pronounced in southern Africa, where South Africa, Namibia, Angola, Zimbabwe, Mozambique, and Tanzania have all experienced government through the lens of only one party since becoming independent states.[43] In these countries, the dominant political party can often become synonymous with the state itself. South Africa is the best-known example, with its storied African National Congress (ANC), formed in 1912 and finally voted into power in 1994 with the end of apartheid and liberation of the country. ANC dominance is fading, and for the first time the party received less than an outright majority of votes in 2024's general elections, but for over twenty years, the real political competition in the country came from intraparty jockeying for power, and the ANC party conference was the most politically significant event in the country.

But other dominant parties play just as ubiquitous a role in political life. Zimbabwe, which emerged as an independent state in 1980 only after an armed struggle against white minority rule, has been politically and economically dominated by one political party, the Zimbabwe African National Union–Patriotic Front, or ZANU-PF, ever since. Throughout Zimbabwe's short history, ZANU-PF has gone to violent extremes to ensure its continued control. From massacres in western areas of the country that supported a rival party[44] in the mid-1980s to the brutal repression of the opposition Movement for Democratic Change in the 2000s, ZANU-PF stopped at nothing to maintain power. Although Robert Mugabe maintained his hold on the presidency for thirty-seven years until he was ousted in 2017, the manner in which he was deposed is illustrative of the party's primacy over even their most famous champion. The coup that ousted him from power was instigated and controlled entirely by ZANU-PF and should not be misunderstood as a fundamental change in the nature of Zimbabwe's politics; its entire purpose was to ensure continuity for the old guard within the party. A long-simmering internal power struggle centering on leadership succession had pitted two ZANU-PF factions against each other, and the group dominated by Emmerson Mnangagwa and the military seized power rather than risk seeing the aged Mugabe transfer power to his wife Grace, who was aligned with other, notably younger, ZANU-PF constituencies.

In Angola and Mozambique, the end of Portuguese colonialism in 1975 ushered in protracted and vicious civil wars fueled in part by Cold War proxy conflict, which ended in 2002 and 1992 respectively. The political party of the victors in both instances—the People's Movement for the Liberation of Angola (MPLA) in Angola, and the Mozambique Liberation Front (FRELIMO) in Mozambique—have been ruling ever since. This history informs the way that forces interested in challenging the status quo are often cast as enemies of the state itself; in both places, major opposition movements are successors to the armed groups that once fought with the now-ruling powers. Against this backdrop, it's unsurprising that political opposition is often met with state repression.

In Angola, Eduardo dos Santos served as president from 1979 to 2017, when his failing health stalled a project to personalize power in his family and prompted him to step down in an MPLA-managed transition. Earlier indicators that dos Santos was interested in a dynastic succession project alarmed the party, and the choice of João Lourenço as the next party flagbearer was an agreement between dos Santos and the rest of the MPLA leadership.[45] While dos Santos's departure from center stage raised collective hopes for change, the same party apparatus in control throughout his tenure remained firmly in charge, and the popular hostility once directed at the dos Santos family now focuses on the ruling party.

Mozambique's FRELIMO party has managed changing personalities for decades, having lost founding President Samora Machel in a plane crash in 1986, forcing the party to manage a transition sooner than expected. The country's first multiparty elections were held in 1994, and a recent round, in 2019, was in keeping with a pattern of flawed elections engineered to guarantee FRELIMO's victory, prompting former US Ambassador to Mozambique, Dennis Jett, to despair that if the population wanted change, "the people of Mozambique are left with the options of armed resistance, Islamist terrorism, emigration, or resignation."[46] The rise of a new political coalition in 2024 led to yet another highly questionable election,[47] widespread popular protests, and a violent state response.

Tanzania's Chama cha Mapinduzi, or CCM, has dominated the east African country since independence in 1961.[48] Originally called the Tanganyika African National Union (TANU), it was founded by Julius Nyerere to advance both independence and socialist principles, borrowing significantly from the Chinese Communist Party (with whom the CCM enjoys enduring close relations). Nyerere led his country from 1961 until 1985 and remained at the party's helm until 1990. Until the very end of his life, he was a fierce advocate for a one-party state, arguing that African political parties "were not formed to challenge any ruling group of our own people; they were formed to challenge the foreigners who ruled over us. They were not, therefore, political 'parties' (i.e., factions) but nationalist movements, and from the outset they represented the interests and aspirations of the whole nation."[49] The advent of multiparty politics in 1992 changed the way CCM retained power, but not the reality of its primacy in Tanzanian political life.

Churn Without Change

Even some countries that have seen democratically driven transfers of power from one party to another have experienced a numbing form of political continuity. The primary political competitors don't change much from election cycle to election cycle, and parties themselves serve as vehicles for identity groups and financial interests rather than entities with discrete policy ideas. Nigeria and Kenya both fit this description. For citizens in these systems, what might look to others like political dynamism can register as stagnation. In Nigeria, where democracy was restored in 1999, presidential elections until 2023 typically featured two candidates who had any chance of success, one representing the People's Democratic Party (PDP), which held power from 1999 to 2015, and one representing an opposing force, which since 2013 had been called the All

People's Congress (APC) and has held the presidency since 2015. In all seven general elections held since the end of military rule, Atiku Abubakar has been a candidate for president or vice president and has done so on behalf of three different parties. Muhammadu Buhari, who led Nigeria from 1983 to 1985 when the country was under military rule, contested for the presidency five times in the new democratic era, finding success twice. The familiar faces are indicative of a static political class engaged in regular electoral contests about the relative slices of "national cake"[50] that different groups would get, but not about fundamental change in the way the state is governed.

It's not just the familiar faces and policy-free party structures that can contribute to an impression of continuity. Extremely fluid partisan identification can be another mechanism for maintaining a surprising degree of continuity in a system where power is transferred in the wake of an election. In Kenya, since 2002, every general election has been won by a different party formation, even in elections in which incumbents were returned to office.[51] A permanent political class cycles in and out of power in an unstable party system, forming new coalitions of identity and regionally based structures with each electoral opportunity, without much in the way of contrasting political platforms. As in Nigeria, there is a great deal of consistency in the names and faces at the top of Kenyan ballots; for example, Raila Odinga has contested for the presidency in five different elections (leading five different political coalitions). By 2022, Kenyan political analysts were using the phrase "elections about nothing"—first coined by John Githongo—to explain the general popular ambivalence that had taken hold in Kenya's electorate. The outcome, in other words, didn't really seem to matter, because the result was presumed to be more of the same.

Political continuity may sound like a stabilizing force, but for the countries experiencing these long periods of consistency, it has not been synonymous with security or economic stability. Political scientist Will Reno found that protracted periods of disorder are often "rooted in decades of personalist rule and the failure of mid-twentieth-century state-building projects."[52] Over the course of long periods of consistent political leadership, Cameroon, Chad, and Nigeria have all experienced armed rebellions. Zimbabwe was the setting for jaw-dropping economic upheaval, at one point becoming the fastest-shrinking economy in the world. Reliable polling is not available in all of the countries discussed above, but where it exists, it often reveals deep popular dissatisfaction with the direction of these countries' overall trajectory, and a lack of trust in political leadership.[53]

Recent African history suggests that when long periods of political consistency end, what follows is unpredictable, but generally characterized by increased political contestation and volatility. When a rare change occurs, it seems to open the floodgates of political demands and ambitions, and the institutions of these states may be ill-prepared to manage and channel those forces. Take, for example, Burkina Faso in 2014, where citizens who were fed up with twenty-seven years of Blaise Compaoré's corrupt presidency—and angered by his attempt to extend it even further while positioning his brother, Francois, to succeed him—rose up in a movement to insist on a change not just in leadership, but in the way that the country was governed. Balai Citoyen (Citizens' Broom) was a civic movement cofounded by popular musicians. They did not just want Compaoré to step down,[54] but also called for an urgent focus on addressing poverty, creating opportunity for young Burkinabe, and building more resilient and unbiased state systems of accountability.[55] Slogans like "our strength is numbers" and "together we are not alone" speak to the generational dynamics at play; Balai Citoyen "provided a hitherto largely alienated and disconnected youth with a means of political mobilization at the same time as it illustrated the relative impotence of regular political parties to genuinely represent the aspirations of Youth."[56]

Ultimately the Burkinabe activists did not get what they were asking for. Their popular uprising prompted elements of the security services to turn on Compaoré, who was forced to relinquish power. Although the military initially played only a brief transitional role and elections in 2015 brought the country new civilian leadership, Burkina Faso's short-lived democracy fell victim to an ever-worsening security situation that was exacerbated by the way Compaoré had both made accommodations with the region's extremists and personalized the country's security services, creating rivalries by favoring those closest to him. Once his system collapsed, the fallout entailed the fragmentation of intelligence capacities, tension and underperformance among defense forces, and ongoing mistrust among security elites at the worst possible time for a country in the Sahel, where violent extremists were looking to expand their reach.[57] The country was plagued by terrorist attacks and the state failed to respond effectively. By early 2022 a coup ushered in a new era of military rule, followed quickly by yet another coup at the end of September 2022. The vision of Balai Citoyen seems a distant memory in today's Burkina Faso, where military leadership persists, and the security outlook grows ever more dire. When one considers the impending end of other personalist regimes in the region, Burkina Faso becomes an alarming cautionary tale.

On the other side of the continent, the Ethiopian People's Revolutionary Democratic Front (EPRDF) tried, and ultimately failed, to manage the leadership transition that began with long-serving Prime Minister Meles Zenawi's death in 2012, resulting in increased state fragility and civil conflict. Meles, representing the Tigrayan faction that held first-among-equals status in the EPRDF, had been an extraordinarily commanding figure in power since 1991, ruthlessly quashing dissent as he pursued his vision of state-led development. Once his dominant personality was gone from the political stage, a popular expectation of profound change became evident in increasing unrest around the country. The EPRDF tried to manage through the sea change in Ethiopian politics by elevating a successor to Meles, Hailemariam Desalegn, who was neither Tigrayan nor a member of one of the country's two largest ethnic groups, the Amhara or the Oromo. But those efforts ultimately buckled under the weight of fractious internal politics, prompting Hailemariam to resign in 2018. When the EPRDF elevated Abiy Ahmed, a youthful, charismatic figure from the Oromo community to succeed Hailemariam, it was the beginning of a political unraveling. Abiy soon formed a new political entity, the Prosperity Party, that absorbed much of the old EPRDF. The Tigrayan elements that had been dominant in the country's politics for so long were isolated, and after a horrific civil war between federal forces and the Tigrayans, the country's politics remain in a state of flux. The civic unrest that led Hailemariam to resign persists, and zero-sum ethnonationalist demands are growing louder as Prime Minister Abiy sets about remaking the state in his image.[58]

In the Gambia, which was led by Yahya Jammeh for over twenty years, political conditions took a more democratic turn, which may be attributable to the surprising circumstances of Jammeh's ouster. His tenure in office was characterized by both violent repression of dissent and increasingly grandiose claims of his genius and popularity—he claimed to have invited a cure for HIV and invented awards and honorifics for himself.[59] Jammeh's delusions may have led him to underestimate the political risk represented by the 2016 elections, which he lost, in part because of the efforts of Gambians within the country and in the diaspora to join forces in support of change—an effort facilitated by digital connection.[60] His attempts to stay in office met with resistance domestically and internationally, and he fled into exile in Equatorial Guinea. Since then, Gambians have enjoyed greater civil and political rights and made it through one relatively sound election cycle. But the work of reforming and shoring up long-neglected institutions is slow going, the opposition coalition that united to oust Jammeh has fractured, and accountability for the abuses of the past remains a work in progress, particularly as members of Jammeh's old regime find their way back into government.[61]

In Sudan, Omar al-Bashir's brutal tenure as president lasted nearly thirty years until a popular uprising prompted the Sudanese military to take him into custody in 2019 and form a short-lived transitional government with civilians. The impetus for getting rid of the Bashir regime came largely from the Sudanese streets, and particularly from young Sudanese demanding a wholesale transformation in the nature of their government. Instead of making way for reform, Sudan's regular and irregular security forces kept a tight grip on power—and on their exclusive access to lucrative business opportunities—before they turned their guns on each other in a fight for supremacy. Citizen activism continues even in the midst of war, but what once was an inspiring story of organic, popular demands for representative, accountable government is now a catastrophic, and entirely man-made, humanitarian crisis.

The pressures and demands animating politics in these states that have experienced a change in leadership after a long period of consistency are as diverse as the states themselves. But two conclusions are clear. First, even changes sparked by popular demands for democracy do not necessarily lead to democratic outcomes, and the legacy of long-dominant systems, whether it is an erosion of the security services in Burkina Faso or ethnic grievances in Ethiopia, casts a long shadow. Second, these watershed moments tend to catch international actors like the United States flat-footed, even when the change occurring was long sought by US policymakers. There is no better example of this than Sudan, where years of focus on eliminating a problem (the Bashir regime) crowded out any space for imagining a durable solution, leaving the United States out of step with the ambitions of Sudanese civilians and slow to grasp the dangers of divisions among armed actors.[62]

These conclusions matter, because more change is coming.

Notes

1. Bobi Wine, "Freedom," June 26, 2018, track 6 on *Kyarenga*, Kamwokya Fire Base Studios, 2018, digital. Used by permission.
2. Gideon H. Chitanga, "Global Broadcast Media is Still Relying on Stereotypical Narratives about Africa" (*Africa No Filter*, 2022), https://africanofilter.org/documents/Gideon-H-Chitanga_Global-broadcast-media.pdf.
3. Nic Cheeseman and Brian Klaas explore this phenomenon in the excellent *How to Rig an Election* (New Haven, CT: Yale University Press, 2018).
4. Steven Levitsky and Lucan A. Way, *Competitive Authoritarianism: Hybrid Regimes after the Cold War* (Cambridge: Cambridge University Press, 2010).
5. Moki Edwin Kindzeka, "Cameroon President Celebrates 89th Birthday," *VOA News*, February 14, 2022, https://www.voanews.com/a/cameroon-president-celebrates-89th-birthday/6440796.html.
6. Amindeh Blaise Atabong, "Cameroon President's 90th Birthday Marked by Cocktail of Woes," *Reuters*, February 13, 2023, https://www.reuters.com/world/africa/cameroon-presidents-90th-birthday-marked-by-cocktail-woes-2023-02-13/.
7. Drew Hinshaw and Joe Parkinson, "Can't Find Cameroon's President? Try Geneva's Intercontinental Hotel," *Wall Street Journal*, November 4, 2018, https://www.wsj.com/articles/where-does-the-lion-sleep-tonight-genevas-intercontinental-hotel-1541368940.
8. Selina Teyie, "Africa's Oldest President Forgets where He is while Addressing Global Summit," *The Star*, January 23, 2023, https://www.the-star.co.ke/news/africa/2023-

01-23-africas-oldest-president-forgets-where-he-is-while-addressing-global-summit/.

9   "Equatorial Guinea: Percentage of Population under 25 Years of Age," World Population Prospects, Department of Economic and Social Affairs Population Division (United Nations, 2022), https://population.un.org/wpp/Graphs/Probabilistic/PopPerc/0-24/226.

10 Very few Eritreans living inside Eritrea have access to the Internet; while data on this is hard to come by, recent estimates predict between 8 and 26 percent; "Eritrea: Universal and Meaningful Connectivity," International Telecommunications Union, 2023, https://datahub.itu.int/dashboards/umc/?e=ERI.

11 Ayenat Mersie, "Eritrean President Sidesteps Questions about Troops in Ethiopia," *Reuters*, last modified February 9, 2023, https://www.reuters.com/world/africa/eritrea-president-says-rights-violations-by-eritrean-troops-ethiopia-fantasy-2023-02-09/.

12 Bukola Adebayo, "Uganda Court Upholds Law That Could Allow Yoweri Museveni to be President for Life," *CNN*, July 27, 2018, https://www.cnn.com/2018/07/27/africa/uganda-presidential-age-limit/index.html.

13 Eyder Peralta, "Uganda's Museveni Faces Tough Challenge in Presidential Election," *NPR*, January 12, 2021, https://www.npr.org/2021/01/12/955938674/ugandas-museveni-faces-tough-challenge-in-presidential-election.

14 Siraje Lubwama and Sadab Kitatta Kaaya, "Museveni Blasts Ministers over Bobi Wine," *The Observer*, May 8, 2019, https://observer.ug/news/headlines/60629-museveni-blasts-ministers-over-bobi-wine.

15 Iain Esau, "Moralising Museveni Chastises Uganda's Youth and Berates European NGOs," *Upstream*, last modified February 11, 2022, https://www.upstreamonline.com/politics/moralising-museveni-chastises-ugandas-youth-and-berates-european-ngos/2-1-1164192.

16 Bradley McAllister, "Rwanda Voters Approve Constitutional Referendum to Extend Presidential Term Limit," *The Jurist*, December 19, 2015, https://www.jurist.org/news/2015/12/rwandans-vote-in-favor-of-extending-presidential-term-limit/.

17 Zack Baddorf, "Rwanda President's Lopsided Re-election Is Seen as a Sign of Oppression," *New York Times*, August 6, 2017, https://www.nytimes.com/2017/08/06/world/africa/rwanda-elections-paul-kagame.html.

18 Reuters, "Ivory Coast President Ouattara's Party Pushes Him to Run Again," *Reuters*, October 1, 2024, https://www.reuters.com/world/africa/ivory-coast-president-ouattaras-party-pushes-him-run-again-2024-10-01/.

19 Ochi (@OchiJnr), "Nigeria's Tinubu has left the Zoom call," comment on X post, July 21, 2024, https://x.com/OchiJnr/status/1815151131053465955.

20 Kenyan Facts (@KResearcher), "African dictators looking at this and wondering why a 'young man' like Biden would willingly not want to continue being president," X post, July 21, 2024, https://x.com/KResearcher/status/1815084790980190403.

21 Uhuru Kenyatta served as the fourth president of Kenya from 2013 to 2022; his father Jomo Kenyatta was independent Kenya's first president, serving from 1964 until his death in 1978. Similarly, Ian Khama served as the fourth president of Botswana from 2008 to 2018; his father Seretse Khama was Botswana's first president, serving from 1966 until his death in office in 1980.

22 For a discussion of the circumstances surrounding Joseph Kabila's selection ascent to the presidency, see Jason Stearns, *Dancing in the Glory of Monsters* (New York: Hachette, 2012), 307–9.

23 Giulia Paravicini, "Congo's Outgoing President Kabila Doesn't Rule Out Running Again in 2023," *Reuters*, last modified December 9, 2018, https://www.reuters.com/article/idUSKBN1O80DU/.

24 Kaniye S. A. Ebeku, "The Succession of Faure Gnassingbe to the Togolese Presidency: An International Law Perspective," *Current African Issues* 30 (2005): 1–33, https://www.diva-portal.org/smash/get/diva2:240415/FULLTEXT02.pdf.

25 Amnesty International, "Togo: Free Participation in Election Process is Made Impossible," Amnesty International public statement, April 20, 2005, https://www.amnesty.org/en/wp-content/uploads/2021/08/afr570102005en.pdf.

26 "Merci, Papa," *Africa Confidential*, April 29, 2005, https://www.africa-confidential.com/article-preview/id/1481/Merci%2c_Papa.

27 "Togo," *Freedom in the World 2020: A Leaderless Struggle for Democracy* (Freedom House, 2020), accessed February 27, 2024, https://freedomhouse.org/country/togo/freedom-world/2020

28 Note 2010 documentary, "la FrancAfrique," that asserted he was not, in fact the winner.

29 Jean Ping, a former Minister of Foreign Affairs under Omar Bongo, ran against Ali Bongo in 2016. Official results suggested he lost by just a handful of votes, but many observers believe those results were manipulated. Ping reportedly fathered two children with Pascaline Bongo. See "Gabon Election: Jean Ping Lays Claim to Presidency Win," *Al Jazeera*, August 29, 2016, https://www.aljazeera.com/news/2016/8/29/gabon-election-jean-ping-lays-claim-to-presidency-win.

30 Khalid Al Mouahidi, "Gabon: Noureddin Bongo Valentin Appointed to a Strategic Position in the Ruling Party," *MedaFrica*, March 11, 2022, https://medafricatimes.com/date/2022/03.

31 "Gabon's Opposition Leader Claims Coup is a 'Family Affair,'" *Africanews* with AP, September 1, 2023, https://www.africanews.com/2023/09/01/gabons-opposition-leader-claims-coup-is-a-family-affair/.

32 "Chad: Pre-Election Crackdown on Opponents," Human Rights Watch, April 8, 2021, https://www.hrw.org/news/2021/04/08/chad-pre-election-crackdown-opponents.

33 Vicky Stark, "Equatorial Guinea Vice President's Superyacht, Properties Seized in South Africa," *Voice of America*, February 16, 2023, https://www.voanews.com/a/equatorial-guinea-vice-president-s-superyacht-properties-seized-in-south-africa-/6966068.html.

34 "Equatorial Guinea Vice President's Superyacht."

35 "Uganda," Freedom on the Net 2022: Countering an Authoritarian Overhaul of the Internet (Freedom House, 2022), https://freedomhouse.org/country/uganda/freedom-net/2022.

36 Job Bwire, "I'm Tired of Waiting, I'll Stand for Presidency in 2026—Muhoozi," *The Monitor*, March 16, 2023, https://www.monitor.co.ug/uganda/news/national/i-m-tired-of-waiting-i-ll-stand-for-presidency-in-2026-muhoozi-4160712.

37 Musinguzi Blanshe, "Uganda: Between Muhoozi and Rwabwogo, Who Will succeed Museveni?" *Africa Report*, September 9, 2024, https://www.theafricareport.com/360778/uganda-between-muhoozi-and-rwabwogo-who-will-succeed-museveni/.

38 "Growing Family Dynasties Undermine Accountability, Encourage Corruption," *ADF Magazine*, last modified December 28, 2022, https://adf-magazine.com/2022/12/growing-family-dynasties-undermine-accountability-encourage-corruption/.

39 NP Admin, "Kagame Appoints Daughter 'presidential advisor,'" *NilePost*, August 2, 2023, https://nilepost.co.ug/news/166914/kagame-appoints-daughter-presidential-advisor.

40 Felix Kipkemoi, "Kagame's Son Ian Joins Presidential Security Team," *The Star*, January 18, 2023, https://www.the-star.co.ke/news/realtime/2023-01-18-kagames-son-ian-joins-presidential-security-team/.

41 Paul Melly, "Africa's Political Dynasties: How Presidents Groom Their Sons for Power," *BBC News*, May 29, 2021, https://www.bbc.com/news/world-africa-57176712.

42 National Intelligence Council, *Sub-Saharan Africa Pitched Contests for Democratization through 2022: A Global Trends Paper* (Washington, DC: National Intelligence Council, February 2018), https://www.dni.gov/files/images/globalTrends/documents/GT-Africa_Democratization_ForPublishing-WithCovers.pdf.

43 Some of these parties have changed names as a result of mergers, but none have ever ceded executive power to another party.

44 ZANU's earliest rival for political power in the new Zimbabwe was the Zimbabwe African People's Union, or ZAPU. Drawing strong support from specific ethnic constituencies in western areas of the country, particularly Matabeleland, ZAPU initially seemed poised to be a check on ZANU-PF's dominance. From 1983 to 1987, the ZANU-PF government neutralized this perceived threat through a campaign named Gukurahundi, in which a special military unit trained by North Korea killed some 20,000 civilians, torturing and detaining many more, in ZAPU strongholds. The current president of Zimbabwe, Emmerson Mnangagwa, was Minister for State Security during this period and is widely understood to have played a key role in executing the Gukurahundi campaign. No one has ever been held accountable for the abuses of the era, and the report of official inquiries into the matter has never been released to the public. The violence ended only with the absorption of ZAPU into ZANU, forming ZANU-PF.

45 Alex Vines, "Angola's Transition to Technocracy Won't Be Victimless," *Foreign Policy*, August 25, 2017, https://foreignpolicy.com/2017/08/25/angolas-transition-to-technocracy-wont-be-victimless/.

46 Dennis Jett, "Mozambique is a Failed State. The West Isn't Helping It," *Foreign Policy*, March 7, 2020, https://foreignpolicy.com/2020/03/07/mozambique-is-a-failed-state-the-west-isnt-helping-it/.

47 International Election Observation Mission, "IRI Preliminary Statement of the 2024 Mozambique General and Provincial Assembly Elections," International Republican Institute, October 11, 2024, https://www.iri.org/resources/iri-releases-preliminary-statement-on-mozambiques-general-election-o-iri-divulga-declaracao-preliminar-sobre-as-eleicoes-gerais-de-mocambique/.

48 The CCM was created in from the merger of TANU, the Tanganyika African National Union, and the Afro Shirazi Party of Zanzibar, in 1977.

49 Julius K. Nyerere, *Democracy and the Party System* (Dar es Salaam: Tanganyika Standard Limited), 1963.

50 "National cake" is a fascinating and widely used term in Nigerian political discourse and analysis, vividly describing the particular type of rentier state politics practiced in the country. See, for example: Jean-François Maystadt and Muhammad-Kabir Salihu, "National or Political Cake? The Political Economy of Intergovernmental Transfers in Nigeria," *Journal of Economic Geography* 19, no. 5 (September 2019): 1119–42, https://doi.org/10.1093/jeg/lby032.

51 Linnet Hamasi, "Political Parties, Democracy, and the 2022 Kenyan Elections," *Kujenga Amani*, August 5, 2022, https://kujenga-amani.ssrc.org/2022/08/05/political-parties-democracy-and-the-2022-kenyan-elections/.

52 William Reno, "Fictional States and Atomized Public Spheres: A Non-Western Approach to Fragility," *Daedalus* 146, no. 4 (Fall 2017).

53 See, for example, recent polling from Uganda highlighting citizens' feelings on the trajectory of the country, run by *Afrobarometer*; Francis Kibirige, "Summary of Results: Afrobarometer Round 9 Survey in Uganda, 2022," *Afrobarometer*, 2023, https://www.afrobarometer.org/publication/uganda-round-9-summary-of-results/.

54 Marianne Saddier, "The Upright Citizens of Burkina Faso," *Africa Is a Country*, October 1, 2014, https://africasacountry.com/2014/10/the-citizens-of-burkina-faso/.

55 Michelle Gavin, "The Roots of Burkina Faso's Crisis," *Africa in Transition*, Council on Foreign Relations, November 19, 2019, https://www.cfr.org/blog/roots-burkina-fasos-crisis.

56 Marie-Soleil Frère and Pierre Englebert, "Briefing: Burkina Faso—The Fall of Blaise Compaoré," *African Affairs* 114, no. 455 (2015): 295–307, https://doi.org/10.1093/afraf/adv010.

57 Gavin, "Roots of Burkina Faso's Crisis."

58 For a discussion of Abiy Ahmed's vision for Ethiopia, see Tom Gardner's *The Abiy Project: God, Power, and War in the New Ethiopia* (London: Hurst Publishers, 2024).

59 Ishaan Tharoor, "5 Crazy Things about the Gambian Dictator Who Just Survived a Coup Attempt," *Washington Post*, January 6, 2015, https://www.washingtonpost.com/news/worldviews/wp/2015/01/06/5-crazy-things-about-the-gambian-dictator-who-just-survived-a-coup-attempt/.

60 Sait Matty Jaw, "WhatsApp, Youth and Politics in the Gambia: An Analysis of 'Democratic Gambia'" in *WhatsApp and Everyday Life in West Africa*, ed. Idayat Hassan and Jamie Hitchen (London: Zed Books, 2022).

61 Thomas Naadi, "Gambia after Yahya Jammeh: 'I'll never get justice,'" *BBC News*, July 13, 2022, https://www.bbc.com/news/world-africa-61864383.

62 Michelle Gavin, "America's Failure of Imagination in Sudan," *Foreign Affairs*, February 4, 2022, https://www.foreignaffairs.com/articles/sudan/2022-02-04/america-sudan-bashir-military-coup.

2

YOUNG, URBAN, AND CONNECTED

[A focus on youth] was a way of accessing broader conversations about power: who had it, who did not, and how to wield it to change the world.[1]

— HOLLY V. SCOTT, *YOUNGER THAN THAT NOW*

When Americans think about young people affecting politics, today we might reflect on youth movements aimed at addressing gun violence or demanding action on climate change. But for most of my life, "youth politics" called to mind images and stories from the counterculture and antiwar movements of the late 1960s, when a portion of the large, "baby boomer" generation publicly and sometimes flamboyantly rejected the social mores of their parents and denounced the draft of the Vietnam War. This is a narrative etched in popular culture that grows more complex with examination; not all young people of the era shared political views or even an interest in political engagement.[2] But the sense of a surging generation, empowered by their sheer numbers and driven by a different vision of American society, clearly animated the politics of the time.

The youth populations in most of Africa today are far larger. In 1968, Americans fifteen to twenty-four comprised about 23 percent of the adult population in the country. In at least a dozen African states, the cohort of people aged fifteen to twenty-four is equivalent to at least 60 percent of the adult population. For comparison, Egypt's fifteen to twenty-four population in 2011, when many analysts were pointing to a youth bulge as a driver of its Arab Spring uprising, was less than a third of the adult population. While other regions of the world have gone through a demographic transition that included a period of low mortality rates and high fertility, Africa's circumstances are unique in their sheer scale. According to UN projections,[3] in the century spanning from 1950 and 2050, Asia's population will nearly quadruple, and Latin America's will grow by about 4.4 times. Africa's will grow by over ten times, from about 228 million

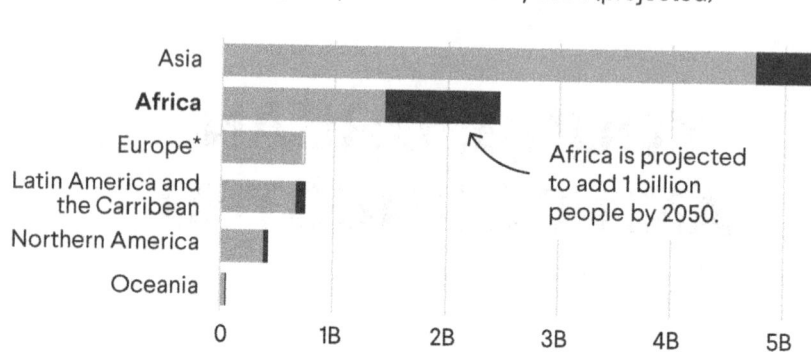

Figure 2.1 Africa is Growing Much Faster than Other Regions.
Credit: Will Merrow, Council on Foreign Relations, Source: UN Population Division, Department of Economic and Social Affairs.

people in 1950 to a projected 2.5 billion by 2050 (see Figure 2.1). At that point, the number of Africans under the age of twenty-four will be roughly equal to the entire region's population today.[4] Over half of the world's total population growth through 2050 will happen in sub-Saharan Africa.[5]

Of course, "youth" can be defined in different ways. Most UN organizations and demographers consider people aged fifteen through twenty-four to fall into this category. The African Union (AU) uses a broader cohort spanning from fifteen though thirty-four. Individual African countries and political parties often use other parameters. But any set of boundaries is imperfect, given the reality that many Africans will enter the labor force sometime during their "youth" years, not to mention the fact that one can be over a dozen years past society's median age and still be considered a youth by the AU. In some societies, formal definitions are less meaningful than social norms, and achieving the social status of "adult" requires financial resources to support oneself and a partner, as well as land or housing. As Honwana wrote, "at ten a child soldier is an adult, at thirty, an unemployed and unmarried man is still a youth."[6] Marc Sommers has written movingly about the plight of young people who cannot amass the resources to "grow up" even as the years tick by, finding themselves stuck in a seemingly endless adolescence.[7] But the conventional definitions are useful for thinking about politics, as political awareness and activism may well precede finishing one's education, getting a job, or even reaching the age of enfranchisement (which is eighteen in most African societies).

The jaw-dropping growth of African populations is not new; it has been happening for decades. As public health measures have greatly reduced infant and child mortality, years of high fertility rates and better disease control have created a population explosion not expected to dissipate for decades to come. That means that despite optimistic approaches to the numbers that paint African demographics as a development opportunity to be seized—the African Union even went so far as to declare 2017 the *Year of Harnessing the Demographic Dividend Through Investments in Youth*—many African countries are nowhere near the moment of opportunity when they might seize upon a "demographic dividend," a phenomenon that swelled labor forces and drove growth in newly industrializing countries of East Asia from 1960 to 2000. The dividend accrues when birth rates come down, creating an age structure in which there are relatively few dependents (children and elders) compared to the most economically productive segment of society, working-age adults. Instead, with high fertility rates persisting, African countries skewed toward the younger end of the age spectrum for many years, with median ages of under twenty (the median age in the United States is about thirty-eight) and roughly 40 percent of the total population composed of children (fourteen and under). This extended period of the demographic transition's youthful phase is recognized for its fundamentally unstable nature. As demographer Richard Cincotta writes, "constrained by an age structure that relentlessly augments that demand for jobs, schooling, and other vital services and infrastructure, countries in the transition's youthful phase typically fail to generate the capacity to meet their citizens' most basic demands."[8]

Of course, there are exceptions. As noted in the introduction, North Africa is distinct, demographically speaking, from the rest of the region, and northern African societies are far less youth-heavy than their neighbors to the south. A number of southern African countries—particularly Botswana, Namibia, and South Africa—demographically resemble the northern tier, with lower fertility and population growth rates (See Map 2.1). This is also true of many island countries in the region. Overall, the fertility rate has been declining throughout sub-Saharan Africa, from 6.3 in 1990 to 4.5 in 2023. This broad trend masks large variations: in 2023 Niger's fertility rate was 6.7; it was less than 3.5 in Kenya and Zimbabwe. So, change is coming, but it is coming slowly, and as long as fertility remains well above the replacement level of 2.1, these societies will continue to grow, and to be disproportionately young.

The pace of population growth cannot help but be dislocating. During Paul Biya's long tenure as president of Cameroon, the country's population has grown from nine million people to about twenty-eight million. President Museveni came to power when Uganda was a country of a little more than fifteen million; today he leads a country of over forty-nine million people. If some of Africa's politics have been stagnant for decades, the same cannot be said of African societies. Africa's burgeoning youth population means that governments confront a colossal education and job-creation challenge, and new strains on natural resources and competition for land.

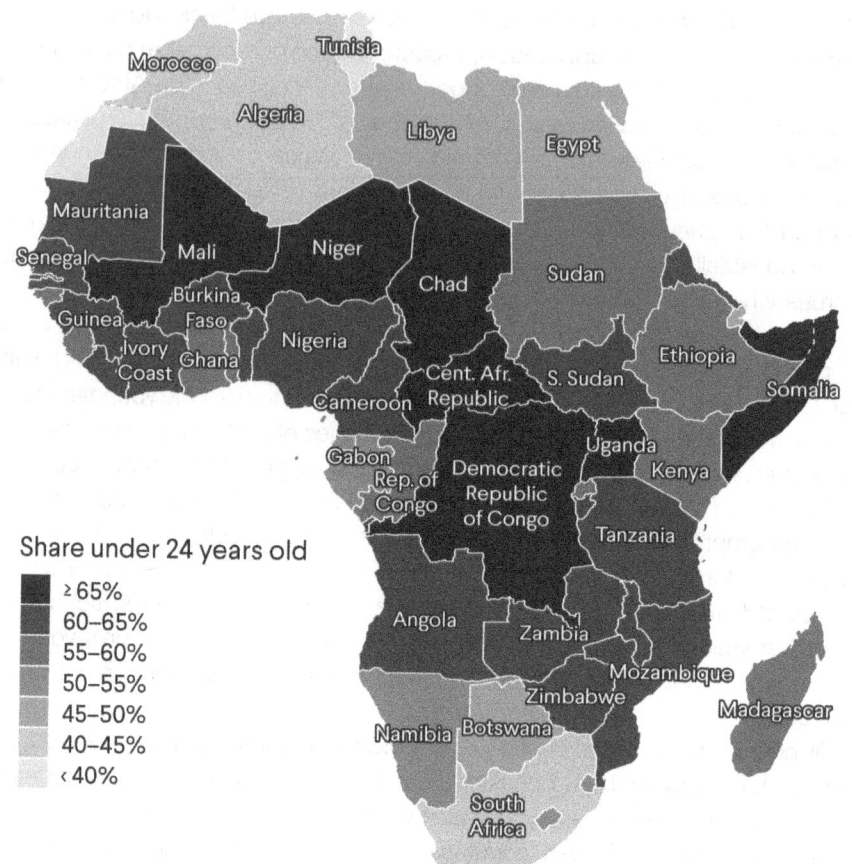

Map 2.1 Which African Countries Have the Youngest Populations?
Credit: Will Merrow, Council on Foreign Relations, Source: UN Population Division, Department of Economic and Social Affairs.

Urban Challenges

These growing populations are also reorganizing themselves, increasingly clustering in urban areas. Africa is not just the fastest-growing region globally; it is also the most rapidly urbanizing. By the end of the century, thirteen of the world's twenty largest cities by population will be African.[9] Far sooner, by 2035, most Africans will live in cities.[10] The OECD projects that the continent's cities will grow by 950 million people by 2050, meaning that two-thirds of population gains in Africa over the next thirty years will be urban,[11] in both mega-cities like Lagos and Kinshasa, and in secondary cities like Kisumu, Kenya and Huambo, Angola. Most of these gains will come from natural population growth, not migration from rural areas driven by manufacturing jobs as occurred in Asia and elsewhere. Even if governments wanted to discourage urban growth, they would be hard pressed to slow it in the decades ahead.

Again, the aggregate numbers conceal vast divergences. Already some 67 percent of Angolans live in cities, while only 14 percent of Burundians do. Some parts of Africa remain predominantly rural. But in addition to Angolans, over half of the populations of Botswana, Cabo Verde, Cameroon, Cote d'Ivoire, Djibouti, Equatorial Guinea, Gabon, Ghana, the Gambia, Liberia, Mauritania, Namibia, Nigeria, the Republic of the Congo, and South Africa live in urban centers by World Bank measurements,[12] with Benin, the Democratic Republic of Congo, Mali, Senegal, Somalia, and Zambia just on the verge of crossing this threshold (see Figure 2.2).

This urbanizing trend creates new governing challenges, as the needs for affordable housing, water and sanitation infrastructure, public health institutions, electricity, viable transportation options, effective policing, and, perhaps most vitally, employment opportunities in the formal sector become more and more urgent on the national agenda. It's not just that a majority of Africans will live in cities by 2035. So too will a majority of Africa's poor.[13] Africa's economic growth has not been accompanied by commensurate job creation, and too many city dwellers are caught in an urban poverty trap, in which poor transportation networks and insufficiently skilled labor create high costs but low incomes.[14] Living in informal settlements and working in the informal economy, city dwellers at the lower end of the socioeconomic spectrum will not be unaware of their

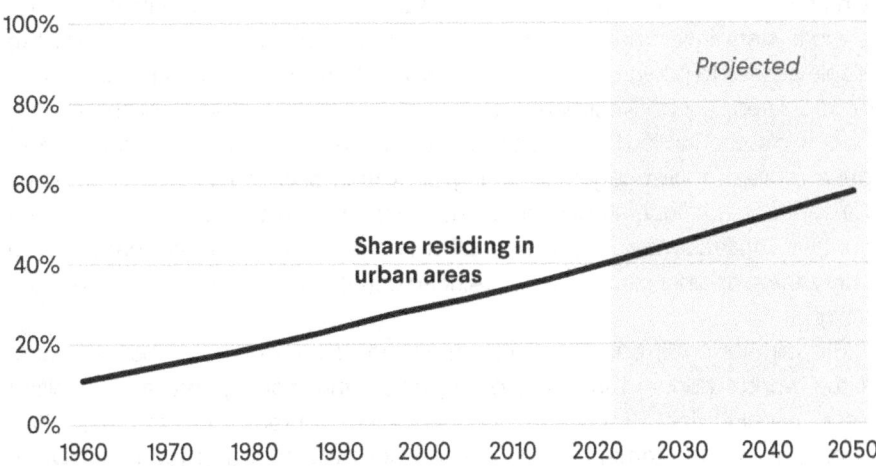

Figure 2.2 By 2050, Africa Will Have a Majority-Urban Population.
Credit: Will Merrow, Council on Foreign Relations, Source: UN Population Division, Department of Economic and Social Affairs.

relative status as they struggle to build a life amid fellow citizens whose standard of living is far higher. Even those fortunate enough to find formal employment struggle, because urban housing markets are underdeveloped and dysfunctional. In all but a handful of countries in the region, teachers or police officers cannot afford the mortgage for even the cheapest newly built house.[15]

The economic context in which these young, urban populations find themselves is tailor-made to accelerate frustration. The rosy, oversimplified forecasts of the "Africa Rising" narrative of the early 2000s era are long gone. Even when GDP growth was strong, surging population growth at the same time made for underwhelming per capita gains. But it is also true that growth rates were falling for the decade before the COVID-19 pandemic and the economic disruption prompted by the crises in Ukraine and Gaza.[16] Those external factors created even more hardship, prompting governments to take out additional loans and households to manage shrinking employment opportunities and eroded savings just as prices were rising, driving up the cost of living. The African Development Bank warned that soaring food and energy prices could trigger significant social unrest, even as the bank predicted solid growth in a number of African countries in the near term.[17]

The disconnect between growth and employment will persist. The industrial sector in Africa grew by only 1 percent as a share of total jobs in the period from 2000 to 2019, while the services sector grew by 9 percent and the agricultural sector shrank a commensurate amount.[18] These numbers do not suggest economies transforming to accommodate massive new labor forces. Such a transformation would require surging increases in the quantity and quality of jobs being created—a particularly challenging task in an age of automation—as well as more state investment in education and investments in infrastructure, like reliable access to power, that raise labor productivity and enable value addition.[19] But too often, such investments are out of reach. In the wake of the COVID pandemic's economic dislocations, many African governments were forced to spend more of their budgets servicing debt than serving citizens.[20] The result is a widespread underemployment and unemployment crisis that affects the youngest Africans most—their unemployment rate is nearly twice that of those twenty-three or older, and in thirteen African countries, it is more than three times as high.[21]

The climate crisis adds another dimension of pressure on urban Africans. Of the world's hundred fastest-growing cities, the majority that are classified "extremely high risk" for climate stress are African. From rising sea levels and flooding in Lagos, Lome, and Abidjan to desertification and food and water shortages threatening Nairobi, changing climatic conditions are heightening the urban competition for resources—even as they drive rural to urban migration, further swelling informal settlements and adding to the challenges of urban governance.[22]

Urban social safety nets require governing capacity, particularly at the municipal level, and resources. But very few African countries allow for direct election of municipal leadership, creating convoluted patterns of accountability between urban residents and governing authorities.[23] Where urban populations have thrown their support to alternatives to the status quo, the existing power structure has pushed back. In 2009, when a breath of political fresh air emerged in the Mozambican city of Beira in the form of a new political party led by the city's directly elected mayor, longtime ruling party Frelimo acted to contain the threat. Mayor Daviz Simango had positioned himself as "the champion of young, educated Mozambicans who face scant chances of getting a job unless they have friends at the top of Frelimo"[24] and eventually he and his party went on to contest national-level elections. But by 2018, Frelimo had pushed through constitutional changes that replaced direct mayoral elections with indirect ones. In Zimbabwe, the opposition Movement for Democratic Change, and its successor, the Citizens Coalition for Change, continue to find success in Zimbabwe's municipal elections, only to then face repeated efforts on the part of the ruling ZANU-PF to thwart their governing authority by having the Minister of Local Government intervene to suspend elected mayors.[25]

Still, despite efforts to squelch cities' desire for change, historically, urban areas in Africa are hotbeds of opposition support. Political organizing is easier in cities than among widely dispersed rural dwellers. Urbanites are more likely to have access to independent media and tend to receive more education than citizens in rural areas.[26] Robin Harding found that from 2005 to 2015, urban residents in African countries surveyed by *Afrobarometer* were between 5 and 7 percentage points less likely to support incumbent authorities than their rural counterparts.[27] Amaka Anku and Tochi Eni-Kalu noted that urban Kenyans, Nigerians, and South Africans were more likely than rural dwellers to identify corruption and economic management as major concerns.[28] As competition for jobs and resources in cities increases, this pattern of anti-incumbent sentiment and frustration with the status quo is likely to persist.

Collective action, like demonstrations and protests, is easier in cities where proximity to sources of political and economic power can also make it more threatening to existing governments.[29] The enduring image of 2024's protest movement in Kenya, which involved mobilizations in cities around the country, will be that of the parliament building aflame. Evidence shows a dramatic increase in protests in the region since 2010. The Armed Conflict Location and Event Data Project recorded 34,513 protest events in Africa from 2011 to 2020, an increase from 5,123 in the previous decade.[30] Lisa Mueller has convincingly argued that this surge is a function of both a desire for political change among protest leaders and a demand for economic opportunity among the urban poor.[31]

It is also possible that cities can make political appeals based on identity politics less compelling, as urban dwellers are more likely to have exposure to fellow citizens with different ethnic, linguistic, or religious backgrounds. Cosmopolitanism can potentially make it harder to drum up support by scapegoating "others" as the source of social or economic ills. In systems where political parties are surrogates for specific identity groups rather than standard bearers for a specific platform of governing ideas, this makes campaigning effectively in cities more challenging—and potentially more incendiary, as it can require pitting neighbor against neighbor rather than a whole community against a distant region. The terror unleashed by youth gangs organized around ethnic lines in Nairobi after the 2007 elections and the violence in Abidjan in 2010 and 2011 remains a notorious example of how wrong these dynamics can go.

New Connections

If young populations and urbanization are driving popular demands that governments cannot meet, technology is providing new tools for political expression and action. According to the International Telecommunications Union, in 2020 only 29 percent of people in sub-Saharan Africa were using the internet—but 92 out of every 100 people had a mobile cellular subscription.[32] Industry group GSMA estimates that 40 percent of the region's adult population are connected to mobile internet services, and another 44 percent live in areas covered by mobile broadband networks.[33] What is not up for debate is the overall trendline; Africa is becoming more digitally connected by the day, and the already rapid pace of growth gained even more momentum in the wake of the COVID-19 pandemic and accompanying shifts to remote work, e-commerce, and virtual interactions (see Figure 2.3).[34] Once again, the figures conceal tremendous variability across the region, from 1 percent of citizens with internet access in closed-off Eritrea to 70 percent in South Africa.[35] But any traveler to one of the region's major cities can see the ubiquity of mobile phones all around them, just as anyone interested in African politics is doubtlessly following a range of African analysts, journalists, and leaders on social media.

While analysts often think of social media as an elite space, conversations that begin in the digital sphere do not stay there (see Figure 2.4). In West Africa, researchers have found that content on WhatsApp is communicated beyond the application's user base, shaping traditional media coverage, and informing community leaders who share messages, and sometimes their phones themselves, with others.[36] Research from Zambia has reached a similar conclusion, indicating that political content on social media reaches far beyond actual social media users, becoming part of word-of-mouth discourse and spreading offline.[37]

Responses to "how often do you use the internet?" in a survey of twenty-nine African countries

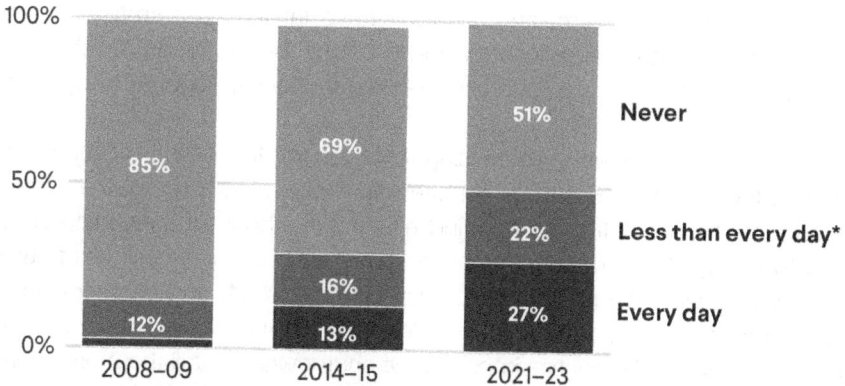

*Includes "a few times a week," "a few times a month," and "less than once a month"

Figure 2.3 An Increasing Share of Africans Use the Internet Daily
(Note: Responses of "don't know" and "refused" are not shown). *Credit: Will Merrow, Council on Foreign Relations, Source: Afrobarometer.*

Responses to "how often do you get news from the followng sources?" in a survey of twenty-nine African countries, by age group

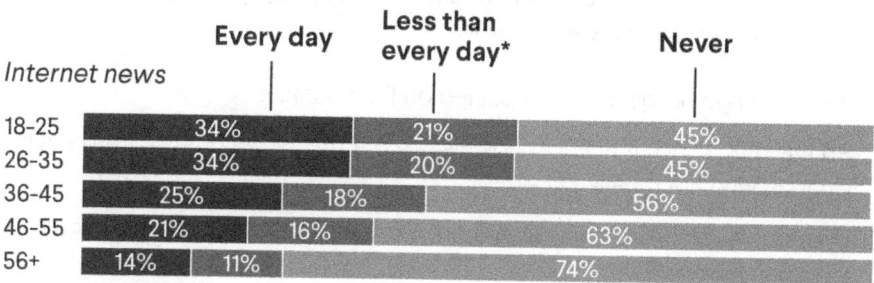

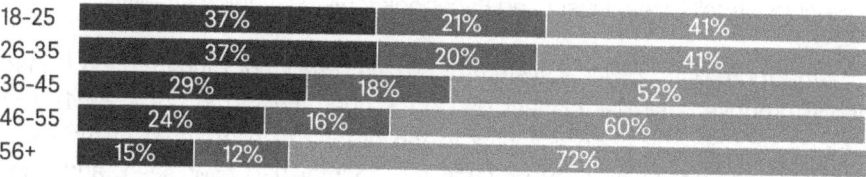

*Includes "a few times a week," "a few times a month," and "less than once a month"

Figure 2.4 Most Young Africans Get News from the Internet and Social Media
(Note: Responses of "don't know" and "refused" are not shown). *Credit: Will Merrow, Council on Foreign Relations, Source: Afrobarometer.*

By the end of 2020, over 233 million Africans subscribed to Facebook,[38] the most popular social media platform in the region (although messaging services like WhatsApp are probably used even more).[39] Other platforms, including X (formerly Twitter), Instagram, and YouTube have far less penetration, but in some countries can be significant; in Kenya, YouTube outpaces Facebook.[40] As of early 2023 TikTok was growing rapidly in Kenya, Nigeria, and South Africa as well.[41]

Repressive governments' increasing enthusiasm for internet censorship and shutdowns[42] indicates how threatening these tools are to the status quo and reveals that citizens often find effective methods of subverting state efforts to control the flow of information. The region experienced twenty-two state-mandated internet shutdowns or disruptions in 2021, and another nine in 2022, a decrease largely attributable to the smaller number of elections slated for that calendar year.[43] Authorities imposed the shutdowns to stall the momentum of protests, or to assert control in times of civil conflict or political challenge. But their attempts to control digital speech had limited effect. President Museveni of Uganda went so far as to ban Facebook outright in early 2021, incensed by the platform's removal of some government accounts found to be manipulating the online discourse in advance of elections.[44] Many Ugandans began using VPNs, and while Twitter/X usage spiked, Facebook remains one of the most popular social media platforms in the country.[45] When Museveni said in December 2022 that Facebook could return if the company would "stop playing games,"[46] the online response in Uganda was derisive.

> Just 4hrs ago his government posted on Facebook.
>
> So this man thinks that Facebook loses more than small business owners in Uganda who are mostly the youth.
>
> Uganda police will post this statement using their official Facebook page (crying laughing emoji)
>
> And he thinks he is in charge when we are using it
>
> Should we tell Mzee. I just used Facebook (crying laughing emoji)[47]

In the more open political system of Nigeria, President Muhammadu Buhari tried to impose a similar blanket ban on X (then Twitter) in June 2021. The platform had already been essential to the organization of some of the most significant anti-police brutality protests the country had ever seen, and one-fifth of the country's massive population has an X account.[48] Twitter removed one of Buhari's own posts, finding that it violated the platform's content rules regarding inciting violence. Buhari had posted, in reference to an insurgency in the country's southeast,

> Many of those misbehaving today are too young to be aware of the destruction and loss of lives that occurred during the Nigerian Civil War. Those of us in the fields for 30 months, who went through the war, will treat them in the language they understand.[49]

Nigerians reacted to the ban by migrating to other platforms or using VPNs; one civil society organization even took the government to a subregional court, where the Economic Community of West African States (ECOWAS) court declared that the ban illegally violated provisions both of the African Charter and the International Covenant on Civil and Political Rights.[50] Seven months after the ban was imposed, it was lifted.

What is clear from these suppression attempts, and legal skirmishes, is that the digital space in the region is both contested and increasingly politically consequential. In Kenya's 2021 election, digital campaign spending surpassed spending on legacy media.[51] As with urban experiences, online experiences have the potential to temper the toxicity of identity politics, providing an opportunity to "allow individuals to publicly surmount differences to create communities of collaboration around various issues which in turn undercuts the apparent immutability of [ethnic] identities."[52] But they can also worsen divisions, creating and reinforcing narratives that vilify others or heighten perceptions of persecution. For Ethiopians, the ethnic demonization that accompanied online discourse domestically and in the diaspora when the 2020–2 Tigray war broke out was a horrifying case in point.[53] As we will see in Chapter 6, Africa's online political discourse is as susceptible to misinformation and disinformation as it has proven to be in the United States and elsewhere.

The digital revolution has brought more access to information—reliable and less so—to more African citizens than ever before, fueling new demands for accountability, enabling political organizing, and creating greater awareness of alternative governance models and practices. From digital tracking of government budgets and expenditures that allows citizens to compare real-life results with funds allocated, to investigative journalism published on social media to evade censorship, tech-savvy young Africans are using the tools at their disposal to shine a light on long-standing practices that do not serve the public interest. During recent elections in Zimbabwe, Nigeria, and the Democratic Republic of the Congo, young voters shared videos of irregular practices at polling places and of precinct-level results in real time, providing a counterpoint to mistrusted electoral authorities. As Nyabola observes, "young Africans are embracing technology and digital platforms as spaces to have their opinions articulated and amplified, as well as to speak directly to Power in their respective societies."⁵⁴

They are also learning from each other in a new, digital, Pan-African conversation. Nigeria's #EndSARS movement prompted activism against police brutality in countries around the continent, and Zambian elections that ousted an increasingly authoritarian incumbent inspired new conversations on how these tactics could be emulated elsewhere. Online coordination can result in offline collective action; protests on March 20, 2023, in Kenya, South Africa, Nigeria, and Tunisia were informed by different political contexts, but were planned to coincide, as a collective show of frustration with existing authorities and the status quo.⁵⁵

Certainly, the Arab Spring protests of 2010–12 inspired activists throughout Africa, just as they alarmed African leaders. African information environments are increasingly globalized,⁵⁶ meaning that Africans are increasingly connected not just to others in their societies, but to others across the continent and around the world. In 2020, Sipho Kings and Simon Allison launched *The Continent*, a PDF newspaper with Pan-African coverage made to be read on a phone and accessible via WhatsApp, Signal, or Telegram. By 2021 it was the most widely read newspaper in Africa, and surveys have shown that 75 percent of readers routinely share the publication with their own WhatsApp networks.⁵⁷

Given the staggering numbers, it's easy to see how appealing to young voters could provide political candidates a strong advantage at the ballot box. From George Weah in Liberia, who effectively used his background as a star soccer player to mobilize youthful excitement for his candidacy in 2017, to William Ruto in Kenya, who vowed to represent the "hustler nation" of young people eking out a living in the informal economy—power seekers are appealing to youth. But delivering on promises and meetings expectations is a far more difficult proposition.

African states are now numerically dominated by young people whose hunger for education, housing, and job opportunities would be difficult for even the most capable and well-resourced government to sate. Polls consistently show that young Africans want their governments to prioritize efforts to address unemployment, followed by health, education, and infrastructure.⁵⁸ They also show that only 28 percent of Africans feel their government is currently doing a good job in responding to the needs of youth, with numbers clocking in as low as 9 percent in Sudan and 11 percent in Gabon.⁵⁹ But most African economies are small relative to the rest of the world, and even the way these small pies are divided often does not reflect the salience of youth issues.

For example, of the fifty countries in the world that spend the smallest portion of their national budget on education, roughly half are African. To be sure, no region of the world is fully hitting the targets agreed upon by UNESCO member states since 2015, namely, 4 to 6 percent of GDP or 15 to 20 percent of total public expenditure. But no region has such a large proportion of school-age citizens, either. On average, sub-Saharan Africa is spending about 3.4 percent of GDP on education. In Uganda, where 44 percent of the population is under the age of fifteen, the state spends 2.6 percent of GDP. In Tanzania, 3.2 percent, and in Angola, 2.4 percent. As always, there is not one African story; Kenya boasts an impressive 5.1 percent.[60] But there is another problem. The resources that are being devoted to education are not delivering the desired results; in fact, the region has the worst education spending efficiency in the world.[61]

Sizable investments in youth priorities may be scarce, but symbolic commitments abound. The African Youth Charter,[62] adopted in 2006, is full of laudable sentiments, and the AU has a Special Envoy on Youth—a somewhat curious development given that youth comprise the vast majority of the entire continent. From marginalizing "youth wings" of political parties to "youth councils" that have no decision-making or budgetary authority and "youth ministries" with relatively small budgets and even smaller ambitions, the formal structures focused on young people are underwhelming at best.

There is little evidence that these youth-focused entities are delivering results. A recent study of "national youth strategies" around the world found that they have very little practical effect in terms of improving the civic and political engagement of young people, in part because implementation is rarely a priority. The same study found that "youth wings" could increase the numbers of young people within a political party, but that the quality of youth political participation was far from guaranteed. "Where political systems are characterized by political patronage or violence, political leaders reward loyalty and control youth wing activity, while denying substantive youth contributions to party agendas."[63] While young, transformative leaders have played an important role in African history,[64] in recent years young people have all too often been marginalized by self-serving elites.

Some countries have experimented with youth quotas in legislatures or on party candidate slates, but the overall level of youth representation in government remains paltry when considered against the backdrop of their demographic might. The International Parliamentary Union reports that as of 2023, only 2.17 percent of parliamentary seats in sub-Saharan African governments were held by people aged thirty or under, and just 20.25 percent were held by those forty or under.[65] Movements like Nigeria's Not Too Young To Run, which helped to lower the minimum age eligibility requirements for officeholders in the country, have had some real success, even spawning similar efforts elsewhere in the region. From its inception in 2016 to the signing of the Not Too Young to Run bill into Nigerian law in May 2018, it was a model of effective youth advocacy. But structural barriers, including the cost of campaigning and opaque party nominating systems, remain serious impediments to youth in government.

Thus, young populations that are solid majorities but treated like a narrow interest group are predisposed to find their governments unresponsive. They have varied political identities and ideologies rather than a cohesive political agenda, but young urban populations will have a set of desires and needs that will be difficult for government to satisfy, prompting more enthusiasm for political alternatives. Dissatisfaction is evident in survey data. Young people across the region indicate that they believe their countries are on the wrong track,[66] and the US National Intelligence Council expects this gloominess to persist, noting that "pessimism is likely to spread in developing countries with large youthful populations but with slowing progress in eradicating poverty and meeting human development needs, particularly Sub-Saharan Africa."[67] With the tools to compare their circumstances to those of others in their digital networks and to learn from others' experiences, young people in these circumstances are natural supporters of "change" agendas.

It's important not to conflate this pessimism and frustration with overall perceptions of Africa or African-ness. Young Africans are as frustrated with media narratives that depict their home continent in undifferentiated, and largely negative, terms as they are with unresponsive governments.[68] The same online discourse that allows young people to commiserate about poor service delivery, out-of-touch leadership, and elite corruption also creates space to skewer stereotypes about the continent, reject patronizing media coverage, and assert Pan-African pride and identity.

If much generational change scholarship is premised on the notion that people value most highly those things that were relatively scarce in their formative years,[69] then it is no surprise that young people coming of age in authoritarian systems like Sudan or the absolute monarchy of Eswatini are fervent supporters of democracy. Or, that those embarking on adulthood in an atmosphere of insecurity—with no lived experience of any past military governments—are less certain about rejecting military rule than their seniors. What passes for democracy in many countries— regular election exercises in authoritarian or competitive authoritarian systems—is not delivering the results young people want to see; they are less satisfied with the way democracy is working than their elders.[70] In places like Gabon and Uganda, democracy, as understood locally, is simply a less attractive form of government to the youngest adults than the rest of the public.[71]

Overall, polls show that young people want government to be more responsive and effective. But in most African countries, young people are less likely to formally participate in the political system. Young Africans vote less than their elders— sometimes by very wide margins, as in Cote d'Ivoire, Tanzania, Cameroon, and Gabon.[72] The scholarship of Daniel Stockemer and Aksel Sundström[73] points to "a paradox of legitimacy" plaguing strategies used around the world ostensibly aimed at increasing the political participation of young people. Stockemer and

Sundström found that distrust can poison the well from the outset in a vicious cycle. "Political elites and institutions are often not responsive to the interests of young citizens. This lack of responsiveness leads to youth disillusionment and disengagement with political and civic institutions, which in turn leads elites to further ignore their demands."[74] Again, because Africa is complex and diverse, there are exceptions. Young people were largely responsible for Zambian President Hakainde Hichilema's electoral victory in 2021, young activists have kept pressure on Sudanese military and political elites in the protracted battle over the country's transition by forming their own formalized, though decentralized, consultative processes, and young Senegalese swept the continent's youngest president into power in 2024.

Opting out of the formalized processes should not be confused with political apathy. As the chapters ahead will demonstrate, young Africans may simply not believe that an electoral process will change anything, having lived through electoral cycles that seemed to have no effect on their lives save, too often, for increased insecurity around the election period. They may believe that the fix is in, and the process is simply theater, or have no desire to support the political choices available to them at the ballot box. It's telling that among the most popular recent tweets in Angola was simply, "The solution for the country is not in the hands of the MPLA or UNITA."[75] Its popularity was boosted by Thiago Costa, an Angolan comedian, who simply responded with a popular GIF of actress Meryl Streep applauding enthusiastically. In a digital space, plucking from a global meme, Angolans embraced the notion that the political solution the country needs is something entirely new, not leadership of the perennially ruling party or its longtime antagonist.

Youth, urbanization, and digitization are changing the makeup of African societies and the way they engage in their political systems. These factors are converging with another powerful trend that points to change: the diminishing potency of established political narratives in the region.

Notes

1. Holly V. Scott, *Younger than That Now: The Politics of Age in the 1960s* (Amherst: University of Massachusetts Press, 2016), 2.
2. For an excellent discussion of the power and limits of "youth" politics in the 1960s, see Scott, *Younger than That Now*.
3. Note that all the demographic numbers come from the UN 2022 Revision of World Population Prospects.

4   For an outstanding discussion of Africa's singular demographic profile, see Edward Paice, *YouthQuake: Why Africa Demography Should Matter to the World* (London: Bloomsbury Publishing, 2023).

5   United Nations, "Global Issues—Population," accessed March 29, 2024, https://www.un.org/en/global-issues/population#:~:text=More%20than%20half%20of%20global,projected%20to%20double%20by%202050.

6   Alcinda M. Honwana, *The Time of Youth: Work, Social Change, and Politics in Africa* (Boulder, CO: Kumarian Press, 2012), 5.

7   Marc Sommers, *Stuck: Rwandan Youth and the Struggle for Adulthood* (Athens: University of Georgia Press, 2012), http://www.jstor.org/stable/j.ctt46nngqw.

8   Richard Cincotta, "Predicting the Rise and Demise of Liberal Democracy: How Well Did We Do?" *New Security Beat*, August 17, 2021, https://www.newsecuritybeat.org/2021/08/predicting-rise-demise-liberal-democracy/.

9   Max Bearak, "How Africa Will Become the Center of the World's Urban Future," *Washington Post*, November 19, 2021, https://www.washingtonpost.com/world/interactive/2021/africa-cities/.

10 OECD/UN ECA/AfDB, *Africa's Urbanisation Dynamics 2022: The Economic Power of Africa's Cities*, West African Studies (Paris: OECD Publishing, 2022), https://doi.org/10.1787/3834ed5b-en.

11 OECD, *Africa's Urbanisation Dynamics 2022*.

12 United Nations, "World Urbanization Prospects 2018," Department of Economic and Social Affairs Population Dynamics, 2022, https://population.un.org/wup/.

13 OECD, *Africa's Urbanisation Dynamics 2022*.

14 Somik Vinay Lall, J. Vernon Henderson, and Anthony J. Venables, *Africa's Cities: Opening Doors to the World* (Washington, DC: World Bank Group, 2017), https://documents1.worldbank.org/curated/en/854221490781543956/pdf/113851-PUB-PUBLIC-PUBDATE-2-9-2017.pdf.

15 *Yearbook: Housing Finance in Africa* (Johannesburg: Centre for Affordable Housing Finance in Africa, 2023), https://housingfinanceafrica.org/app/uploads/2023/10/2023-CAHF-Yb_Compressed-14.11.2023.pdf.

16 Mayowa Kuyoro, Acha Leke, Olivia White, et al., "Reimagining Economic Growth in Africa: Turning Diversity into Opportunity," McKinsey Global Institute, June 5, 2023, https://www.mckinsey.com/mgi/our-research/reimagining-economic-growth-in-africa-turning-diversity-into-opportunity.

17 African Development Bank, *Africa's Macroeconomic Performance and Outlook January 2024* (Abidjan: African Development Bank, 2024), 29, https://www.afdb.org/en/documents/africas-macroeconomic-performance-and-outlook-january-2024.

18 Kuyoro, Leke, White, et al., "Reimagining Economic Growth."

19 Valerijs Rezvijs, Satyam Panday, and Tatiana Lyseno, *Sub-Saharan Africa's Demographic Transition: A Window of Opportunity for Growth* (New York: S&P Global Ratings, August 2021), 7, https://www.spglobal.com/_assets/documents/ratings/research/100344423.pdf.

20 United Nations, *A World of Debt: A Growing Burden to Global Prosperity* (Geneva: United Nations Global Crisis Response Group, July 2023), https://doi.org/10.18356/29589304-4.

21 Mo Ibrahim Foundation, *2022 Ibrahim Index of African Governance—Index Report* (London: Mo Ibrahim Foundation, January 2023), https://assets.iiag.online/2022/2022-Index-Report.pdf.

22 "Particularly Exposed to Climate Shocks, African Cities Are Turning to Adaptation and Resilience," African Development Bank, November 14, 2022, https://www.afdb.org/en/news-and-events/particularly-exposed-climate-shocks-african-cities-are-turning-adaptation-and-resilience-56462.

23 Most African states use indirect elections, and a few rely on presidential appointments; see Danielle Resnick, "Realizing the New Urban Agenda in Africa: The Centrality of Local Politics," *Brookings*, June 22, 2022, https://www.brookings.edu/blog/africa-in-focus/2022/06/22/realizing-the-new-urban-agenda-in-africa-the-centrality-of-local-politics/.

24 Marina Lopes, "Mozambique Mayor Puts Fear in Frelimo," *Reuters*, last modified September 20, 2012, https://www.reuters.com/article/us-mozambique-politics/mozambique-mayor-puts-fear-in-frelimo-idUSBRE88J0ST20120920.

25 Andrew Kunambura, "Zimbabwe: Harare Circus Rages On, Capital Run by Two Mayors," *allAfrica*, https://allafrica.com/stories/202206040079.html.

26 OECD, *Africa's Urbanisation Dynamics 2022*, 14.

27 Robin Harding, *Rural Democracy: Elections and Development in Africa* (Oxford: Oxford University Press, 2020), 1–192.

28 Amaka Anku and Tochi Eni-Kalu, "Africa's Slums Aren't Harbingers of Anarchy—They're Engines of Democracy," *Foreign Affairs*, December 16, 2019, https://www.foreignaffairs.com/africa/africas-slums-arent-harbingers-anarchy-theyre-engines-democracy.

29 Jeremy Wallace, "Cities, Redistribution, and Authoritarian Regime Survival," *Journal of Politics* 75, no. 3 (July 2013): 632–45, http://pscourses.ucsd.edu/ps200b/Wallace%20Cities,%20Redistribution,%20and%20Authoritarian%20Regime%20Survival.pdf.

30 Timothy Lay, "ACLED 2021: The Year in Review," Armed Conflict Location and Event Data Project, March 8, 2022, https://acleddata.com/2022/03/08/2021-year-in-review/#conclusion.

31 Lisa Mueller, *Political Protest in Contemporary Africa* (Cambridge: Cambridge University Press, 2018), https://doi.org/10.1017/9781108529143.

32 International Telecommunications Union, "Mobile-Cellular Telephone Subscriptions per 100 Inhabitants, by Region, 2023," ITU Facts and Figures 2023, accessed April 1, 2024, https://www.itu.int/itu-d/reports/statistics/2023/10/10/ff23-subscriptions/.

33 GSMA Intelligence, "The Mobile Economy Sub-Saharan Africa 2023," GSMA, October 17, 2023, https://www.gsma.com/solutions-and-impact/connectivity-for-good/mobile-economy/sub-saharan-africa/.

34 Libuseng Malephane, "Digital Divide: Who is Africa in Connected and Who is Not," *Afrobarometer Dispatch* No. 582, December 14, 2022, https://www.afrobarometer.org/wp-content/uploads/2022/12/AD582-PAP18-Digital-divide-Who-in-Africa-is-connected-and-who-is-not-Afrobarometer-Pan-Africa-Profile-14dec22.pdf.

35 Hannah Ritchie, Edouard Mathieu, Max Roser, and Esteban Ortiz-Ospina, "Internet," *Our World in Data*, April 13, 2023, https://ourworldindata.org/internet#internet-access.

36 See multiple examples throughout: Idayat Hassan and Jamie Hitchen, *WhatsApp and Everyday Life in West Africa* (London: Bloomsbury Publishing, 2022).

37 Gabrielle Lynch and Elena Gadjanovaa, "Overcoming Incumbency Advantage: The Importance of Social Media on- and offline in Zambia's 2021 Elections," *Journal of Eastern African Studies* 16, no. 4 (2022), https://doi.org/10.1080/17531055.2023.2232241

38 Bridget Boakye, "Social Media Futures: How to Change the African Narrative," Tony Blair Institute for Global Change, April 19, 2021, https://www.institute.global/insights/tech-and-digitalisation/social-media-futures-how-change-african-narrative.

39 For more on how Facebook used its Free Basics initiative to become so popular in the region, see Toussaint Nothias, "The Rise and Fall . . . and Rise Again of Facebook's Free Basics: Civil Society and the Challenge of Resistance to Corporate Connectivity Projects," Global Media Technologies and Cultures Lab, April 21, 2020, http://globalmedia.mit.edu/2020/04/21/the-rise-and-fall-and-rise-again-of-facebooks-free-basics-civil-and-the-challenge-of-resistance-to-corporate-connectivity-projects/.

40 Maureen Kimotho, "More Men than Women Use Social Media: Report," *NTV*, February 21, 2023, https://ntvkenya.co.ke/news/more-men-than-women-use-social-media-report/.

41 Newton Adika, "Social Media Usage Trends in Africa: GeoPoll Report,"*GeoPoll*, September 6, 2023, https://www.geopoll.com/blog/social-media-usage-trends-in-africa-geopoll-report/.

42 "Despots and Disruptions: Five Dimensions of Internet Shutdowns in Africa," *CIPESA* (February 2019), 1–13, https://cipesa.org/wp-content/files/briefs/report/Despots-And-Disruptions_March-20.pdf.

43 Zach Rosson, Felicia Anthonio, Sage Cheng, et al., "Weapons of Control, Shields of Impunity: Internet Shutdowns in 2022," *AccessNow*, February 28, 2023, https://www.accessnow.org/wp-content/uploads/2023/03/2022-KIO-Report-Africa.pdf.

44 Abdi Latif Dahir, "Uganda Blocks Facebook ahead of Contentious Election," *New York Times*, January 13, 2021, https://www.nytimes.com/2021/01/13/world/africa/uganda-facebook-ban-elections.html.

45 Ambrose Gahene, "Use of Facebook Still Illegal Says Uganda Communications Commission," *CIO Africa*, March 5, 2022, https://cioafrica.co/use-of-facebook-still-illegal-says-uganda-communications-commission/.

46 Daily Monitor (@DailyMonitor), "Facebook are arrogant. They are being used to attack us," X post, December 23, 2022, https://twitter.com/DailyMonitor/status/1606242894112620544.

47 Daily Monitor (@DailyMonitor), "Facebook are arrogant."
48 "Nigeria's Twitter Ban Unlawful: W. African Court," *France 24*, July 14, 2022, https://www.france24.com/en/live-news/20220714-nigeria-s-twitter-ban-unlawful-w-african-court.
49 "Muhammadu Buhari: Twitter Deletes Nigerian Leader's 'civil war' Post," *BBC News*, June 2, 2021, https://www.bbc.com/news/world-africa-57336571.
50 The Community Court of Justice of ECOWAS, "The Registered Trustees of the Socio-Economic Rights and Accountability project (SERAP) v. Federal Republic of Nigeria," Judgement no. ECW/CCJ/JUD/08/21, April 26, 2021, http://www.courtecowas.org/wp-content/uploads/2021/08/JUD-ECW-CCJ-JUD-08-21-Registered-Trustees-of-the-Socio-Economic-Accountability-Projet-SERAP-vs.-FED.-REP.-of-NIGERIA-26_04_21.pdf.
51 Karen Allen, Jean le Roux, and Bonface Beti, *A Question of Influence? Case Study of Kenyan Elections in a Digital Age* (Pretoria: Institute for Security Studies, July 3, 2023), 5, https://issafrica.org/research/east-africa-report/a-question-of-influence-case-study-of-kenyan-elections-in-a-digital-age.
52 Nanjala Nyabola, *Digital Democracy, Analogue Politics: How the Internet Era is Transforming Politics in Kenya* (London: Bloomsbury Publishing, 2018), 204.
53 Tessa Knight, "Ethiopian Diaspora Groups Organize Click-to-Tweet Tigray Campaigns amid Information Scarcity," DFR Lab via *Medium*, April 23, 2021, https://medium.com/dfrlab/ethiopian-diaspora-groups-organize-click-to-tweet-tigray-campaigns-amid-information-scarcity-7e8d7ed73e2f.
54 Nyabola, *Digital Democracy*.
55 Faustine Ngila, "Protests against Government Policies Are Roiling All Four Corners of Africa," *Quartz*, March 20, 2023, https://qz.com/protests-rock-south-africa-kenya-tunisia-and-nigeria-1850242880.
56 According to the KOF Information Globalization index, Africa ranks at 61 on a 100-point scale; Savina Gygli, Florian Haelg, Niklas Potrafke, and Jan-Egbert Sturm, "The KOF Globalisation Index—Revisited," *Review of International Organizations* 14, no. 3 (2019): 543–74, https://doi.org/10.1007/s11558-019-09344-2.
57 Simon Allison, "Chapter 10: Reinventing the Newspaper for the WhatsApp Age," in *WhatsApp and Everyday Life in West Africa*, ed. Idayat Hassan and Jamie Hitchen (London: Bloomsbury Publishing, 2022).
58 *Afrobarometer*'s polling defines youth as respondents aged eighteen to thirty-five.
59 Gildfred Boateng Asiamah, Ousmane Djiby Sambou, and Sadhiska Bhoojedhur, "AD486: Africans Say Governments Aren't Doing Enough to Help Youth," *Afrobarometer*, November 4, 2021, https://www.afrobarometer.org/publication/ad486-africans-say-governments-arent-doing-enough-help-youth/.
60 "Government Expenditure on Education, Total (% of GDP)—Sub-Saharan Africa," World Bank open data, World Bank, September 19, 2023, https://data.worldbank.org/indicator/SE.XPD.TOTL.GD.ZS?locations=ZG.
61 Dhruv Gandhi, "Figures of the Week: Public Spending on education in Africa," *Brookings*, February 13, 2020, https://www.brookings.edu/articles/figures-of-the-week-public-spending-on-education-in-africa/.

62 African Union, "African Youth Charter," July 2, 2006, https://au.int/sites/default/files/treaties/7789-treaty-0033_-_african_youth_charter_e.pdf.

63 Aaron Azelton, Bret Barrowman, and Lisa Reppell, "Raising Their Voices: How Effective are Pro-Youth Laws and Policies?" *Consortium for Elections and Political Process Strengthening* (2019): 1–112, https://www.iri.org/wp-content/uploads/legacy/iri.org/iri_proyouth-report_.pdf.

64 To cite just a few examples: Thomas Sankara was in his early thirties when he became the President of Burkina Faso in 1983; Steve Biko was in his early twenties when he helped to found the influential South African Students Organization; Patrice Lumumba was thirty when he became the Prime Minister of what is today known as the Democratic Republic of the Congo.

65 "Data on Age: Global and Regional Averages," Interparliamentary Union, updated March 2023, https://data.ipu.org/age-brackets-aggregate?month=3&year=2023.

66 Asiamah, Sambou, and Bhoojedhur, "AD486."

67 "Emerging Dynamics—Societal: Disillusioned, Informed, and Divided," *Global Trends 2040: A More Contested World*, Office of the Director of National Intelligence, March 2021, https://www.dni.gov/index.php/gt2040-home/emerging-dynamics/societal-dynamics.

68 "Corruption Is the Most Common Story Africa's Youth Hear about the Continent," *African Media Agency*, November 20, 2021, https://africanmediaagency.com/corruption-is-the-most-common-story-africas-youth-hear-about-the-continent/.

69 Ronald Inglehart, "The Silent Revolution in Europe: Intergenerational Change in Post-Industrial Societies," *American Political Science Association* 65, no. 4 (December 1971): 991–1017, https://doi.org/10.2307/1953494.

70 Afrobarometer Network, "Africans Want More Democracy, but Their Leaders Still Aren't Listening," *Afrobarometer Policy Paper* No. 85, January 2023, 1–44, https://www.afrobarometer.org/wp-content/uploads/2023/01/PP85-PAP20-Africans-want-more-democracy-but-leaders-arent-listening-Afrobarometer-Pan-Africa-Profile-17jan23.pdf.

71 Afrobarometer Network, "Africans Want More Democracy."

72 Afrobarometer Network, "Africans Want More Democracy."

73 Daniel Stockemer and Aksel Sundström, *Youth without Representation: The Absence of Young Adults in Parliaments, Cabinets, and Candidacies* (Ann Arbor: University of Michigan Press, 2022).

74 Azelton, Barrowman, and Reppell, "Raising Their Voices."

75 Thiago Costa//T.C (@ti_ticii) "For the people in the back," X post, January 19, 2023, https://twitter.com/ti_ticii/status/1615977631358545931.

3
TIRED OLD STORIES

This is proof that Angola is a country frozen in time, and that the fault of all this was not the war but rather the War Lords.[1]
— COMMENT ON SOCIAL MEDIA POST ON HOW POOR LIVING CONDITIONS FEATURED IN POPULAR MUSIC FROM 2005 PERSIST IN 2023.

Most African countries hold regular elections, although the quality of those exercises, and the depth of the democracy they are intended to embody, is as varied as the continent itself. Across the board, however, victory at the ballot box matters to political leaders, as being "duly elected" is seen as a signifier of legitimacy on the global stage and reflects the African Union's own principles, enshrined in the Charter on Democracy, Elections, and Governance.[2] But in many states, whether the fix is in, or an electoral exercise holds some genuine element of suspense, the prevailing narrative around *why* a given leader or party is entitled to victory is not ultimately about their superior policy plans, or their governing track record.

Perhaps the most infamous example comes from Liberia's 1997 elections, in which voters made plain that the real selling point of candidate Charles Taylor was the well-founded fear that he would unleash hell upon the remaining population if he did not win. This sentiment was embodied in the heartbreaking refrain of his supporters: "You killed my ma, you killed my pa. I'll vote for you."[3] Faced with the certainty that the powerful warlord contesting the elections would never accept defeat peacefully, a majority of Liberians, traumatized after eight years of gruesome civil war, cast their ballots for Taylor. In the end, their efforts to placate him at the ballot box only bought the country a brief respite, as war erupted again in 1999.

But there are numerous other, less sensational examples of claims to power that deviate substantially from conventional notions about a contest of ideas, or even from identity politics, which are so often invoked to explain African political systems. While appeals to ethnic, regional, linguistic, and religious identity are very much a part of the region's political landscape,[4] and clientelism underpins political dynamics in many states,⁵ overriding national narratives grounded in history play a powerful role in underpinning the legitimacy of many African governments. These narratives often speak to the role an individual or party played in bringing some past national trauma to an end. They frame political power as a reward owed to heroic victors, or a logical entitlement for the only trustworthy option before voters. But those painful pasts are increasingly distant from the lived experience of voters, making them far less compelling to the young populations that constitute a majority of citizens.

In many of the continent's youngest countries, legitimacy narratives revolve around the struggle for independence, self-determination, and majority rule. South Africa's African National Congress (ANC) is the most celebrated of the region's liberation movements, but for those born after the end of minority rule in 1994, known as the "born free" generation, the liberation is incomplete. For South Africans who did not personally struggle in the apartheid era, but grew up in its aftermath, the ANC's historic achievements sit alongside internal party power struggles, persistent inequality, "state capture" scandals in which state and party officials collude to enrich themselves,⁶ and failing public services that have been features of the political landscape under thirty years of ANC leadership. In 2023, official statistics reflected a youth unemployment rate of 61 percent, which rises to 71 percent when also accounting for young people who have stopped even trying to find work.⁷ The storied ANC has seen its political dominance erode substantially, even as it continues to rely on an assumption that its role at the forefront of the liberation struggle should continue to command the loyalty of South African voters. Launching the ANC's first campaign rally in advance of the country's 2024 elections, South African President Cyril Ramaphosa implored voters not to be guided by their assessment of his first term in office, but rather the progress the country had made since the end of apartheid.

> Many people keep spreading this false narrative that the ANC has done nothing. Our people know what the ANC has done. They are the ones who have seen the work of the ANC. They are the ones who see the work that is in progress. They see what has already been achieved. And they know that South Africa is a better place than it was when we were under apartheid.⁸

The theme was quickly echoed by several of Ramaphosa's cabinet ministers, who blamed apartheid for everything from a devasting building fire in Johannesburg in 2023⁹ to the country's crumbling rail infrastructure.¹⁰

The South African electorate wasn't buying it, as evidenced by several viral TikTok videos in which South African shoppers flip through a book entitled *Reasons to Vote ANC* only to find all of the pages blank.¹¹ After all, the choice at the ballot box was not between supporting the ANC or resuming apartheid.

Recent *Afrobarometer* polling found that more than half of South Africans do not feel a strong affinity to any political party. Notably, a majority of the people expressing that view were young South Africans living in urban areas.[12] Some 67 percent of South Africans aged eighteen to thirty-five also expressed willingness to give up democratic rights—the very rights their parents fought for in resisting apartheid—in exchange for a government that could deliver security, jobs, and housing. A significantly smaller percentage of older South Africans were willing to make the same trade.[13] It likely redounds to the ANC's benefit that South Africa's population is less youth-heavy than most of the region, including its neighbor to the northeast. But the party of Mandela still absorbed an unprecedented blow in the 2024 elections, losing its outright majority and forcing it into a coalition government with other political parties.

Zimbabwe shook off British colonial and white minority rule after an eight-year civil war to achieve internationally recognized independence in 1980. In his inaugural address, founding leader Robert Mugabe told citizens, "my party recognizes the fundamental principle of that, in constituting a government, it is necessary to be guided by the national interest rather than by strictly party considerations."[14] But in practice, distinctions between the party's interest and the national interest were quickly, and brutally, erased. By the beginning of 1983, Mugabe had deployed North Korean–trained soldiers to Matabeleland to eliminate any political threat from his strongest rival and fellow liberation fighter, Joshua Nkomo, primarily by massacring his supporters. An estimated 20,000 people were killed in the genocidal campaign,[15] until what was left of Nkomo's political party was subsumed into Mugabe's Zimbabwe African National Union (ZANU) to become ZANU-PF in 1987.

Recent decades have been ruinously hard for most Zimbabweans. In ten of the years between 2000 and 2022, the country's economy shrank, even as the population size grew by more than 30 percent.[16] Today, over half of the population lives in poverty. Young people confront staggering levels of unemployment, and the collapse of its once-admired education system means that prospects for the next generation are ever more grim. Repeated episodes of hyperinflation have upended economic life. The state uses fear and violence with impunity to intimidate opposition politicians and independent journalists.[17] This misery has been overseen by ZANU-PF, which has continued to dominate government.[18] The country is in such shambles that it's hard to imagine a compelling ZANU-PF campaign pitch for yet another term. Indeed, when Justice Minister Ziyambi Ziyambi explained that ZANU-PF would not be publishing a new manifesto ahead of 2023's general elections but would instead run on its record (see Figure 3.1), stating that "our work is our manifesto,"[19] he was met with widespread derision online by Zimbabweans decrying living conditions and speculating that the ruling party was simply "tired of lying to the people."[20]

Figure 3.1 Cartoon Laying Out ZANU-PF's "Work."[21]
Credit: ZimDaily Newspaper, August 25, 2023.

In a country in which over 85 percent of people indicate that their government is doing badly at keeping prices stable and creating jobs, running on the record does seem to be a strange choice.[22] But in the contemporary rhetoric of the ruling party, economic conditions are not really the point. As Zimbabwean President Emerson Mnangagwa told a rally in the Midlands region in June 2023,

> ZANU-PF is the only party which has a history and a legacy for this country. We will not allow zvimbwasungata* to rule this country. The current freedom we are enjoying, the current liberation, the current independence, and sovereignty, the current respect and dignity we are enjoying as people, it came at a cost. It came as a result of some daughters and sons who sacrificed their lives and limbs for us to get independence.[23]

Former State Security Minister, Owen "Mudha" Ncube was even more direct in September of 2022, going so far as to announce the presidential election result a year in advance.

---

*Zvimbwasungata roughly translates as "sellouts."

Our President has won the 2023 presidential election. It is only ZANU-PF which must rule this country not the opposition because liberation fighters sacrificed for this country.[24]

The idea is not that ZANU-PF is good at governing the country. The idea is that ZANU-PF deserves to be in charge, and will be in charge, because they delivered the country independence from white minority rule at modern Zimbabwe's founding in 1980. The majority of Zimbabweans, of course, were born well after that date. But in the framing of ZANU-PF leaders, the people still owe the party their loyalty, and presumably always will; President Mnangagwa has often repeated that, "ZANU-PF will keep on ruling and ruling and ruling for eternity."[25] Young Zimbabweans are expected to continue paying political debts to the party institution associated with the liberators, despite being impoverished and abused, even as that generation of independence leaders fades away.

Increasingly, they decline to do so. Zimbabwe's growing urban centers have been opposition strongholds since 2000, and the young adults in Harare and Bulawayo tend to support challengers to ZANU-PF or to decline to participate in voting at all, given low levels of confidence in the integrity of the process.[26] In order to prevail in the 2023 election, ZANU-PF had to heavily influence both the preelection climate and election day itself, to the point that the typically toothless Southern African Development Community (SADC) observer delegation declined to give the proceedings its seal of approval.[27]

A related dynamic plays out in Angola, a former Portuguese colony where independence in 1975 kicked off long periods of civil war as competing factions, and their great power patrons, fought for supremacy. In Angola, the underlying political narrative about legitimacy is not about just the ruling party's role in resisting colonial oppression, but military victory over domestic rivals that delivered the country from brutal civil war. The ruling party brought clarity to the violently contentious question of who was in charge, making it ill equipped to transition to a political marketplace of ideas associated with democratic governance. Indeed, Angola was not an early adopter of multiparty democracy, waiting until 1992 to open the political system, at least in theory. As Ricardo Soares de Oliveira wrote in his examination of the state-building project in Angola, "emphasis on political order and authority contained few hints of a social contract, with the MPLA's sense of legitimacy emanating primarily from the war victory."[28] The long hangover from the civil war was exacerbated by the transformation of the MPLA's main domestic rival on the battlefield, the National Union for the Total Independence of Angola, or UNITA, into a political opposition party. As late as 2022, the MPLA's electoral campaigns were as much about equating the opposition with the "enemy" as describing a vision for the country's future.[29]

Invoking the war is a persistent theme outside of the electoral cycle as well; at an MPLA rally in 2023 the governor of the Luanda province described UNITA thusly,

> They were against Angola and the Angolan people when they violated the 1994 Lusaka protocol,[30] and they returned to war . . . They show once again that they are against Angola and the Angolan people, when through subversion they try to take power through non-democratic means.[31]

And when UNITA's parliamentarians attempted to initiate impeachment proceedings against President Lourenço, the MPLA released a statement warning that UNITA's leaders had reached a "CLEAR UNDERSTANDING THAT THE ARMED INSURGENCY OF THE PAST CAN NOW BE DISGUISED AS A POSSIBLE POPULAR INSURGENCY."[32] Yet the reaction among many young Angolans on social media was not one of alarm about UNITA's nefarious agenda, but bemusement that the MPLA's statement was issued entirely in capital letters, the digital equivalent of shouting. Angolans on Twitter/X noted that the statement came across as "scolding" and "screaming," and speculated that "the nervousness was so much that the finger could not leave the shift key."[33] The contrast between the urgent and indignant tone of the statement and its reception in the digital sphere could not be more stark.

But the disconnect is about more than style. Angolan society as a whole is extremely young; with a median age under seventeen. It is also increasingly impatient with the ruling party, rendering elections a fraught exercise. Over half of the population lives below the international poverty line for lower middle-income countries,[34] and youth unemployment exceeds 50 percent.[35] Extreme income inequality means that urban Angolans are keenly aware of the difference between the lifestyles of those at the top of the pyramid and the prevailing conditions endured by a majority of citizens. Relatively low investment in education and healthcare disadvantages Angolan youth compared to their peers in neighboring countries.[36] The socioeconomic divide in Angola is sometimes expressed in generational terms. When the National Assembly building flooded in December 2023, one social media user described the scene as "older people tasting their own medicine."[37]

In fact, by 2022, the MPLA was barely clinging to power, winning only 51 percent of the vote and losing its two-thirds majority in parliament despite a playing field tilted heavily in its favor. The voters' roll was stacked with the names of deceased citizens. Media coverage overwhelmingly favored the MPLA. Domestic observers were denied access to polling sites.[38] A quarter of those serving on the National Election Commission declined to sign off on the announced results because of their concerns about the process.[39] Security forces maintained a prominent presence in urban areas in the aftermath of the polling to dissuade citizens from protesting.⁴⁰ Yet the results still indicated softening support for the MPLA, and analysts noted that the polls revealed an inversion of the old Angolan political formula, in which the MPLA dominated the center and UNITA enjoyed rural support. Today, the opposite appears to be true.⁴¹

The gulf between the official understanding of what underpins the government's legitimacy and popular views is on display every April 4, when Angolans celebrate "Peace Day," marking the anniversary of the 2002 agreement that ended the country's twenty-seven-year civil war. For those who remember the brutality of the conflict or have heard stories of suffering from their elders, the day is undoubtedly meaningful. But for most Angolans, the notion that they are not at war is cold comfort. Waves of protest sparked by the soaring cost of living swept through Angolan cities in 2023, and the violent police response prompted some to question whether the much-celebrated "peace" really prevailed.

> When they realize that the peace of Angola is no longer related to the war that happened, we will be at peace.
>
> Gains of peace is the only song these old incompetent politicians have to play. Over and over again. Aren't they tired? Peace without having food on the table and other basic conditions, is pure illusion that runs far away from the suffered reality many Angolans face everyday. Sad.⁴²

Angola is not alone in appealing to the electorate based on the notion that incumbent powers should be retained because they delivered the country from a violent past. In Uganda, independence in 1962 ushered in decades of violent contestation for control of the state, a period dominated by the regimes of Idi Amin and Milton Obote and punctuated by three successful military coups in 1971, 1980, and 1985. Current President Yoweri Museveni's National Resistance Army ultimately prevailed, seizing the capital city of Kampala and installing itself in power. When he was sworn in to office in 1986, Museveni promised Ugandans nothing less than "a fundamental change in the politics of our country." He went on,

> In Africa, we have seen so many changes that change, as such, is nothing short of mere turmoil. We have had one group getting rid of another one, only for it to turnout to be worse than the group it displaced. Please do not count us in that group of people.⁴³

He and his National Resistance Movement (NRM) were going to deliver the country from all that tumultuous chaos, offering stability and security to the population. In practice, despite talk about democracy, this meant that Ugandans would have no elections at all for a decade, and that multiparty politics would be resisted until 2005 on the grounds that they could be too "polarizing" and risk the country's hard-won peace. When the first elections were held, one of Museveni's campaign ads read, "Don't forget the past. Over one million Ugandans, our brothers, sisters, family and friends, lost their lives. YOUR VOTE COULD BRING IT BACK."[44]

For over thirty years, the underlying justification for Museveni's leadership has been the idea that by maintaining consistency at the top, and imposing "discipline"—a favorite word that he employs regularly in his exhortations to citizens[45]—on security forces and society as a whole, he holds back the fractious forces that resulted in the deaths of well over half a million Ugandan civilians in the country's first decades of independence. His government created memorials consisting of mounds of skulls and other human remains in the Luwero Triangle to underscore the terrible nature of the conflict that preceded his tenure.[46] As private secretary to the president David Mafabi told *The Monitor* newspaper after thirty years of Museveni's tenure in 2016, "you may say the President has overstayed, but his longevity has been the longevity of peace and stability. We now have a predictable government and peace."[47]

Certainly, Museveni and the NRM have also touted their development gains, but this is often framed, and executed, in a securitized context, in which men in fatigues (often led by relatives of Museveni himself) are in the lead.[48] The president's campaign slogan in 2021 was "Securing your Future." That same year, NRM-aligned youth like Jacob Eyeru, then the leader of the government's National Youth Council, continue to echo the prevailing political narrative, noting "If you come from the north and east you will understand that a big achievement of peace has been brought. For 20 years those regions were engulfed in war."[49] The reminders are persistent and sometimes bizarre. Celebrating his seventy-ninth birthday in Katonga, site of a historic NRM victory in 1985, Museveni posted to X (formerly Twitter) a photo of himself slicing into an enormous cake decorated with camouflage frosting and edible photos of soldiers firing rifles, writing,

> I am glad the Bazzukulu[†] agreed with the idea to unite my 79 years of life celebration with our struggle. In this case, the battles of September 1972 and 1985 (Katonga). I want to thank all those who fought in Katonga and the battles before. All the past wars in Uganda were unnecessary because there was always another way of solving the problems peacefully. Since 1962, we could have had peaceful politics, but some people didn't want to. They decided to go for violence and sectarianism.[50]

[†]Bazzukulu means "grandchildren" in Luganda.

But Uganda's population is one of the youngest in the world; the median age is under sixteen. The vast majority of the population was born after Museveni assumed office. They did not live through the chaotic years of Obote and Amin, and only a fraction of young adults benefit from NRM-sponsored positions like Eyeru does. For many of these Ugandans, the current government's success in stopping the country's cycles of political violence in the 1970s and 1980s feels less relevant and urgent than their day-to-day struggles, and there is a terrible irony in Museveni's early promise of "a fundamental change." Survey data from 2022 indicates that in the county's sprawling capital, Kampala, over 62 percent of citizens believe the country is going in the wrong direction. These Ugandans want the government to prioritize fighting corruption, health, and education, and addressing unemployment. Political violence and ethnic tensions—the demons supposedly kept at bay by Museveni—are among the lowest priorities among Kampala's 3.8 million people. Urban dwellers throughout the country also strongly support term limits for the presidency; they are more than 10 percent more likely to do so than rural Ugandans.[51]

Unsurprisingly, in recent years many of Uganda's urban youth have been strong supporters of Robert Kyagulanyi, better known as Bobi Wine, a musician and opposition politician who ran for president against Museveni in Uganda's deeply flawed elections of 2021. Unlike the previous opposition stalwart, Kizza Besigye, Wine is of a different generation than Museveni and was never a part of the NRM. Sometimes known as the "ghetto president" because of his origins and support base among poor urbanites, Wine's cultural capital, gained in part through song lyrics that decry corruption and champion youth empowerment, helped to propel his political rise. It began with a successful campaign for a parliamentary seat in 2017, just as debate was underway regarding a ruling-party proposal to abolish the constitutional age limit for the presidency (which was necessary to enable President Museveni to run in the 2021 elections). His supporters' appreciation for Wine's vocal opposition to that maneuver, and willingness to challenge Museveni for the presidency in 2021, were grounded in frustration with the status quo and the personalization of the state. Rather than speaking to a national longing to ensure predictability in government, his political movement, the National Unity Platform, focuses on demands for change; its manifesto states clearly that it was "formed to spearhead the first ever inclusive, non-violent transition of political power in Uganda."[52] Describing his reason for seeking the presidency, Wine has been explicit about his belief that leadership change is the essential linchpin in any effort to make government function for his supporters. For his party, regime change is the ultimate goal.

Having seen that the parliament, just like the judiciary, were firmly captured by General Museveni, and all the power is concentrated in the presidency, our only solution is to remove General Museveni, so that we can again take back power to the institutions. General Museveni remains the singular problem to democracy. He remains the single disempowerment to the institutions. And we believe that without General Museveni, who uses the military and the national resources to arm-twist all these institutions, we can achieve servant leadership.[53]

In 2021, over the course of the campaign Wine and other challengers were threatened, arrested, and assaulted, and some supporters were killed by the state's security forces. Tanks were deployed in Kampala, leaving domestic and international observers skeptical about the credibility of the general election result, in which President Museveni was returned to office with just under 59 percent of the vote. As will be discussed in Chapter 6, Museveni and his allies continue to adapt their governing tactics to contain the threat posed by self-styled "change agents." Whether a movement whose "political base has always been made up largely of subsistence farmers who live in remote and somewhat isolated areas of Southern Uganda in which political mobilization and information could be most easily controlled by party-state officials"[54] can continue to parry the challenges of the country's demographic shifts remains to be seen.

Political appeals based on defining national events are certainly not unique to Africa. But the region's youthful demographics render these appeals less compelling, and more vulnerable to widespread criticism, than they might be otherwise. Different interpretations of the lessons and salience of national history help to define generational fault lines throughout the region. This is as true in authoritarian states as it is in more democratic countries. In some of the latter, young people with no lived experience of hard-fought struggles for political liberalization are more skeptical about democratic governance than their elders. Stories about how democracy will improve their lives are wearing thin.

Each year in July, Kenyans celebrate Saba Saba Day, commemorating the watershed 1990 demonstration of resistance to Daniel arap Moi's autocratic rule.[55] The organized mass movement, or "second liberation," (the first being the end of colonialism) that kicked off on Saba Saba would continue to pressure Moi into restoring term limits and multipartyism a year and a half later. This eventually led to a constitutional overhaul in 2010, although not without significant costs, including lives lost, for activists. While political elites worked to manage Kenya's transition to ensure their continued access to state coffers,[56] Kenya did transform from an authoritarian state to one characterized by close political competition and lively political expression.

But by 2022, disillusionment with Kenya's political system led to the lowest voter turnout in fifteen years, despite the population of eligible voters having increased by 10 percent from the previous election.[57] The lackluster turnout was largely attributed to an anemic youth vote.[58] Young people under the age of thirty make up about 70 percent of Kenya's population, but the right to make political choices at the ballot box that was at the heart of Saba Saba no longer seems as meaningful to many Kenyans. Young, urban Kenyans want their government to prioritize fighting unemployment and corruption,[59] but it was not clear to many that the choices on offer in the political marketplace were suited to that agenda. For some, formal politics seemed to be an obstacle to progress toward those goals rather than a vehicle for achieving them.[60] In the 2022 contest, the notion that daily life would not change regardless of the outcome was given a boost by the fact that the primary contenders were known political quantities, one the clear choice of the outgoing president and the other an incumbent deputy president. Despite differences in style and personal biography, the campaign spotlighted very few clear differences in policy substance. In his influential essay about the contest, "2022: Kenya's First Ever Election About Nothing," John Githongo offered a glimpse into the developments that might explain the lack of youthful enthusiasm for formal political participation:

> The truth is that we are going into an election believing in nothing, standing for nothing. At best, we are searching. All the leading political formations are born of each other and birthed by many profound compromises, and this in part explains the blankness . . . An entire generation below 35 years of age has grown up that finds watching our political leaders on the seven o'clock news boring and, some even argue, detrimental to mental health. They catch the outrageous highlights on Twitter, WhatsApp and Instagram. The thundering statements of ministers, the head of state and his deputy have been reduced to fleeting minutes of entertainment to be taken as seriously as a Nollywood thriller . . . The con has been exposed as a con, an empty debe* making noises that are incoherent and sometimes amusing.[61]

Many young Kenyans still mobilize on Saba Saba Day to protest their economic conditions and police brutality—and in 2024 the day was marked with memorial concerts in honor of those who lost their lives protesting government—but the connective tissue between that agenda and the formal electoral politics of the state has weakened. Kenyans still support democracy, but between 2002 and 2018, the percentage of Kenyans rejecting authoritarianism and demanding democratic governance fell by 14 percent.[62] By 2021, polls showed that the youngest cohort of enfranchised Kenyans, aged eighteen to thirty, are 10 percent less likely to support democracy than Kenyans sixty or older.[63] The Gen

---

*"Debe" here refers to a tin container.

Z protests that exploded across the country in 2024, which will be explored in Chapter 5, were the manifestation of political demands that do not correspond to the electoral choices on offer.

Likewise, in Nigeria, a country under military rule for nearly thirty years since independence in 1960, the struggle for democracy was long and costly, and the country's elites—in this case the military—carefully managed the transition.[64] As in so many African states, youth dominate Nigeria's population; roughly three-quarters of all Nigerians are under the age of thirty-five, giving the country the largest youth population in the world. But today, the youngest cohort of politically enfranchised citizens, who have little to no lived experience of life under a junta, are the least likely to express support for democracy (64 percent, compared to 70–77 percent among their elders), and as of 2022, less likely to vote or identify with a political party.[65]

What went wrong? When democratic governance was restored in 1999, President Olusegun Obasanjo spoke to the high expectations of citizens, noting in his inaugural address that during the dark days of military rule, "the citizens developed distrust in government, and because promises made for the improvement of the conditions of the people were not kept all statements by government met with cynicism . . . Government and all its agencies became thoroughly corrupt and reckless." But all of this was going to change, a "New Dawn" was coming, and by changing "our ways of governance and doing business," Nigerians would be able to "ensure progress, justice, harmony and unity and above all, to rekindle confidence amongst out people. Confidence that their conditions will rapidly improve and that Nigeria will be great and will become a major world player in the near the future."[66]

Many things did improve, particularly relating to civil and political rights. But taking stock in 2024, few Nigerians would say that the "New Dawn" delivered on its promises. Corruption at a grand scale, and the cynicism it engenders, abounds.[67] In disparate parts of the country, the Nigerian government has proven unable to provide security for its citizens.[68] Vote buying and impunity for violations of the country's laws have been hallmarks of Nigerian elections,[69] and few Nigerians have confidence in the electoral commission or the judiciary.[70] Nigeria's youth are collectively better educated than older generations, but less likely to be employed.[71] The democratic governance they have known throughout most of their lives has not impressed them, and it is unsurprising that their experiences and observations might lead to skepticism about the potential for their governing system to deliver better results.

While Nigeria's 2023 general elections saw a significant uptick in youth voter registration and an energized urban youth movement in parts of the country organized around a maverick third party campaign, in the end, voter turnout was the lowest in Nigerian history, at 27 percent.[72] The disappointing turnout was largely attributed to security threats and practical constraints (the polling took place amid simultaneous fuel and currency shortages), but the ultimate result of the election was a further erosion of trust in the democratic nature of the state.[73] Results conflicted with preelection polls, electoral reforms intended to enhance transparency failed to meet expectations, and outright rigging in some constituencies[74] cast a pall over the process as a whole.

As in Kenya, youthful skepticism about formal political participation and election fatigue should not be conflated with apathy, as subsequent chapters will discuss. In states like Kenya and Nigeria, it is not the stories of individual or party heroics that many young people are questioning. Instead, it is the political system as a whole, and the idea, dear to their elders who made sacrifices in the fight against autocracy, that democratic politics, at least as they have been practiced to date, can deliver results. In many parts of Africa, democracy's legitimacy and value is under the microscope.

Notes

1. Comment on post by ANKARA YARINE (@iusimperii18), "The songs on this album prove that Angola has not changed at all," X post, December 18, 2023, https://twitter.com/Egocentricpapi/status/1736844079042883616.
2. African Union, "African Charter on Democracy, Elections and Governance," January 30, 2007, 3, https://au.int/sites/default/files/treaties/36384-treaty-african-charter-on-democracy-and-governance.pdf.
3. "Taylor Still Looms Large as Election Countdown Begins," *The New Humanitarian*, June 30, 2005, https://www.thenewhumanitarian.org/report/55205/liberia-taylor-still-looms-large-election-countdown-begins.
4. See for example Francis M. Deng, "Ethnicity: An African Predicament," *Brookings*, June 1, 1997, https://www.brookings.edu/articles/ethnicity-an-african-predicament/; Ian Taylor, "Chapter 6: The Role of Identity in African Politics," in *African Politics: A Very Short Introduction* (Oxford: Oxford University Press, 2018), https://doi.org/10.1093/actrade/9780198806578.003.0006.
5. Nicolas van de Walle, "The Path from Neopatrimonialism: Democracy and Clientelism in Africa Today," *Working Paper* 3, no. 7, Mario Einaudi Center for International Studies, June 2007, https://ecommons.cornell.edu/server/api/core/bitstreams/493ab0c8-9d08-42fc-816b-7b4ac1a23859/content.
6. Republic of South Africa, "The Judicial Commission of Inquiry into Allegations of State Capture, Corruption and Fraud in the Public Sector including Organs of State," June 22, 2022, https://www.statecapture.org.za/site/information/reports.
7. Statistics South Africa, "South Africa's Youth Continues to Bear the Burden of Unemployment," June 1, 2022, https://www.statssa.gov.za/?p=15407.
8. "South Africa: Ramaphosa Launches First Campaign Rally for 2024 Elections," *Africanews*, last modified September 4, 2023, https://www.africanews.

com/2023/09/04/south-africa-ramaphosa-launches-first-campaign-rally-for-2024-elections/.

9   Kyle Zeeman, "'Whether we like it or not, this is the result of apartheid' — Lindiwe Zulu on Joburg CBD Fire," *The Citizen*, September 1, 2023, https://www.citizen.co.za/news/south-africa/results-of-apartheid-lindiwe-zulu-on-joburg-cbd-fire/.

10 Angela Tuck, "After 20 Wasted Years, a Single Arrow Remains in the ANC's Quiver," *Vryeweekblad*, September 8, 2023, https://www.vryeweekblad.com/en/opinions-and-debate/2023-09-08-20-wasted-years-and-the-ghost-of-apartheid/?utm_source=substack&utm_medium=email.

11 See, for example, Kgosi (@Kgosi__sa), "Best selling book," TikTok, May 15, 2024, https://www.tiktok.com/@kgosi__sa/video/7369319210910043398?lang=en.

12 Jamy Felton, "Increasingly Non-Partisan, South Africans Willing to Trade Elections for Security, Housing, Jobs," *Afrobarometer*, October 30, 2018, https://www.afrobarometer.org/wp-content/uploads/2022/02/ab_r7_dispatchno248_south_africa_elections1.pdf.

13 Dominique Dryding, "Are South Africans Giving Up on Democracy?" *Afrobarometer*, July 14, 2020, https://www.afrobarometer.org/wp-content/uploads/2022/02/ab_r7_dispatchno372_are_south_africans_giving_up_on_democracy.pdf.

14 "Mugabe's Promise: A Transcript of the Late Leader's Address to the nation on March 4, 1980," *Foreign Policy*, https://foreignpolicy.com/2019/09/06/mugabes-promise/.

15 International Association of Genocide Scholars, "Resolution on State Repression in Zimbabwe," June 7, 2005, https://genocidescholars.org/wp-content/uploads/2019/04/IAGS-RESOLUTION-ON-ZIMBABWE-7-June-2005.pdf.

16 World Bank, "GDP Growth (annual %) — Zimbabwe," World Development Indicators, 2022, https://data.worldbank.org/indicator/NY.GDP.MKTP.KD.ZG?locations=ZW.

17 For a powerful illustration of the role of political violence in independent Zimbabwe, see Peter Godwin, *The Fear: Robert Mugabe and the Martyrdom of Zimbabwe* (New York: Hachette Book Group, 2011).

18 Farai Shawn Matiashe, "Zimbabwe: With its Two-Thirds Majority, How Far Will ZANU-PF Go?" *The Africa Report*, February 15, 2024, https://www.theafricareport.com/336371/zimbabwe-with-its-two-thirds-majority-how-far-will-zanu-pf-go/.

19 Zvamaida Murwira, "Our Work is Our Manifesto," *The Herald*, July 24, 2023, https://www.herald.co.zw/our-work-is-our-manifesto/.

20 See, for example, the replies to Zimbabwean journalist Hopewell Chinono's tweet regarding ZANU-PF's decision to forgo a written manifesto, Hopewell Chinono (@daddyhope), "For the first time in the history of post colonial Zimbabwe, ZANUPF has no election manifesto, it has nothing to sell at all," Twitter post, July 24, 2023, http://twitter.com/daddyhope/status/1683377840551501824.

21 Zimbabwe Daily (@ZimDaily), "Our Work Is Our Manifesto," Twitter post, July 25, 2023, https://twitter.com/ZimDaily/status/1683786736822788096.

22 Asafika Mpako and Simangele Moyo-Nyede, "Zimbabweans Offer Bleak Outlook on the State of the Economy," *Afrobarometer*, June 24, 2023, https://www.afrobarometer.org/wp-content/uploads/2023/06/AD658-Zimbabweans-offer-bleak-assessments-on-the-economy-Afrobarometer-23jun23.pdf.

23 "'We will deal with them,' says Mnangagwa as He Vows Zanu PF Will Never Surrender Power to Opposition 'sellouts,'" *New Zimbabwe*, June 25, 2022, https://www.newzimbabwe.com/we-will-deal-with-them-says-mnangagwa-as-he-makes-it-clear-zanu-pf-not-ready-to-surrender-power/.

24 "Chamisa is the enemy, says Mudha, declares Zanu-PF must 'rule forever,'" Nehanda Radio, September 16, 2022, https://nehandaradio.com/2022/09/16/chamisa-is-the-enemy-says-mudha-declares-zanu-pf-must-rule-forever/.

25 Gabriele Steinhauser, "'Life Was Better under Mugabe:' Disappointment, Fear Cloud Zimbabwe Election," *Wall Street Journal*, August 23, 2023. https://www.wsj.com/world/africa/life-was-better-under-mugabe-disappointment-fear-cloud-zimbabwe-election-8ac63d5f.

26 "Young Zimbabweans Less Likely than Their Elders to Cast Their Ballots on Election Day, New Afrobarometer Survey Shows," *Afrobarometer*, August 22, 2023, https://www.afrobarometer.org/wp-content/uploads/2023/08/News_release-Young-Zimbabweans-less-likely-to-vote-Afrobarometer-22aug23.pdf.; "Zimbabwe: Apathy Derails Young Prospective Voters," *The Africa Report*, April 7, 2023, https://www.theafricareport.com/298317/zimbabwe-apathy-derails-young-prospective-voters/.

27 Southern African Development Community, "SADC Electoral Observation Mission Preliminary Statement to the Harmonised Election to the Republic of Zimbabwe," August 25, 2023, 10, https://www.sadc.int/document/sadc-electoral-observation-mission-preliminary-statement-harmonised-election-republic.

28 Ricardo Soares de Oliveira and Susan Taponier, "'O Governo Está Aqui': Post-war State-Making in the Angolan Periphery," *Dans Politique Africaine* 130 (2012/13): 165–87, https://www.cairn.info/revue-politique-africaine-2013-2-page-165.htm.

29 In an interview just after the election, Catarina Antunes Gomes and Cesaltina Abreu of the Social Sciences and Humanities Laboratory of the Catholic University of Angola described the dark tenor of the campaign:

> The electoral campaign should be a time when candidates share their ideas with us, debate their parties' proposals and tell us their thoughts about Angola's future. But this was not what happened. The ruling party had a strong negative discourse, treating the other parties as enemies rather than adversaries. They didn't present any ideas on how to make the country progress.

"ANGOLA: 'Much effort was put into excluding people from the electoral process,'" CIVICUS, September 12, 2022, https://www.civicus.org/index.php/media-resources/news/interviews/6024-angola-much-effort-was-put-into-excluding-people-from-the-electoral-process

30 The 1994 Lusaka Protocol the second peace deal that attempted to end the Angolan civil war; like the first, it failed due to violations by both parties; United Nations Security Council, "Lusaka Protocol," December 22, 1994, https://peacemaker.un.org/sites/peacemaker.un.org/files/AO_941115_LusakaProtocol%28en%29.pdf.

31 "'O MPLA não tem medo' da destituição," *Angonoticias*, July 27, 2023, https://www.angonoticias.com/Artigos/item/74438/o-mpla-nao-tem-medo-da-destitucao.

32 MPLA, "Press Release," Facebook, July 20, 2023, https://www.facebook.com/photo/?fbid=816907599804171&set=a.461826221978979.

33 César Chiyaya (@cesarchiyaya), "O BP do MPLA escreveu o comunicado com o caps lock ligado?" Twitter post, July 21, 2023, https://twitter.com/cesarchiyaya/status/1682360855965446147.

34 Liliana D. Sousa, "Poverty & Equity Brief: Africa Eastern & Southern Angola," *World Bank Group* (April 2023): 1–2, https://databankfiles.worldbank.org/public/ddpext_download/poverty/987B9C90-CB9F-4D93-AE8C-750588BF00QA/current/Global_POVEQ_AGO.pdf.

35 "Angola: Overview," World Bank, last modified September 24, 2023, https://www.worldbank.org/en/country/angola/overview.

36 Sousa, "Poverty & Equity Brief."

37 Thiago Costa//T.C. (@ti_ticii), "Malta, the WATER FOR ALL project has finally reached the Assembly," X post, December 12, 2023, https://twitter.com/ti_ticii/status/173463672453998942.

38 "Angola: The Democratic Transition that Never Was," Civicus Lens, September 13, 2022, https://lens.civicus.org/angola-the-democratic-transition-that-never-was/.

39 Alex Vines, "Angola's Political Earthquake: The Aftermath of the August 2022 Elections," ISP online, September 7, 2022, https://www.ispionline.it/en/publication/angolas-political-earthquake-aftermath-august-2022-elections-36067.

40 *Freedom in the World 2023*: "Angola," Freedom House, accessed March 19, 2024, https://freedomhouse.org/country/angola/freedom-world/2023.

41 Peter Fabricius, "UNITA Shakes the Foundations of MPLA Rule in Angola," Institute for Security Studies, September 2, 2022, https://issafrica.org/iss-today/unita-shakes-the-foundations-of-mpla-rule-in-angola.

42 See comments (second comment since deleted); César Chiyaya (@cesarchiyaya), "Dia da #PAZ," Twitter post, April 3, 2020, https://twitter.com/mr_chiyaya/status/1642997019298996225.

43 Bart Kakooza, "Museveni swearing ceremony 1986," YouTube video, 36:07, May 23, 2023, https://www.youtube.com/watch?v=ygFtVOe7C2o.

44 "A Memoir of the Bush War and the Press in Uganda—Review," *The Elephant*, June 20, 2019, https://www.theelephant.info/analysis/2019/06/20/combatants-a-memoir-of-the-bush-war-and-the-press-in-uganda-review/.

45 "President Museveni Cautions the Youths against Wrong Ideology and Indiscipline," Uganda Media Centre, Ministry of ICT and National Guidance, August 18, 2023, https://www.mediacentre.go.ug/media/president-museveni-cautions-youths-against-wrong-ideology-and-indiscipline.

46 Pauline Bernard, "The Politics of the Luweero Skulls: The Making of Memorial Heritage and Post-Revolutionary State Legitimacy over the Luweero Mass Graves in Uganda," *Journal of Eastern African Studies* 11, no. 1 (2017): 188–209, https://doi.org/10.1080/17531055.2017.1288959

47 Yasiin Mugerwa, "Has Museveni Delivered the Fundamental Change?" *Monitor*, last modified May January 26, 2024, https://www.monitor.co.ug/uganda/special-reports/has-museveni-delivered-the-fundamental-change–1650042.

48 Sam Wilkins and Richard Vokes, "Transition, Transformation, and the Politics of the Future in Uganda," *Journal of Eastern African Studies* 17, no. 1–2 (June 2023): 1–18, https://doi.org/10.1080/17531055.2023.2236848.

49 Patience Atuhaire, "Uganda's Yoweri Museveni: How an ex-Rebel Has Stayed in Power for 35 Years," *BBC News*, May 10, 2021, https://www.bbc.com/news/world-africa-55550932.

50 "Museveni Hails Katonga Heroes, Roots for Education and Wealth Creation," *New Vision*, September 9, 2023, https://www.newvision.co.ug/category/news/museveni-hails-katonga-heroes-roots-for-educa-NV_169679.

51 Francis Kibirige, "Summary of Results: Afrobarometer Round 9 Survey in Uganda, 2022," *Afrobarometer*, August 8, 2023, https://www.afrobarometer.org/publication/uganda-round-9-summary-of-results/.

52 "National Unity Platform 2021–2026," National Unity Party, December 23, 2020, https://issuu.com/kyagulanyi/docs/final_manifesto_2021-26.

53 Mvemba Phezo Dizolele, "Bobi Wine on Youth Movements and Liberation," Center for Strategic and International Studies, August 24, 2023, https://www.csis.org/podcasts/africa/bobi-wine-youth-movements-and-liberation.

54 Wilkins and Vokes, "Transition, Transformation, and the Politics of the Future in Uganda."

55 For a brief, excellent recounting of Saba Saba's history, see Kwamchetsi Makokha, "Saba Saba and the Evolution of Citizen Power," *The Elephant*, July 7, 2020, https://www.theelephant.info/features/2020/07/07/saba-saba-and-the-evolution-of-citizen-power/.

56 Nic Cheeseman, Karuti Kanyinga, and Gabrielle Lynch ed., *The Oxford Handbook of Kenyan Politics* (Oxford: Oxford University Press, 2020).

57 George Maringa, "Election 2022 to Feature Highest Number of Registered Voters, Polling Stations in Kenya's History," *The Standard*, https://www.standardmedia.co.ke/national/article/2001448421/election-2022-to-feature-highest-number-of-registered-voters-polling-stations-in-kenyas-history.

58 Luke Anami, "Kenya Election: Lowest Turnout in 15 Years as Youth Stay Away," *The East African*, August 14, 2022, https://www.theeastafrican.co.ke/tea/news/east-africa/lowest-turnout-in-15-years-as-youth-stay-away-3913984.

59 "Summary of Results: Afrobarometer Round 9 Survey in Kenya, 2022," Afrobarometer (2022): 1–85, https://www.afrobarometer.org/wp-content/uploads/2022/08/KEN-_-AB-R9_-Summary-of-Results-16aug22.pdf.

60 Interview with Jacob Ouma in Nairobi in March 2022.

61 John Githongo, "2022: Kenya's First Ever Election about Nothing," *The Elephant*, March 11, 2022, https://www.theelephant.info/op-eds/2022/03/11/2022-kenyas-first-ever-election-about-nothing/.

62 Robert Mattes, "Democracy in Africa: Demand, Supply, and the 'dissatisfied democrat,'" *Afrobarometer Policy Paper* No. 54, February 2019, 1–30, https://www.afrobarometer.org/wp-content/uploads/migrated/files/publications/Policy%20papers/ab_r7_policypaperno54_africans_views_of_democracy1.pdf.

63 "Africans Want More Democracy, but Their Leaders Still Aren't Listening," *Afrobarometer Policy Paper* No. 85, January 2023, 1–44, https://www.afrobarometer.org/wp-content/uploads/2023/01/PP85-PAP20-Africans-want-more-democracy-but-leaders-arent-listening-Afrobarometer-Pan-Africa-Profile-17jan23.pdf.

64 John Campbell, *Nigeria: Dancing on the Brink* (Lanham, MD: Rowman & Littlefield, 2013).

65 Amara Galileo, Raphael Mbaegbu, and Sunday Joseph Duntoye, "Nigerians Want Democracy, though Dissatisfaction Rises amid Worsening Economic Conditions," *Afrobarometer Dispatch* No. 606, February 2023, 1–14, https://www.afrobarometer.org/wp-content/uploads/2023/02/AD606-Nigerians-want-democracy%5ELLLJ-though-dissatisfaction-rises-in-worsening-economy-Afrobarometer-22feb23.pdf.

66 Olusegun Obasanjo, "President Obasanjo's Inaugural Address to the Nation—May 29, 1999" (speech, Abuja, May 29, 1999), accessed March 19, 2024, https://www.dawodu.com/obas1.htm.

67 Matthew T. Page, "A New Taxonomy for Corruption in Nigeria," Carnegie Endowment for International Peace, July 2018, https://carnegieendowment.org/files/CP_338_Page_Nigeria_Brief_FINAL.pdf.

68 "Nigeria," Global Organized Crime Index, accessed March 19, 2024, https://ocindex.net/country/nigeria.

69 Leena Koni Hoffman and Raj Navanit Patel, "Vote-selling Behaviour and Democratic Dissatisfaction in Nigeria," Chatham House, July 2022, https://www.chathamhouse.org/sites/default/files/2022-07/2022-07-28-vote-selling-nigeria-hoffmann-patel.pdf.

70 "Summary of Results: Afrobarometer Round 9 Survey in Nigeria, 2022," compiled by NOI Polls, *Afrobarometer*, August 26, 2022, 39, https://www.afrobarometer.org/wp-content/uploads/2022/08/Nigeria-Afrobarometer-R9-Summary-of-Results-26august2022.pdf.

71 Sunday Joseph Duntoye and Raphael Mbaegbu, "Young Nigerians Prioritise Security, Jobs, and the Economy for Government Action," *Afrobarometer Dispatch* No. 708, September 2023, 1–11, https://www.afrobarometer.org/wp-content/uploads/2023/09/AD708-Young-Nigerians-prioritise-security%5ELLLJ-jobs%5ELLLJ-economy-for-govt-action-Afrobarometer-29sep23.pdf.

72 Idayat Hassan and Alex Vines, "Nigeria: Trust and Turnout Define 2023 Elections," Chatham House, March 31, 2023, https://www.chathamhouse.org/2023/03/nigeria-trust-and-turnout-define-2023-elections.

73 Toyin Akinniyi, "Interview: How Can Nigeria Build Trust in Public Institutions?" *Luminate*, August 7, 2023, https://www.luminategroup.com/posts/story/interview-how-can-nigeria-build-trust-in-public-institutions.

74 Friday Olokor, "Elections: Imo, Rivers Results Manipulated, says Yiaga Africa," *The Punch*, March 2, 2023, https://punchng.com/elections-imo-rivers-results-manipulated-says-yiaga-africa/.

4
CAMOUFLAGE COMES BACK IN STYLE

The research shows in a compelling manner that tolerance for ongoing inequality, government under-performance and elite self-enrichment is sharply waning across the continent.
　　　　　　　　　　　　　—UNITED NATIONS DEVELOPMENT PROGRAM
　　　　　　　　　　　　　　　　　　SOLDIERS AND CITIZENS REPORT[1]

In some parts of Africa, the era of volatility has already arrived. Just after midnight, in the early hours of August 19, 2020, citizens of Mali who were watching state television saw their president, Ibrahim Boubacar Keita, resign while in the custody of mutineers. "Do I really have a choice?" he asked plaintively behind his surgical mask, explaining that he wished to avoid bloodshed.[2] He had come to power with a convincing victory in the 2013 elections, which were intended to restore democracy after an earlier coup had occurred in 2012. But seven years after crowds celebrated his electoral victory in the streets, equally jubilant masses of people came out to cheer on the military for ousting him, some snapping pictures with their phones of the armed convoy whisking him away to the military base where he would issue his televised resignation.[3]

The coup in Mali did not surprise many; mass demonstrations had been held for months decrying corruption, insecurity, and the dubious legitimacy of the country's 2018 and 2020 elections.[4] But, at the time, few predicted that so many dominoes would fall in similar fashion, creating the so-called coup belt of countries in which the military has seized control of the state stretching across the continent from the Atlantic Ocean to the Red Sea. Since 2020, Africa has experienced over a dozen coups and coup attempts,[5] a significant uptick from the frequency of coups since 2000. At that time, only four countries were headed by juntas. Today, military governments control Guinea, Mali, Burkina Faso, Niger, Chad, Sudan, and Gabon. While it is true that this region has long experience with putschists—collectively these seven countries have experienced over sixty coups and coup attempts[6]—dismissing the recent developments as business-as-usual would be a mistake. Some of these states had experienced significant periods of political consistency in recent years. Idriss Déby was the president of Chad for over thirty years until his death triggered the military's 2021 seizure of power. Guinea was led by the same man, Lasana Conté, from 1984 until the end of 2008, then by Alpha Condé for nearly eleven years until the 2021 coup d'etat. Burkina Faso was governed by Blaise Compaoré from 1987 until a popular uprising forced him to step down in 2014; the country has since churned through over half a dozen interim leaders, and one democratically elected president who held on for six years before being deposed in 2022.

With all the hand-wringing among supporters of democracy about the latest trends, it's important to acknowledge that a solid majority of Africans consistently support democratic governance in polls. In fact, the ousted leaders of Mali, Guinea, and Burkina Faso were once popular elected figures who had "delivered" their countries from periods of military rule through victory at the ballot box.[7] International journalists reported that cries of "Long live democracy! Long live change!" rang out on the streets of Guinea's capital when Condé's victory was announced in 2010.[8] When Burkina Faso's electoral commission announced that Roch Kaboré had won the 2015 election, "crowds celebrated the news in the streets of the capital, Ouagadougou, honking car and motorbike horns."[9] But the numbers have been slipping over time. Between 2015 and 2022, support for democracy dropped by 36 percent in Mali, by 26 percent in Burkina Faso, and by 15 percent in Guinea.[10] By the time the military took over in these states, the press coverage was all about the crowds cheering for the uniformed replacements of the once-popular civilian leaders.[11] It's not just the throngs of jubilant youths celebrating juntas in the streets that give observers a sense that military takeovers have their supporters. Young people have also used online spaces to express their disdain for the political leadership of yesterday. When photos surfaced of a disheveled Alpha Condé lounging on a couch surrounded by heavily armed men in fatigues shortly after Guinea's 2021 coup,[12] young Guineans initiated the "Alpha Conde challenge," posting pictures of themselves sprawling glumly on couches in satirical imitation of the deposed president across social media.[13] Likewise, when Gabon's ousted president, Ali Bongo, posted a video while under house arrest, calling on the friends of Gabon to "make noise" to protest his detention, young Africans set his plea to music and shared amusing TikTok and YouTube videos of themselves dancing along.[14] It wasn't just that they could not take seriously a call to rush to Bongo's defense; it's that they were more inclined to celebrate his reversal of fortune. The videos and memes should be taken with several grains of salt; rarely do disapproving but cautious civilians generate much in the way of press coverage or viral digital content. But at the same time, there is real evidence indicating that in many

African states, young people are not just dissatisfied with the way democracy is working;[15] they are more willing than their elders to entertain the idea of a military takeover.

Of course, coups d'etat are only one manifestation of volatility and frustration, and specific domestic dynamics, as well as individual incentives and decision-making, are all involved in setting the stage for a military takeover. Tinkering with term limits and holding dubious elections helped to tip the balance in Guinea and Gabon. The unexpected death of the president triggered Chad's coup, as military and political elites sought to manage the sudden transition without reference to the constitution. Mass protests and largely peaceful civilian demands for change prompted Sudan's military to oust the government in an attempt to control the sea change enveloping the country. Persistent insecurity combined with long-standing frustrations with the political class in Mali, Burkina Faso, and Niger laid the groundwork for their multiple coups, but so too did military reshuffles that left some ambitious soldiers embittered. No country is destined to experience a coup d'etat. But in many countries, converging trends across Africa create fertile ground for the kind of dramatic change that military seizures of power typically promise (even if they rarely deliver).

In 2022 and 2023, the United Nations Development Program (UNDP) conducted a survey of citizens in several African states that have experienced recent military coups as well as those in countries with generally positive democratic trajectories.[16] Researchers found that a decline in civic trust in government capacity and commitment to provide dignity and opportunity, combined with anger at corruption and electoral manipulation, have created a "grievance base," noting that this is "especially true for younger generations."[17] This aggrieved population is primed to embrace change, and willing to entertain the ideas of those who purport to offer it. Of several proposed rationales for supporting a coup d'etat in the UNDP study, "time for change" was the most popular reason, cited by 44 percent of respondents.

Other polling data points in the same direction. *Afrobarometer* has found that young adults are also more open to military intervention in government when leaders abuse power (56 percent for eighteen to thirty-six-year-olds versus 46 percent of those fifty-six and older).[18] As E. Gyimah-Boadi noted, "Given their numerical superiority across the continent, it must be deeply concerning that younger Africans are more likely than their elders to express their readiness for military intervention."[19] Part of this may be about different generational experiences, insofar as older generations may remember the downsides to former military regimes. But for the majority with no memory of life under a junta, only life in weak, deeply flawed democracies, the story is different. In systems where the trappings of democracy do not seem to equate to any accountability for bad leadership or real power for voters, citizens lose faith in their mode of governance. They no longer expect the democratic system, as they have experienced it, to lead to any significant change, and research shows that wide gaps between aspirations and expectations can tip people toward radical solutions.[20] This scenario isn't a hypothetical; in many African states, it has already happened. Frustration with government performance, insecurity, perceptions of widening inequality, and disgust with pervasive corruption have all corroded public trust in the state. A radical solution has appeal.

Part of this has to do with how citizens see democracy function domestically. Surveys in the region show that people want government to tackle unemployment, management of the economy (which usually means bringing down the cost of living), and the provision of public goods like healthcare, water, and infrastructure.[21] But as the UNDP report noted, the countries experiencing coups over the last five years, with the exception of Gabon, have ranked near the bottom of human development, economic freedom, and multidimensional poverty indices. Clearly, citizens' most urgent needs were not being met.[22]

Perceptions of relative deprivation are also strongly associated with low trust in government institutions.[23] If the prevailing system seems to value others disproportionately, one quickly concludes that the system is rotten. Researchers measured young people's political inclusion and participation at some of the lowest levels on the continent in the countries that recently experienced coups, and found that 80 percent of people agreed that more young people were needed in leadership positions, compared to 62 percent in relatively stable democracies.[24] The appeal of several junta leaders is helped by the fact that they are notably younger than their predecessors. As of early 2024, the military leaders of Mali, Burkina Faso, Chad, and Guinea were all born in the 1980s. This relative deprivation association may also be a part of why urban residents, who can more readily see the inequities of their society, are more skeptical about the capacity of elections to hold leaders accountable than their rural counterparts,[25] and why overall, their support for elections has declined over the past decade.[26]

Concerns about corruption are another, related part of the picture. Polling from 2021 to 2023 found that a majority of Africans believed that corruption was increasing in their country. Over two-thirds of respondents thought that their government did a poor job fighting corruption.[27] Even a casual glance at the social media discourse throughout the region confirms that perceptions of corruption are widespread and create an oppositional dynamic between beleaguered citizens and a predatory state.

Take, for example, the viral "math" discourse of 2023. What many young Americans experienced as a commentary on gender and consumer culture ("girl math" and "boy math")[28] many young Africans turned into a critique of corrupt officials. In response to an online prompt, "What's Nigerian politics math?" commenters expressed their certainty that public servants were only serving themselves.

Enter office with one car. Leave office with mansions and properties in Lagos, Abuja, Dubai, UK, & US. Billions in various bank NGN accounts + offshore Swiss accounts with millions of dollars stashed. This maths will favour me and my family. Amen

Sell VOTES/POSITIONS to highest bidder

(Nigerian - integrity) * corruption = presidency/governorship[29]

The same consensus around predatory government was evident in online discourse in Cameroon, when a social media account announcing the yearly budget for different government ministries drew scores of suspicious comments, in particular for the budget of the Ministry of Youth and Civic Education:

They are already rubbing their hands

For the youth of his family or else?[30]

The multiplicity of scandals surrounding assistance intended to combat the COVID-19 pandemic, from inflated medical supply contracts to missing millions earmarked for pandemic response,[31] only made a bad situation worse.

It would be one thing if governments that underperformed were certain to face consequences at the ballot box. But often incumbents manipulate the rules to stay in power, altering constitutions to avoid term limits, ensuring that opponents cannot organize, and holding elections in conditions so unsafe that many cannot come out to vote. The number one reason respondents gave the UNDP research team for why non-democratic government can sometimes be preferable was that democracy can be abused or simply does not work.[32] The relationship between governments that never seem to change and military takeovers is so clear that the Africa Center for Strategic Studies described term limit evasions and military takeovers are "two sides of the same coin."[33] Frustration builds, and a toxic stew of dissatisfaction, mistrust, resentment of those who seem to benefit from the status quo, and cynicism about democracy combines to build the "grievance base" that can be tapped into by ambitious men in fatigues.

That sense of grievance was on full display in Mali in the months leading up to Keita's middle-of-the-night resignation at gunpoint. The capital city of Bamako had been the site of massive protests organized by a coalition of opposition parties, religious leaders, and civil society organizations demanding governance reform, decrying corruption among ruling elites, and calling for Keita's resignation.[34] Those protests were met with a heavy-handed state response, further fueling popular anger.[35] Likewise, in Sudan, protests preceded the military's takeover. They started in Khartoum and followed in other cities by the end of 2018. While initially focusing on bread and fuel prices, within weeks they morphed into spirited calls for the end of Bashir's rule and democratic reform. In Guinea, the National Front for the Defense of the Constitution mobilized before the coup to resist Alpha Condé's attempts to stay in power. Less than a year after the Guinean military's seizure of power, the same coalition would take to the streets again to push for a democratic transition, only to be formally dissolved by the ruling junta that had once capitalized on their movement.[36] These movements were not taking to the streets to call for military intervention, but they were indicators that an aggrieved population would welcome change.

In 2019, data across thirty-four countries showed that on average, only 34 percent of Africans were satisfied with the way democracy works in their countries. In Gabon, only 6 percent were satisfied.[37] It should come as no surprise that the Gabonese weren't eager to "make noise" to restore the government that had so let them down. Indeed, if a lack of trust in governing institutions, a sense of pervasive corruption in government, and a mismatch between citizen and government priorities help to create conditions for a coup, Gabon was ripe for the taking. A 2021 survey indicated that only 14 percent of Gabonese citizens believed elections held officials accountable, and less than a third of citizens believed the 2016 elections were free and fair.[38] The decades of Bongo family dominance seemed like an anachronism for Gabonese well aware of other countries that experienced real political change. Around 76 percent of Gabonese believed that corruption was increasing in the country, a 24 percent increase from a decade prior.[39] With roughly 80 percent of the country living in urban areas, a median age below twenty-two, internet penetration above 60 percent, and a youth unemployment rate of about 35 percent,[40] the desire for change was palpable enough to make the risk of the coup worth it to the perpetrators.

The sense of possibility that being in the midst of a watershed moment brings can be invigorating. Indeed, UNDP researchers found that the biggest difference in responses about the overall direction of the country between those who lived in countries that had recently experienced a coup d'etat and those in countries deemed to have a positive democratic trajectory was that 49 percent of citizens living under military rule felt "excited" about the future, versus 25 percent expressing the same feeling in democracies.[41] The citizens who lived through military seizures of power expressed more optimism that positive change would occur in their countries by a margin of 24 percent.[42]

In contrast, people in countries that by most metrics have positive governance trajectories "cited higher levels of frustration and skepticism about government than were reported in the coup-affected countries. This discrepancy seems to suggest both higher expectations in these settings, as well as challenges that persist even in contexts with relative development progress." The citizens in countries that are stable and making marginal development gains are pessimistic about their futures, perhaps because marginal gains cannot meet the growing demands of the population. There is no breakthrough moment in the offing, only gradualism. As the authors of the report write, the dissatisfaction of Africans in these countries speaks to "aspirations left unmet despite the overall development gains registered."[43]

But willingness to give the men in fatigues a chance is not the same everywhere. Sudan's recent history clearly illustrates how military takeovers are not always perceived as advancing the citizenry's desire for change. In late 2018, a popular movement developed in Sudan that was unrelenting in its demand for something new. Fed up with crippling inflation, angry about years of economic mismanagement, and eager to see an end to the violent brand of authoritarianism that was a specialty of the Sudanese leadership, they took to the streets en masse to insist the existing government step down and make space for an inclusive democracy.[44] The predominantly young members of a "leaderless" movement had assets that the repressive state did not. "These groups—urban, linked to the diaspora, often led by women—were a new force in Sudanese politics, and played to a tune that the gerontocrats behind the walls of the military headquarters simply couldn't understand."[45] Demonstrators persisted in the face of a lethal state response, rejected misleading state media reports aimed at discrediting the movement, and found ways to express solidarity even when the state shut down social media. By 2019, the political situation had become untenable, and Sudan's military moved to oust President Bashir and seize control of the country, lest their interests be damaged by the changes afoot.

When the military seized power in 2019, the streets celebrated the removal of the Bashir regime but kept protesting to insist on civilian government. The Sudanese protesters wanted change but immediately rejected the notion that a military takeover fit the bill, in part because Bashir himself had come to power via coup, though he subsequently sought to legitimize his rule through periodic elections devoid of either integrity or suspense. Sudan's population never had a chance to grow cynical about democracy because they never experienced anything even close to it. After a tenuous transitional period in which the military and civilians shared power, another October 2021 coup confirmed the Sudanese military's unwillingness to give up power.

Indeed, a majority of Sudanese understood the coup as a negative development, and "youth representatives described how the coup constituted a deep shock to young people in particular. They said events plunged many into a state of fear and depression, shattering their dreams of building a modern national state after the overthrow of the previous regime."[46] Military rule in Sudan arrested the process of change young people in the streets wanted to see, rather than ushering it in.

By 2024, as Sudan's security forces continued to fight with each other, the country had become the source of the world's largest displacement crisis and site of horrifying war crimes along with humanitarian catastrophe. But many of the young people who had organized to topple Bashir, despite being at the mercy of armed actors, continued their civic activism. The resistance committees that were at the heart of the uprising pivoted to providing services to their fellow citizens as the state and international aid operations all but disappeared. From community food pantries to finding fuel for makeshift ambulances to facilitating evacuations from neighborhoods under fire, Sudan's youth-led movement persists.

A Story to Match the Grievances

Several of the recent coup leaders have tried to establish new legitimacy narratives, invoking revolutionary giants like Thomas Sankara, echoing the words of Patrice Lumumba,[47] or invoking Jerry Rawlings,[48] sporting red berets or striking Pan-African poses to buttress the notion that they are the new liberators, and that their seizure of power represents "real" independence.* Burkina's military government even took formal steps to elevate Sankara to the rank of "hero of the nation."[49] These reference points serve several useful purposes. First and most obviously, they place the military leaders in the company of figures with near-universal name recognition and a great deal of public admiration. But they also establish a framing that suggests the grievances of the population relate to a form of colonial oppression that never ended. Ousted governments are painted as the feckless puppets of external actors intent on extracting the wealth of the country and keeping its citizens powerless. The primary villains in this story are external; former colonial powers (particularly the French and more generally the "West") and international institutions like the United Nations. In some ways, these military leaders are co-opting the narrative of the continent's dominant liberation parties in a back-to-the-future gambit.

Looking into why young people get involved in violent extremist groups, researchers Mats Utas and Henrik Vigh found that youth engaged not out of total conviction or agreement with the group's agenda, but as a way to express "both a local and a global critique of the dominant orders that they are caught in" and

---

*Thomas Sankara was a coup leader himself, having seized power in what is now Burkina Faso in 1983. His anti-imperialist, Pan-African philosophy emphasized African self-reliance. He was assassinated in the course of a countercoup in 1987, but is remembered and even idolized in many quarters as a champion of African dignity and resistance. See Brian J. Peterson's excellent biography *Thomas Sankara: A Revolutionary in Cold War Africa* (Bloomington: Indiana University Press, 2021). Patrice Lumumba was the first Prime Minister of the Democratic Republic of the Congo and another important Pan-African intellectual. He was killed in 1961 after a US-backed coup d'etat in the country. Jerry Rawlings was Ghanaian leader who came to power via coup d'etat and ruled by fiat for over a decade but eventually steered Ghana back to democracy, was elected president twice, and stepped down in 2001 in accordance with constitutional term limits.

to find "alternative avenues to social worth and recognition."[50] The same may well be true for the youths enthusing over military takeovers—they can reject the status quo domestically, push back on the global forces that seem to them both arrogant and cruel, and recast themselves as proud revolutionaries. It is notable that junta leaders make frequent reference to "restoring the dignity" of the people in their justifications for seizing power. In his first speech as the country's leader, Guinea's Colonel Doumbouya claimed,

> Our gesture is therefore nothing other than the expression of our desire for dignity which you certainly share with us. However, it is because respect for our dignity has been flouted since 1958 by a minority which confiscates power and its economic advantages that we have taken the initiative, summoned by a sense of duty, to create the conditions for a new political and social departure.[51]

Likewise, General Oligui Nguema of Gabon told journalists that his purpose was nothing less than "to restore our institutions and the dignity of the Gabonese people."[52] Burkina Faso's Ibrahim Traoré has closed speeches calling for "Glory to our peoples, dignity to our peoples, victory to our peoples."[53]

The degree to which the neo-liberation narrative was conceived and drafted in Moscow is well worth investigating, and there is ample evidence that Russia has deployed all of the tools in its formidable disinformation arsenal to this effect;[54] but focusing on Russia's role alone risks missing the point that its information campaigns easily gained traction in several countries because of ample home-grown frustrations and resentments. The "grievance base" was fertile ground for a story that offered a simple explanation about why the status quo was so unsatisfying. In this telling, rather than self-serving governing elites combining with a set of unwieldly structural factors and global economic shocks to create stifling conditions, a cabal of outsiders and their agents within deliberately created the deeply frustrating context in which so many young Africans have found themselves. This sounds like a far easier problem to solve, and one calling for radical action rather than long-term, incremental strategies. The appeal, particularly to young people, is undeniable.

The liberation framing also provides a ready scapegoat for the inevitable persistence of dissatisfaction after a coup. Powerful external forces will continue to exist, and thus can continue to be blamed for all manner of security and economic problems, rather than bad domestic choices. Speaking for the military government of Mali at the UN General Assembly in 2022, interim Prime Minister Abdoulaye Maiga used his platform to vehemently denounce the French government, insisting that France, which had deployed forces to combat terrorists in Mali for nearly a decade, had "provided intelligence and arms to terrorist groups," and that this was "the basis for the worsening insecurity and destabilization in Mali." After leveling this implausible accusation, he offered advice to French officials, urging them,

> Look at how the world changes. Move on from the colonial past. Look at the anger, the frustration, the rejection of this in African towns and rural areas. Understand that this movement is inexorable. Your intimidation, your subversive action, are just increasing the number of Africans who want to preserve their dignity.[55]

Through this lens, the fact that security in Mali significantly worsened since the military seized power in 2020—with annual jihadist attacks increasing by roughly 40 percent between 2020 and 2022[56]—could be explained by diabolical French agendas, and the regional leaders pressuring Mali's junta were traitors to the cause of African agency and dignity. When Maiga returned to Bamako from New York, he was greeted with a hero's welcome.[57] Certainly, Mali's information environment is constricted and distorted by the military government and its Russian supporters. But it is also true that young people who have felt humiliated and frustrated were thrilled by the idea of their country unabashedly asserting itself on a global stage.

Similarly, Ibrahim Traoré, Burkina Faso's uniformed leader, chose his speech at the Russia-Africa Summit held in St. Petersburg in July 2023 both to underscore his youthfulness—he was thirty-four when he seized power—and to drive these points home, first apologizing "to the elders. Please, forgive me if I have wronged you in any way. My generation is asking many questions without getting any answers." Then he moved on to speculate about the bright new dawn coming when outside forces could be defeated, wondering aloud,

> What will happen tomorrow in this new, free world which we are striving for, a world without interference in our internal affairs? . . . We, the heads of African states, must stop acting as puppets ready to act whenever the imperialists pull the strings.[58]

The speech was a social media sensation—doubtlessly helped along by Russian bots, but also because it felt cathartic to many on the continent frustrated with their prospects. The irony of condemning interference in other's affairs while speaking in Russia before President Putin, who has overseen a massive foreign influence operation during his tenure, was lost on Traoré's admirers.

Guinea's junta leader, Colonel Mamadi Doumbouya, took note and sought out his own viral moment at the UN General Assembly later in 2023, pushing back against critics of coups by asserting that "the real putschists" are leaders who "cheat to manipulate the text of the constitution in order to stay in power eternally." Having already appointed himself the leader of Guineans without consulting them, he decided to speak for all of Africa in rejecting democratic governance as a whole, which he claimed was imposed by the West, suggesting that it is ill-suited to African "realities, our customs and environment."[59]

Ephemeral Euphoria

But pointing to external forces can only go so far in fending off simmering dissatisfaction domestically. Researchers have found a waning of optimism about the potential for coups to drive positive change as time goes on, leading those interested in power to stage yet another intervention. Indeed, the coup that ousted President Keita in Mali was followed by another, led by the same military officer in charge of the first putsch, who found that having a civilian interim president was not to his liking. Burkina Faso's January 2022 coup was followed less than a year later by another, ostensibly because the first junta wasn't making enough progress on security issues. The countercoups in Mali and Burkina Faso illustrate how quickly pressure can build, creating fresh opportunities to hit the reset button on the promise of a new dispensation. Surveys show a decrease in excitement and pride several months after an unconstitutional transfer of power, and an increase in worry. As the UNDP research team noted, "this sensitive interplay between hope, delivery and expectation contributes to the risk of prolonged turbulence in transitional contexts."[60]

Enthusiasm for military governance appears to have had a short shelf life in Guinea, where despite initial indicators that the population welcomed the 2021 coup d'etat, citizens have been pushing back, often at great risk to their safety.[61] Several rounds of sizable street protests have featured complaints about the cost of living, calls for the release of political prisoners, and demands for a speedier return to civilian rule. A general strike in 2024 ground the struggling economy to a near-standstill until the junta met at least some of the opposition demands.[62]

Who's Next?

After Gabon's coup, speculation about which country might come next had become a familiar topic of conversation for anyone interested in African politics. Several governments undertook "coup-proofing" measures aimed at staving off a putsch; shortly after Gabon's coup, military reshuffles involving promotions, transfers, and retirements were announced in both Cameroon and Rwanda.[63] Nigeria's Chief of Defense Staff felt compelled to scold those calling for a military takeover publicly, urging his fellow Nigerians to be patient through "trying periods."[64] *The Economist* magazine ran an October 2023 article titled "Where Will the Next Coup Be in Africa?" complete with a graphic showing high-risk countries.[65]

A great deal of attention has focused on Cameroon, where the long-serving President Biya has carefully maneuvered to reduce threats from the military ever since an attempted coup in 1984. Young Cameroonians, who have no lived experience of any type of government other than one dominated by President Biya, are more than twice as likely as their elders to support military intervention in government.[66] In 2023, false rumors that Biya was under house arrest circulated online days after Gabon's coup, and were met with many approving responses, though also with a healthy dose of skepticism, particularly about the idea that Biya would even be in the country.

> I think it is just wishful thinking.
>
> Too good to be true[67]
>
> Paul Biya does not reside in Cameroon. How is this possible.
>
> Paul Biya spends most of his time outside Cameroon so the unconfirmed reports are probably just that.[68]

Eventually Cameroon's Minister of Information, Rene Emmanuel Sadi, threatened that anyone "speculating" about a possible coup in the country and drawing "senseless and preposterous parallels" risked arrest and prosecution.[69] This, too prompted a dismissive digital discourse.

> . . . and then he gets toppled next week! It would really prove that nature has a very wicked sense of humour!
>
> With this statement, he's set the ball rolling. There will surely be a coup that will oust his government; just a matter of time.[70]

For these digitally connected young Africans, a coup seems not only like a viable possibility, but a potential source of relief, a way out of the political waiting room that offers little reason to believe their circumstances will improve. Political change is sought as a kind of pressure release, but it does not have to come dressed in fatigues. There is no single trajectory that African states will follow, which makes old arguments about Afro-pessimism or Afro-optimism beside the point. The unifying factor is a quest for governance that works better than the status quo.

Notes

1. United Nations Development Programme, *Soldiers and Citizens: Military Coups and the Need for Democratic Renewal in Africa* (New York: UNDP, 2023), https://www.soldiersandcitizens.org/assets/UNDP_Soldiers_and_citizens_ENG.pdf.
2. "Mali President Resigns after Military Mutiny: Live Updates," *Al Jazeera*, August 10, 2020, https://www.aljazeera.com/news/2020/8/19/mali-president-resigns-after-military-mutiny-live-updates.
3. Voice of America, "Footage of Mali Soldiers Detaining President," YouTube Video, 0:56 sec, August 19, 2020, https://www.youtube.com/watch?v=TBwSUHQ10rE.
4. Alex Vines, "Why the Mali Coup Should Matter to the UK," Chatham House, August 20, 2020, https://www.chathamhouse.org/2020/08/why-mali-coup-should-matter-uk.
5. Successful coups occurred in Mali in 2020; Guinea, Chad, Sudan, and Mali again in 2021; Burkina Faso twice in 2022; and Niger and Gabon in 2023. Unsuccessful attempts were documented in the Gambia, Sao Tome and Principe, Guinea Bissau, Niger, and the Central African Republic.
6. "Frequency of Coup Events from 1945 to 2023, by Country," Cline Center for Advanced Social Research, University of Illinois, Accessed April 2, 2024, https://clinecenter.illinois.edu/project/research-themes/democracy-and-development/coup-detat-project/freq-table.
7. Alexis Arieff and Lauren Ploch Blanchard, "'An Epidemic of Coups' in Africa? Issues for Congress," *Congressional Research Service*, February 11, 2022, https://crsreports.congress.gov/product/pdf/IN/IN11854.
8. James André, "Alpha Conde Declared Winner in Guinea Presidential Run-off," *France24*, last modified November 16, 2010, https://www.france24.com/en/20101115-guinea-alpha-conde-wins-presidential-vote-electoral-commission-diallo-politics-africa-cnei.
9. Mathieu Bonkoungou and Nadoun Coulibaly, "Kabore Wins Burkina Faso Presidential Election," *Reuters*, last modified November 30, 2015, https://www.reuters.com/article/us-burkina-election/kabore-wins-burkina-faso-presidential-election-idUSKBN0TJ0QT20151201/.
10. *Afrobarometer*, "Afrobarometer Data Show Worrying Trends for Democracy in Africa, Prof. Gyimah-Boadi Warns," news release, June 16, 2023, https://www.afrobarometer.org/wp-content/uploads/2023/06/News-release-Afrobarometer-data-show-worrying-trends-for-democracy-in-Africa-bh-16june23.pdf.
11. See, for example, "Mali Coup: Thousands Take to Bamako Streets to Celebrate," *BBC News*, August 21, 2020, https://www.bbc.com/news/world-africa-53868236; "In Pictures: Many Guineans Celebrate as Soldiers Seize Power," *Al Jazeera*, September 6, 2021, https://www.aljazeera.com/gallery/2021/9/6/many-guineans-celebrate-as-soldiers-seize-power; Anne Mimault and Thiam Ndiaga, "Burkina Faso Crowd Celebrates West Africa's Latest Coup," *Reuters*, January 25, 2022, https://www.reuters.com/world/africa/burkina-faso-crowd-celebrates-west-africas-latest-coup-2022-01-25/.

12. "Guinea Coup Leader to Form New Government in Weeks," *BBC News*, September 6, 2021, https://www.bbc.com/news/world-africa-58461436.
13. Mouhamed Camara, "Guinée: Un challenge inspiré de la photo de Alpha Condé fait sensation sur les réseaux sociaux (photos)," *Sene.News*, last modified September 10, 2021, https://www.senenews.com/senenews-people/insolites-buzz/guinee-un-challenge-inspire-de-la-photo-de-alpha-conde-fait-sensation-sur-les-reseaux-sociaux-photos_367791.html.
14. *Al Jazeera English*, "Ali Bongo's 'make noise' Plea Turns into Meme," YouTube video, 1:25, September 4, 2023, https://www.youtube.com/watch?v=K5Bv1IVRZMc.
15. Josephine Appiah-Nyamekye Sanny, Shannon van Wyk-Khosa, and Joseph Asunka, "Africa's Youth: More Educated, Less Employed, still Unheard in Policy and Development," *Afrobarometer Dispatch* no. 734, November 15, 2023, https://www.afrobarometer.org/wp-content/uploads/2023/11/AD734-PAP3-Africas-youth-More-educated-less-employed-still-unheard-Afrobarometer-18nov23.pdf.
16. The UNDP *Soldier and Citizens* survey questioned 8,000 respondents, 5,000 in Burkina Faso, Chad, Guinea, Mali and Sudan, and another 3,000 in the Gambia, Ghana, and Tanzania.
17. UNDP, *Soldiers and Citizens*, 16.
18. Sanny, van Wyk-Khosa, and Asunka, "Africa's Youth."
19. *Afrobarometer*, "Afrobarometer Data Show Worrying Trends."
20. Jeremy Chevrier, *Exploring the Connections Between Poverty, Lack of Economic Opportunity, and Violent Extremism in sub-Saharan Africa* (Washington, DC: USAID Center for Resilience, November 2017), 9, https://pdf.usaid.gov/pdf_docs/PA00WQ7X.pdf.
21. Christiaan Keulder and Robert Mattes, "Why Are Africans Dissatisfied with Democracy? Think corruption," *Afrobarometer*, November 25, 2021, https://www.afrobarometer.org/articles/why-are-africans-dissatisfied-democracy-think-corruption/.
22. UNDP, *Soldiers and Citizens*, 102.
23. Thomas Isbell, "WP196: Keeping Tabs? Perceptions of Relative Deprivation and Political Trust in Africa," *Afrobarometer Working Paper* 196, February 21, 2023, https://www.afrobarometer.org/publication/wp196-keeping-tabs-perceptions-of-relative-deprivation-and-political-trust-in-africa/.
24. UNDP, *Soldiers and Citizens*.
25. Fredline M'Cormack-Hale and Mavis Zupork Dome, "AD551: Support for Elections Weakens among Africans; Many See Them as Ineffective in Holding Leaders Accountable," *Afrobarometer Dispatch* no. 551, September 16, 2022, https://www.afrobarometer.org/publication/ad551-support-for-elections-weakens-among-africans-many-see-them-as-ineffective-in-holding-leaders-accountable/.
26. There are some notable exceptions to this, including in the Gambia and Liberia; see M'Cormack-Hale and Dome, "AD551."
27. Keulder and Mattes, "Why Are Africans Dissatisfied with Democracy?"

28 Dani Di Placido, "'Boy Math' and 'Girl Math' Meme, Explained," *Forbes*, September 29, 2023, https://www.forbes.com/sites/danidiplacido/2023/09/29/boy-math-and-girl-math-meme-explained/?sh=3262c94568b1.

29 X-Daily (@X_Dailly), "What's Nigerian politics maths?" X post, October 3, 2023, https://twitter.com/X_Daily/status/1709221578309857473.

30 The Cameroonian (@TheCameroonianZ), "27 milliards FCFA: Budget 2024 pour le ministère de la Jeunesse et de l'Education Civique," X post, December 3, 2023, https://twitter.com/TheCameroonianZ/status/1731536617678991728.

31 Enoch Randy Aikeins, "Corruption in Africa Deepens the Wounds of COVID-19," Institute for Security Studies, May 19, 2022, https://issafrica.org/iss-today/corruption-in-africa-deepens-the-wounds-of-covid-19.

32 UNDP, *Soldiers and Citizens*, 85.

33 "Term Limit Evasions and Coups in Africa: Two Sides of the Same Coin," Africa Center for Strategic Studies, October 24, 2023, https://africacenter.org/spotlight/term-limit-evasions-coups-africa-same-coin/.

34 Associated Press, "Tens of Thousands Protest in Mali amid Growing Opposition to Keita Presidency," *New York Times*, last modified August 19, 2020, https://www.nytimes.com/2020/06/19/world/africa/mali-protests-keita.html.

35 "Mali: Security Forces Use Excessive Force at Protests," Human Rights Watch, August 12, 2020, https://www.hrw.org/news/2020/08/12/mali-security-forces-use-excessive-force-protests.

36 "Guinea: Government Dissolves Opposition Coalition," Human Rights Watch, August 11, 2022, https://www.hrw.org/news/2022/08/11/guinea-government-dissolves-opposition-coalition.

37 Robert Mattes, "Democracy in Africa: Demand, Supply, and the 'dissatisfied democrat,'" *Afrobarometer Policy Paper* No. 54, February 2019, 1–30, https://www.afrobarometer.org/wp-content/uploads/migrated/files/publications/Policy%20papers/ab_r7_policypaperno54_africans_views_of_democracy1.pdf.

38 M'Cormack-Hale and Dome, "AD551."

39 Boniface Dulani, Gildfred Boateng Asiamah, and Patrick Zindikirani, "Amid Rising Corruption, Most Africans Say They Risk Retaliation if They Speak Up," *Afrobarometer Dispatch* No. 743, December 6, 2023, 1–25, https://www.afrobarometer.org/wp-content/uploads/2023/12/AD743-PAP5-Amid-rising-corruption-Africans-say-they-risk-retaliation-if-they-speak-up-Afrobarometer_3dec23.pdf.

40 "Unemployment, Youth Total (% of total labor force ages 15–24) (modeled ILO estimate)—Gabon," World Bank, accessed February 4, 2024, https://data.worldbank.org/indicator/SL.UEM.1524.ZS?locations=GA.

41 UNDP, *Soldiers and Citizens*.

42 UNDP, *Soldiers and Citizens*.

43 UNDP, *Soldiers and Citizens*.

44 "Protesters Call on Sudan's President Bashir to Step Down," *BBC News*, January 4, 2019, https://www.bbc.com/news/world-africa-46761119.

45 Willow Berridge, Justin Lynch, Raga Makawi, and Alex de Waal, *Sudan's Unfinished Democracy: The Promise and Betrayal of a People's Revolution* (London: Hurst Publishers, 2022), 22.

46 UNDP, *Soldiers and Citizens*, 131.

47 See, for example, Patrice Lumumba, "Speech at the Opening of the All-African Conference in Leopoldville," (speech, Leopoldville, August 25, 1960), Patrice Lumumba Archive, https://www.marxists.org/subject/africa/lumumba/1960/08/25.htm.

48 See, for example, Thomas Naadi, "Gabon Coup Leader Brice Nguema Vows Free Elections—but No Date," *BBC News*, September 4, 2023, https://www.bbc.com/news/world-africa-66705693.

49 *Rédaction Africanews* with AFP, "Burkina Faso: Former President Thomas Sankara Elevated to the Rank of 'national hero,'" *Africanews*, last modified October 5, 2023, https://www.africanews.com/2023/10/05/burkina-faso-former-president-thomas-sankara-elevated-to-the-rank-of-national-hero/.

50 Mats Utas and Henrik Vigh, "Radicalized Youth: Oppositional Poses and Positions," in *Africa's Insurgents: Navigating and Evolving Landscape*, ed. Morten Bøås and Kevin C. Dunn (Boulder, CO: Lynne Rienner Publishers, 2017), 25.

51 WOMEN's TV—Liberia, "FULL SPEECH by Col. Mamady Doumbouya, Coup Leader Conakry, Guinea," Facebook, September 6, 2021, https://www.facebook.com/womentvlib/posts/full-speech-by-col-mamady-doumbouya-coup-leader-conakry-guinea-dear-compatriots-/377706300694212/.

52 Marwane Ben Yahmed, "[Exclusive] Gabon's Brice Clotaire Oligui Nguema: 'This is not a coup d'état, but an act of liberation,'" *Africa Report*, September 22, 2023, https://www.theafricareport.com/322833/exclusive-gabons-brice-clotaire-oligui-nguema-this-is-not-a-coup-detat-but-an-act-of-liberation/.

53 "'A slave who cannot assume his own revolt does not deserve to be pitied,' says Ibrahim Traoré of Burkina Faso," *Peoples Dispatch*, August 2, 2023, https://peoplesdispatch.org/2023/08/02/a-slave-who-cannot-assume-his-own-revolt-does-not-deserve-to-be-pitied-says-ibrahim-traore-of-burkina-faso/.

54 Mark Duerksen, "Disinformation Drilling into Africa's Information Ecosystems," Africa Center for Strategic Studies, February 8, 2023, https://africacenter.org/experts/disinformation-drilling-africa-information-ecosystems/.

55 United Nations, "Mali—Prime Minister Addresses General Debate, 77th Session," UN Web TV, 34:58, September 24, 2022, https://webtv.un.org/en/asset/k1y/k1ya9lo5mi.

56 "Mali Catastrophe Accelerating under Junta Rule," Africa Center for Strategic Studies, July 10, 2023, https://africacenter.org/spotlight/mali-catastrophe-accelerating-under-junta-rule/.

57 "Malians Celebrate Return of Interim PM," *Africanews*, September 28, 2022, https://www.africanews.com/2022/09/28/malians-celebrate-return-of-interim-pm//.

58 "Interim President of Burkina Faso Traoré Speaking at Russia-Africa Summit: Russia Is Part of the Family for Africa," *Special Dispatch* no. 10742, Middle Eastern Media Research Institute, https://www.memri.org/reports/interim-president-burkina-faso-traore-speaking-russia-africa-summit-russia-part-family.

59 Michelle Gavin, "A Dispiriting UNGA," *Africa in Transition*, Council on Foreign Relations, September 27, 2023, https://www.cfr.org/blog/dispiriting-unga.

60 UNDP, *Soldiers and Citizens*, 19.

61 "Guinea's Suppression of Protests Stokes Anger against Military," *Al Jazeera*, May 25, 2023, https://www.aljazeera.com/news/2023/5/25/guineas-suppression-of-protests-stokes-anger-against-military.

62 Le Monde with AFP, "Guinea Capital Brought to Standstill by General Strike against Junta," *Le Monde*, February 26, 2024, https://www.lemonde.fr/en/international/article/2024/02/26/guinea-capital-brought-to-standstill-by-general-strike-against-junta_6560870_4.html.

63 Nalova Akua, "Central Africa's Dinosaur Regimes and the Art of Coup-proofing," *African Arguments*, November 27, 2023, https://africanarguments.org/2023/11/central-africas-dinosaur-regimes-and-the-art-of-coup-proofing/.

64 Dennis Naku, "Military Vows to Go after Advocates of Coup," *The Punch*, February 22, 2024, https://punchng.com/military-vows-to-go-after-advocates-of-coup/.

65 "Where Will the Next Coup Be in Africa?" *The Economist*, October 9, 2023, https://www.economist.com/graphic-detail/2023/10/09/where-will-the-next-coup-be-in-africa.

66 The two youngest cohorts, 18–25 and 26–35, have 13.3% and 14% approval for military intervention, versus 5–6% for older groups; see Sanny, van Wyk-Khosa, and Asunka, "Africa's Youth."

67 Responses to BLA SNIPER SQUAD (@MatthewEkong), "Breaking News: Military Coup in Cameroon," X post, September 5, 2023, https://twitter.com/MatthewEkong/status/1698988481144672315

68 Responses to Chief Ikukuoma (@IkukuomaC), "Unconfirmed reports are stating that Paul Biya has been placed under house arrest by Cameroon soldiers," X post, September 3, 2023, https://twitter.com/IkukuomaC/status/1698457302284619802.

69 "Cameroon Threatens Prosecution against Coup Speculators," *Qiraat Africa*, September 27, 2023, https://qiraatafrican.com/en/9292/cameroon-threatens-prosecution-against-coup-speculators/.

70 Responses to Kennedy Wandera (@KennedyWandera_), "Cameroon President Paul Biya's government to arrest, prosecute and jail citizens who speculate his regime will face a coup," X post, September 29, 2023, https://twitter.com/KennedyWandera_/status/1707663562359947674.

5
IMPATIENT POLITICS

Sorry for the delay. Uprooting a regime.
—SIGNS POSTED IN KHARTOUM BY DEMONSTRATORS APOLOGIZING FOR TRAFFIC DISRUPTIONS[1]

A history of military intervention in politics increases the likelihood of coups going forward, but the change young people seek doesn't have to be dressed in fatigues. Mass protests can shake governments and force reforms. Change can also come through the ballot box—or at least, that still appears to be a viable path to some African publics. But convincing young Africans that engaging with the formal political system is worth their time is only half the battle. The challenge of delivering on campaign promises to an ever-growing labor force frustrated with the status quo can reverse political fortunes quickly.

Consider developments in Senegal, a country often held up as an exemplar of how civic action can protect democracy. In 2012, a massive, youthful citizens' movement—mostly famously embodied by the Y'en a Marre, or "fed up" campaign—organized to resist then-President Abdoulaye Wade's attempts to extend his tenure into a constitutionally dubious third term. This rejection of Wade's machinations benefited Macky Sall, who defeated Wade at the polls in 2012, and was reelected in 2019.

But Sall's popularity waned as Senegal's young people continued to struggle with unemployment, the cost of living, and corruption. Sall's own flirtation with the prospect of a third term incensed many Senegalese, as did his increasingly heavy-handed approach to governance. During Sall's second term, scores of political protesters were killed, over a thousand were arrested, and internet shutdowns became relatively commonplace. Many suspected politically motivated prosecutions as Sall's political rivals experienced an epidemic of legal trouble.

Meanwhile, a rising political star, the relatively young Ousmane Sonko, captured the zeitgeist with his denunciation of cozy relations between Senegalese and French elites, attacks on corruption, the promise to review fishing, oil, and gas agreements to ensure citizens are benefiting from the country's resources, and an antiestablishment messaging aimed directly at unemployed youth. Like other opposition figures, he soon found himself in court. Sonko was charged with rape and convicted in 2023 on lesser charges of "corrupting a minor" as well as defamation of a minister.[2] As the 2024 elections approached, and Sall finally announced that he would not seek a third term, Sonko's political party was disbanded by the government, and the state leveled new charges against him of criminal conspiracy and planning insurrection. His legal woes regularly prompted street protests as his supporters claimed that the government was trying to silence him and derail his political ambitions.

Tensions rose to a boiling point as Sall's preferred successor, a technocrat in his sixties, failed to generate popular enthusiasm and Sonko's close political ally, the even younger Bassirou Diomaye Faye, emerged as challenger for the presidency in Sonko's stead. With mere days to go before the election slated for February 25, Sall announced that he was postponing the polls indefinitely, ostensibly because of ongoing disputes about which candidates would qualify to be on the ballot. True to form, Senegal's citizens took to the streets, insisting on elections as soon as possible. The courts rejected Sall's power play and he backed down, hastily granting amnesty to many jailed demonstrators, and agreeing to step down at the end of his constitutionally mandated term. On March 24, 2024, registered voters in Senegal came out in impressive numbers to vote in the country's presidential election and made Faye, forty-four, the youngest elected leader on the continent. Just ten days before his victory, he was in prison, having been charged with defamation over a Facebook post critical of the government. He had never held an executive office before.

For Senegal, where polls show that young adults are better educated than their elders but have higher rates of unemployment (three in ten are out of work),[3] the popular impetus for change found an outlet, at least for the moment. It took years of demonstrations and protests, including several that resulted in the deaths of civilians, a well-timed display of judicial independence, an election that reflected the will of the people, and a charismatic leader able to rally the discontented to affect political change. In his victory speech, Faye stressed that his election represented a break—a "rupture"—from the past. Days later, in his inaugural address, he underscored the point again, "I am aware that the results at the ballot box express a profound desire for systematic change."[4]

But the changes citizens seek can be hard to come by, particularly in the short term. No one can conjure dignified jobs out of thin air and promises to renegotiate oil and gas contracts will have to contend with market realities. With public debt in Senegal at more than 70 percent of GDP around election time, there is not a great deal of space to increase spending on job-creating projects, and young Senegalese continue to risk their lives in rickety boats in hopes of reaching Europe and economic opportunity. Less than a year into his tenure, President Faye released a twenty-five-year development plan aimed at establishing "the foundations for economic sovereignty."[5] Most Senegalese citizens haven't been alive for twenty-five years yet. If Kenya is any guide, Faye's honeymoon will be brief.

Hustlers in a Hurry

William Ruto campaigned on promises to help Kenya's "hustlers"—the young people just getting by, often in the informal economy, without powerful connections or the advantages of wealth and status. Despite being deputy president at the time, he positioned himself as an outsider, having fallen out with President Uhuru Kenyatta, who campaigned for Ruto's main opponent. In Ruto's telling, he would end the era of political dynasties and govern with the hardworking, youthful masses in mind. While an alarming number of young people declined to participate at all in the 2022 elections, turned off by the familiar cast of characters, many of those who did mobilize for Ruto found his recognition of their socioeconomic plight compelling.

There was another reason Ruto was able to attract enough votes to secure victory. As Peter Lockwood found, voters wanted to punish his predecessor for unmet promises.[6] He writes about a "backlash" driven by a collective sense that Uhuru Kenyatta "meant to create prosperity and yet failed to do so whilst enriching himself in the process."[7] Noting that Kenyatta had presented himself as a champion of youth focused on "prosperity for all" during his first campaign, Lockwood's fieldwork illustrates how the bitterness of young Kenyans' dashed expectations in central Kenya moved many to support Kenyatta's political nemesis, Ruto.

But as soon as he secured the presidency, Ruto was in the same position as his predecessor, trying to make good on campaign promises with only limited success. The mismatch between expectations and reality was apparent at the outset. A few weeks into Ruto's presidency, county governors were being overwhelmed with job applications from young Kenyans eager for the jobs that were promised on the campaign trail, and publicly questioning whether they should fire existing civil servants to accommodate the new demands.[8]

It didn't take long for those masses to express disappointment with the pace of change. The much-touted and undeniably popular "Hustler Fund" Ruto's government established to provide widespread access to cheap credit felt like a drop in the bucket compared to the soaring cost of living. The economic blows of a regional drought, the COVID-19 pandemic, and supply chain disruptions related to the war in Ukraine piled atop the consequences of years of profligate borrowing to raise the debt burden and squeeze Kenya's fiscal space. Rising food and fuel prices took the heaviest toll on low-income earners—the very constituency expecting to benefit from a Ruto administration. But to garner support from international financial institutions, Ruto had to prioritize cutting subsidies and raising revenue.[9] His government is so attuned to the political peril associated with inadequate job creation that they have announced their intention to find a million job opportunities per year *outside* of Kenya. The idea is that young Kenyans can work abroad and send much-needed foreign exchange in the form of remittances back home.[10]

Scarcely six months after he took office, massive street protests began, organized by his main political opponent but fueled by popular outrage over cost-of-living increases. The protests surged again in July 2023, and a violent police response led to dozens of civilian deaths.[11] The situation grew so precarious that the country's leading newspapers issued a joint warning of the risk of "genocide or civil war."[12] In the wake of the protests and the state's violent response, even some prominent pro-Ruto social media personalities expressed a sense of betrayal.

> The Anger is real. The Angst of the people is palpable; we the ones who fought hard for this Administration; we must raise our voices and let them deal with us. They only understand one language—Chaos. B'coz they're tyrannical, incorrigible LIARS. Let the country BURN now.[13]

Increasingly, Kenya's leaders sounded like they were playing for time. When Deputy President Rigathi Gachagua delivered a commencement address at Jomo Kenyatta University of Agriculture and Technology in 2023, he told the graduates,

> I'm an honest man. I don't want to sit here and lie that we have jobs for you. These jobs we are going to create together with you. Our MPs worked very gracefully for two nights and passed the Finance Bill to create a housing fund that will be used to construct houses every year. Among those houses, you will have an opportunity to earn a living.[14]

It did not go over well. The new tax to create the housing fund was highly controversial, and the linkage to urgent employment needs dubious. On social media, young Kenyans expressed their dismay.

> The hustler's suffering starts. Who told Gachagua that everybody wants to be a construction worker in non-existent housing project?

> You lot are the ones who promised jobs in sijui [roughly] 100 days, Kenyans did not ask you to say that, you did, of your own accord. Just say you can't keep the promise, no more of this honest man bullshit.[15]

The Ruto administration reversed course on some subsidies and worked on accommodating the political opposition to calm the violence. But while senior opposition figures can be appeased, Kenya's youthful population is another matter. Nearly one year into his presidency, surveys found that roughly half of Kenyans felt he had not achieved anything.[16] The online response to Ruto's November 2023 State of the Nation speech included a lot of regret and frustration.

> The worst part is, he's not even listening to those he conned into voting for him?

> The people who voted for Ruto have to remind us every three days how they made a mistake.[17]

Days after the speech, the Federation of Kenyan Employers announced that 70,000 Kenyans had lost their jobs since October 2022, blaming tax increases for the downturn.

> We are moving from the frying pan into the fire. By the time Ruto will be leaving office, everyone else will be jobless except for those working in government.[18]

In January 2024, a group of boda-boda (motorcycle taxi) drivers went so far as to file a lawsuit against the Kenyan government, claiming that the campaign that brought Ruto's government to power did so by associating closely with their members, and that as a result those members were suffering because of the "hostility of the people of Kenya who are clearly dissatisfied with the government's inability to bring down the cost of living."[19]

It's easy to look at voter turnout and conclude that young Kenyans are either dissatisfied with politics or disinterested. But the evidence does not point to apathy. Turned off by the lack of internal democracy in major political parties and the absence of clear policy differences among leading candidates, many young Kenyans eschew formal political participation. Instead, many continue to discuss issues of governance in person and digitally—often with great wit and creativity—creating a shared community that recognizes the absurdity of some political practices. In so doing, they collectively create a consensus that renounces the status quo in both form and substance.

But they do more than sit back and satirize. Some engage in do-it-yourself governance, banding together to provide basic service delivery, such as access to clean water, to their urban communities where the government has failed, as members of Shining Hope for Communities do in the densely populated Kibera neighborhood of Nairobi. Many also mobilize around specific causes where they believe change is within their grasp. Young Kenyan women have organized around sexual harassment and assault with the #MyDressMyChoice campaign[20] and Legal Sisters' efforts to regulate the boda-boda industry,[21] grabbing the attention of senior leaders and demanding that the police and judicial system take these issues seriously. One civil society leader told me that he sees fundamental generational change in the nature of activism in the country.[22] Whereas established nongovernmental organizations used to anchor civil society, often with foreign funders, now he sees "wildcat" organizing, with coalitions forming and dissolving around specific issues, using their digital savvy to attract attention and force political elites to respond. Some of those elites find this burdensome; in early 2024 Kenyan Member of Parliament Gideon Kimaiyo tweeted,

> I don't know how we created this activist country, everybody is an activist . . . We have over-exaggerated our entitlement to rights.[23]

This observation was met with anger online.

> In a country where politicians like yourself steal with impunity and no recourse, activism is the only available alternative. We can't have a country where corrupt politicians have their way and the public has no say.
>
> In fact everyone should be an activist in this country, you're oppressing us and you have the audacity to say we have too much freedom of speech? Let us speak about our problems bana.
>
> This is because elected leaders abscond their duty of representation and abandon the masses for selfish interests.

In June of 2024, Kenya's sleeping giant—its urban youth—woke up in a big way. Fed up with a seemingly endless parade of new taxes and unconvinced that revenue generated by the state would be spent in the public interest, young Kenyans organized online, using digital tools to educate fellow citizens in local languages about the finance bill and about dubious spending decisions by their government.[24] They shared video explainers and eye-catching graphics about soaring state expenditures on cars for top officials, contrasting these increases with cuts in youth development programs.[25] Then, mobilized by hashtags #RejectFinanceBill2024, #OccupyParliament, and #RutoMustGo, which were mentioned in twenty-five million posts on X in the second half of June, and even crowdfunded in digital space, they took to the physical streets in urban centers around the country.[26] Calling themselves "tribe-less, party-less, and fear-less,"[27] these young protesters persevered despite the state's efforts to throttle internet speeds, intimidate activists, and even open fire on unarmed demonstrators.

The 2024 Gen Z protesters forced Ruto to scrap his unpopular finance bill and to dissolve his cabinet in an effort to quell the unrest. But the energy online and on the streets was not just about objectionable legislation; it was about endemic corruption, and a political class that expected citizens to buy into a system that serves elites well and the public poorly. While Ruto has vacillated between efforts to vilify and mollify protesters, many are still calling for him to step down, unconvinced by arguments that they should wait for the next election cycle. Ruto has brought opposition leaders into his new government to recalibrate his political coalition, but for many young Kenyans, these maneuvers miss the point. They don't want a reshuffling of the deck of ethnic constituencies. They want a sea change in accountability and a whole new governing class that can plausibly earn their trust, and they continue strategizing about how to get there.

Ruto won the presidency by promising to be a change agent, then found that young Kenyans had a far more ambitious agenda than he did. How that tension will be reconciled remains to be seen, but it certainly provides a cautionary tale for other African leaders seeking to harness popular hunger for transformative change. Ambitious new leaders like Faye and his supporters might take more heart from the relatively patient people of Zambia.

Managing Expectations

Zambia, like Senegal, has experienced democratic transfers of power, from one party to another, since multiparty elections were introduced in 1991. But it also has a history of political repression, and by 2016, the then-ruling Patriotic Front (PF) was employing tactics designed to prevent such a transfer from occurring again.

The PF's base had originally been the urban poor, and its charismatic leader Michael Sata campaigned on promises of more jobs, lower taxes, improved urban housing, and an end to the harassment of street vendors.[28] But when he and the PF finally won at the polls in 2011, it was difficult to deliver on these promises, and the party showed little tolerance for criticism.[29] The situation devolved when Sata died in office, and a snap election in 2015 narrowly brought another PF politician to the presidency, Edgar Lungu.

Lungu did not have Sata's political skills, but he did have a taste for power, presiding over new restrictions on freedom of expression, such as the closure of the popular newspaper *The Post* in 2016 and Prime TV in 2020. The 2016 elections were widely seen as a step backward for Zambian democracy, and featured a biased media and police force that distorted the preelection environment.[30] The tilt toward authoritarianism continued into 2017, when Lungu's main political rival, Hakainde Hichilema of the United Party for National Development (UPND), was arrested on treason charges, ostensibly because his motorcade failed to yield to Lungu's. He was in custody for 100 days before officials from the commonwealth helped to negotiate his release.

But the campaign that preceded the 2021 Zambian election was different. Although the COVID pandemic offered new reasons to deny the opposition opportunities to assemble, and violent party cadres had been empowered and widely deployed, both the realities of Zambians' quality of life and the lessons learned by the political opposition nudged the country in a different direction. As the PF's urban base struggled with the rising cost of living and the impossible-to-ignore consequences of poor economic management in the form of Zambia's default on its foreign debt in 2020,[31] Lungu's party had to wrestle with the challenges of incumbency. These included factors beyond their control, like the global drop in price of Zambia's most important export, copper, and those within it, such as the level of corruption in government and eye-popping additions to the country's debt burden. Campaigning for reelection, the PF was in the position of touting their infrastructure projects and telling the population how well things were going, contradicting people's lived experience.

At the same time, the political opposition was poised to take advantage of the disappointment, and a largely youth-led, digitally savvy movement coalesced around Hakainde's UPND in the hopes of triggering change. In 2016 and 2021, they borrowed a tactic the PF had employed to bring Sata to power, encouraging their supporters to behave outwardly as though they supported the incumbents, but to vote their conscience. This method of addressing ruling-party intimidation was coined the "watermelon" strategy when used by the UPND, as it entailed urging supporters to dress outwardly in the color of the PF (green) but to vote for the UPND, associated with the color red.[32] Particularly in 2021, minimal investments in posters and billboards and a constrained capacity to hold rallies were offset with an intensive, but far less visible campaign.

Young UPND supporters started referring to Hichilema as "Bally"—a slang reference to a father figure.[33] The term acknowledged the age gap between the candidate and the masses but wielded the language of youth to turn it into a positive with the humanizing, informal moniker. In contrast, the PF sometimes came off tone deaf. Hoping to shore up a critical ethnic constituency, Lungu chose a running mate notorious for having eliminated university meal allowances as Minister of Higher Education.[34] Unaccountable PF cadres shook down market vendors, creating resentment among the urban poor[35] and offending struggling citizens by showing off wads of cash on social media,[36] while the government employed heavy-handed tactics with journalists and civil society.[37]

Online organizing was essential and spilled over into face-to-face conversations countrywide.

Young Zambians did not just broadcast political messages on social media; they used Facebook Live and Twitter Spaces to interact directly with peers. As

Lynch and Gadjanovaa noted, while political space in Zambia was shrinking, digital space still offered the opportunity to build a sense that change was possible, even as the government tried to rein in digital speech by passing a controversial Cyber Security and Cyber Crimes Act in the months leading up to the election. "Social media provided a space in which ordinary citizens could display their frustrations with the PF and support for the UPND in ways that helped to foster a sense that Hichilema was an electorally viable alternative."[38] Meticulous attention to voter protection efforts—much of it driven by committed young volunteers—reinforced the idea that participating in the election would not be a waste of time and energy. Some twenty thousand UPND election agents fanned out across the country's polling stations on election day, using a phone app and satellite system to monitor fraud.[39]

It worked; turnout went from roughly 57 percent of eligible voters in 2016 to 71 percent in 2021. On election day, WhatsApp, Facebook, Twitter, and Instagram were all disrupted, but civil society was well organized, and the Christian Churches Monitoring Group was able to conduct a solid parallel vote count.[40] When early results showed Hichilema's support dwarfing that of the incumbent, Lungu released a statement declaring that the election was not free and fair and that isolated incidents of violence "rendered the whole exercise a nullity."[41] But with the Zambian Electoral Commission as well as domestic and international monitors disputing his claims, eventually Lungu backed down and conceded the election.

Hichilema acknowledged the central role that young people played in his victory early in his inaugural address, and indicated his grasp of their desire for a new direction and the urgency of job creation:

> This victory is not mine but for all the citizens of our great country, especially the youth who turned out to vote in great numbers with great energy and passion, and made this day possible . . . The people decided it was time for a change, and we can boldly say, change is here! . . . To the jobless youths, a new dawn is here where you will be skilled and find opportunity to work or do business in an economy that we will revive.[42]

When I met with a group of young, politically active Zambians in Lusaka in 2022, they described a mentality of do-or-die around the 2021 campaign as they looked toward the future. One prominent online organizer told me that he was well aware that being identified with the opposition meant closing doors to some opportunities, but "there was nothing to lose."[43] Sounding a similar note, one influential musician told me, "we want more than survival."[44] There was obvious pride in recounting how young Zambians had layered their own communications strategies over traditional political organizing to build momentum, but also a sober reflection on how little opportunity awaited them without political change. They also talked about the difficulty of remaining patient and managing expectations around the pace of change.

In the wake of the election, Zambia was an outlier in African polling as one of only two countries in which a majority—some 72 percent—said that the government was doing well in creating jobs,[45] and over half of urban dwellers thought the country is moving in the right direction. But the truth is that since coming to office, President Hichilema had very limited capacity to alter the economic realities that had motivated so many Zambians to vote for a change in course. Zambia did not strike a deal with creditors on debt restructuring until 2024. The help offered by the International Monetary Fund (IMF) came with requirements to end fuel subsidies and cut government spending—not exactly a recipe for bolstering the urban poor. New challenges keep emerging as well. By the time the debt restructuring deal was finalized, Zambia had suffered a cholera outbreak and a drought in southern Africa had taken a toll on the agricultural sector and the hydroelectric power supply.

Even in optimistic Zambia, there are small reminders that popular patience is not limitless. When President Hichilema posted on social media marking the two-year anniversary of his victory, commenters offered encouragement, but also pointed messages.

> Happy two years . . . hope it's a reminder of how fast time is flying & hope you fulfill the promises you made . . . otherwise we are watching & saying out what we see wrong.

> This is to be a joyous day indeed Mr. President but then I am one of those that are still far from really being joyful as you still got much to do. Many things are not going well especially for the youths sir.[46]

When Hichilema tried to put a positive spin on the country's difficult conditions, promising to use the inflection point of the drought "to change Zambia forever," the social media reaction was cynical.

> This man is all talk. He thinks he is talking to children we are tired of your rhetorics bwana.

> Zambians wake up. We have heard this one before. Busy promising as if they are still in opposition. Mr. President, find time to tour around especially in markets and see the trajectory prices of things.

> I really woke up at 2 in the morning to go and vote for this, bally.

> Comments suggest things are not looking good.[47]

Looking for a Messiah

The hope invested in leadership change is often unrealistic, since no individual, no matter how well-intentioned or capable, can do away with the structural challenges facing so many African societies. But perceived change agents can be powerful symbols and rallying points around which to imagine a different future.

In Nigeria, what began as a movement rejecting police brutality morphed into a campaign to challenge the governing status quo. Police, as the representatives of governing authorities that urban citizens are most likely to encounter in their daily lives, are a flashpoint across much of Africa. *Afrobarometer* found that majorities in sixteen countries believe most or all police to be corrupt,[48] and extrajudicial killings by police are a prominent feature of human rights reporting in the region. For example, Amnesty International published a report in 2016 on the practices of a particularly notorious Nigerian police unit, the Special Anti-Robbery Squad or SARS. It makes for harrowing reading.

> The Special Anti-Robbery Squad (SARS), a special branch of the Nigeria police created to fight violent crime, is responsible for widespread torture and other cruel, inhuman or degrading treatment or punishment (other ill-treatment) of detainees in their custody. Amnesty International's research shows that detainees, both men and women, are subjected to various methods of torture and ill-treatment in order to extract information and "confessions." Such methods include severe beating, hanging, starvation, shooting in the legs, mock executions and threats of execution.[49]

Nigerian activists began campaigning for the disbanding of SARS in 2017, in person and online. But the movement surged to new prominence in early October 2020, when a widely circulated online video purporting to show police shooting an unarmed youth fueled fresh outrage, leading to an outpouring of activism in cities across the country. Because the surge of the #EndSARS movement came just months after George Floyd was murdered by police in the United States, triggering demonstrations around the world against racial injustice and police brutality, it resonated beyond Nigeria's borders quickly. Over a ten-day period in October 2020, forty-eight million #EndSARS tweets were posted on Twitter.[50]

Within days, the Nigerian authorities agreed to disband SARS.[51] But in part because they had made several similar pledges in the past, and because the general police force had used excessive force in response to the early waves of protest, momentum continued to build. While continuing to focus on policing, the agenda of the protesters became more expansive. "Youths also used that opportunity to protest bad governance, unemployment, insecurity, and poor infrastructures among others. They were also protesting the existing political climate which enthroned mediocrity in governance. Some of the youths even called for the resignation of President Muhammadu Buhari."[52] This cohort of young Nigerians has been called the Soro Soke generation, using the Yoruba term for "speak up."[53]

On October 20, police and military units opened fire on protesters gathered at the Lekki Toll Gate in Lagos State, the commercial capital of the country. The death toll is disputed, but most reports indicate that fifteen people were killed and dozens more wounded.[54] The massacre cast a pall over #EndSARS, but the energy that fueled the protests remained. Although the movement was diffuse and "leaderless" by design (though there were numerous instances of young people taking on critical responsibilities, including members of the Feminist Coalition that provided a helpline, fundraising, and transparent accounting),[55] some of that latent energy found new expression in the run-up to Nigeria's 2023 elections. One Nigeria-watcher summed it up. "Arguably, the most consequential result of the #EndSARS movement was to mobilize a segment of the population that had long shown high levels of political apathy: young people."[56]

It initially looked as though Nigeria's general elections would be business as usual, with the country's two major parties, both of which had held power at various points since the country's return to multiparty democracy in 1999, facing off. The cast of characters was familiar, pitting former Vice President Atiku Abubakar against former governor of Lagos State Bola Tinubu, both septuagenarians against whom numerous charges of corruption had been leveled over the years. But youthful momentum began to coalesce around a third-party contender, former governor of Anambra State Peter Obi. Obi, at sixty-one years of age, defected from the People's Democratic Party (PDP), dissatisfied with the primary process that saw Atiku emerging as the PDP's presidential candidate, and joined the marginal, largely politically insignificant Labor Party. Yet his campaign caught fire, in part because of his political messages about combating corruption, addressing insecurity, and creating jobs, but also because he represented an alternative to a choice that seemed to represent more of the same. In his indictment of the political elite, many young Nigerians heard echoes of their own frustrations.[57] Many of the social media posts boosting Obi in the preelection period also carried the #EndSARS hashtag.

A change agent had presented himself, and a movement of so-called Obi-dients energetically worked to amplify his message digitally, trying to compensate for the Labor Party's anemic organizing apparatus on the ground with efforts in cyberspace. When a former chair of one of Nigeria's two dominant political parties cast doubt on the significance of Obi's online popularity, musing, "obedient or disobedient, time will tell. Time will tell. We now live in a world where you can have just ten young men or women in one room, whether motivated or not motivated, and they can churn out one million stories using different names,"[58] he set up the oppositional generational dynamic embraced by so many of Obi's supporters. The Obi campaign often seemed like a collective exercise in political imagination built around the candidate's encouraging but unspecific idea that "a new Nigeria is possible." Nearly ten million new voters registered to participate in the election, the vast majority of them young people, helping to fuel a narrative that the youth vote could set Nigeria on a new course.

In the end, it was not enough. Bola Tinubu—a candidate who told Nigerians that "it is my turn"[59] and whose age and health raised so many questions during the campaign that he released a much-mocked video of himself pedaling a stationary bicycle in an attempt to quiet the concerns—was elected president of Nigeria with 37 percent of all votes cast. Obi came in third, although he made far more gains than any previous third-party contender, winning 25 percent of votes and emerging as the top choice in urban centers like Lagos and Abuja.[60] The surge of new voter registrations did not translate into greater participation; the election saw the lowest voter turnout in the country's history, presumably due to a combination of deliberate voter suppression, logistical snafus, and the combined effects of a fuel and currency crisis that made travel extremely difficult. A country in which 90 percent of citizens reported feeling that the country was moving in the wrong direction[61] voted to keep the ruling party in power. The aftermath of the election left a bitter taste for many. Because the Obi-dients had been so bullish, they struggled to accept the results, and since election day itself was flawed,[62] mistrust in the process deepened.

As scholar Ebenezer Obadare has written, not only did the Obi-dient movement fail to overcome the absence of a countrywide party apparatus; it also contained elements within it that were both inspiring and alarming.

> Holding up Obi as a moral paragon, it refused to entertain any legitimate criticism of the candidate, and in a few instructive cases went as far as attempting to "cancel" those who refused to bend the knee. As it hardened into a political cult more or less, it alienated those who tended to be sympathetic to Obi but had reservations about the rush to beatify him.[63]

The notion that one man, who was no stranger to politics as usual in Nigeria, could change the nature of governance in the vast, complicated country only focused more attention on the Igbo and Christian elements of Obi's identity, which came at a political cost.

In the wake of the election, many young Nigerians sounded notes of resignation and frustration on social media, echoing this prescient sentiment from the hopeful days of the campaign.

> If Obi lose hope dash out.[64]

#TinubuIsNotMyPresident was the top trending hashtag on Nigerian X (formerly Twitter) on inauguration day. The mood was not improved by the shocks of two major policy changes that Tinubu's government introduced, an end to the fuel subsidy that was draining the national coffers, and removal of foreign exchange restrictions. Despite widespread consensus that these reforms were essential to the long-term health of the Nigerian economy, they took a toll on citizens, adding to the cost of transporting supplies to urban areas and sending inflation rates soaring. Demonstrations sprang up around the country demanding that the government address the cost of living. The economic pressures, ongoing security crises, and political disappointment were apparent in the strains of nihilism that emerged in Nigerian online discussions.

I'm sorry, but I'm slowly getting to the point where I believe that a disintegration of Nigeria is the only solution. The people of the middlebelt cannot continue to be at the mercy of Islamic jihadists, while successive presidents do absolutely nothing about it. This happens because elected officials care more about politics & elections than actually securing the lives and property of the citizens. The disunity in Nigeria along ethno-religious lines is the reason the whole country hasn't stood up in unison to demand that these people do their jobs. This disunity has gotten even worse over the last 10 years since the APC started to exploit our fragile fault lines. If we cannot speak in one voice, then let as many homogenous small countries as can be birthed from this contraption emerge.

You don't have to be sorry cuz realistically #Disintegration is the ultimate solution What's the benefit of one Nigeria other than pain, lies, hatred, suffering, bigotry, terrorism looting and backwardness? #EndNigeriaToSaveLives

I am right here at that point waiting for you. We at this end are not abnormal people. Neither are we hateful of anyone. Rather, our message is predicated on love and the need for Nigerians to know and appreciate that Self Preservation is most paramount. Don't flinch.

U are just coming welcome, all this one Nigeria talk is a waste of time, I am of the opinion that they split this country, the whole thing is a mistake to begin with.[65]

In contrast to the activism implied by Soro Soke, a different Yoruba term made it into the global mainstream—japa, literally meaning to run away or escape. Migration has always been an option, particularly for the educated and skilled, but polls and visa applications in Europe and North America show that the trend was on a steep upward trajectory even before the anticlimactic elections of 2023.[66] As Nigerian journalist Ugonna-Ora Owoh noted, Obi himself appeared to endorse the phenomenon when he posted on social media that the brain drain that may "look like a loss today" will redound to the country's benefit "when we start doing the right things and taking the governance of our nation more seriously."[67]

Of course, most young Nigerians eager for change will not leave. They will remain as a latent political force, waiting for a moment that motivates them to overcome their cynicism and resignation. The longer that takes, the more many grow increasingly willing to experiment.

The Pan-African Laboratory

Thanks to digital connection, a Pan-African laboratory is up and running, and best practices are being shared and updated in real time. Young Africans draw lessons and inspiration from each other, and in many cases are in direct contact with peers in other settings. In 2015, Senegalese and Burkinabe activists worked with Congolese civil society on strategies aimed at forcing then Congolese President Joseph Kabila to step down as the constitution required. In the run-up to the 2023 elections in Zimbabwe, young Zimbabweans regularly made express references to the tactics successfully used in neighboring Zambia to unseat an incumbent leader. Zambians too explicitly referenced developments in other African states as sources of inspiration, singling out two in particular. First, they pointed to Malawi's 2019 and 2020 elections, in which initially the incumbent president was declared the victor. That announcement was met with mass protests, a continuation of demonstrations against corruption, police brutality, and poor service delivery that had begun before the polls. A rerun was held after the country's highest court determined that ubiquitous and blatant irregularities in the process nullified the result. On the second attempt, the opposition united, and, buoyed by popular distaste for the ruling party's attempts to steal the election the first time around, won the day.

But Zambians also pointed to the example of Bobi Wine's campaign in Uganda, despite the fact that he did not prevail in the 2021 polls. The momentum and energy he created online embodied a potent idea about speaking truth to power and taking young people seriously. Likewise, young Ugandans online pored over video of the South African opposition's "practice protest," discussing what lessons they might take from the exercise.[68] As one Zambian civic leader said, "young people with access to technology can compare what is happening in other spaces and what is happening in our space."[69]

That was certainly the case with the 2024 Kenyan Gen Z protests, which sparked political conversations around the continent and prompted similar protest movements in Uganda and Nigeria. Uganda's #StopCorruption protests met with threats and violence before they even got off the ground,[70] but Nigeria's

#EndBadGovernance campaign, which mobilized protesters angry about surging fuel costs and profligate government spending across over twenty-four cities prompted some government action. Hoping to stave off the protests, the Nigerian government announced an increase in the minimum wage. When that failed to stall protesters' momentum, the president promised a cabinet reshuffle. Nigeria's protests, which were also met with violence, fizzled as muddled messages overtook the discourse, creating distractions over Russian influences and calls for military takeovers.[71] Yet the sense of grievance remained, and additional protests marked Nigeria's 64th Independence Day. It's notable that those protests prompted President Tinubu to plead for "patience"—a trait rarely associated with frustrated young people.[72]

The porous borders of the digital sphere help drive home that the status quo is not the only option. When Macky Sall finally announced that he would not run for a third term in Senegal, it sparked online conversation in Cameroon about Biya's seemingly endless reign. Similarly, Angolans held up Senegalese protesters as a model for Angolan youth.[73] Liberians online followed the Obi campaign in Nigeria with great interest, while Nigerians in turn tracked Kenya's 2022 elections with care, along with peers in Uganda and Ethiopia.[74] Congolese and Zimbabweans online tried to extract lessons and inspiration from Senegal's 2024 election.[75] The ANC's failure to maintain its majority in government in 2024 elections likewise prompted intense discussion across the continent, with commenters weighing in from Angola, Ghana, Tanzania, Uganda, Mozambique, and Nigeria to express their hope that their own leaders might learn from the ANC's cautionary tale.[76]

The Zambian government's attempts to root out self-dealing public servants have attracted particular attention. When Zambian Foreign Minister Stanley Kakubo announced that he would resign from the cabinet because he was being investigated for corrupt practices and did not wish to become a distraction, people chimed in to note that officials in their countries never seemed to lose power in this way.

> In Nigeria . . . he'd run for office of governor.
>
> Can never happen in Ghana.
>
> At least he can resign. In Kenya an appeal to the tribe will be made and ideology of tribalism taken a notch higher to the point of a higher office instead of resignation.[77]

Kenyans admired a viral video of Zambian President Hichilema scolding MPs who purchase cars with state funds.[78] Even a post of a road sign in Zambia triggered a pointed response from an online Ugandan.

> Road sign posts of the Zambian President reminding citizens that corruption is enemy of development. In Uganda M7 [Museveni] tells IGG [Inspector

General of Government] not to scare away the thieves because they build 5-star hotels.[79]

Digital connectivity also links diaspora communities to the debates happening in their homelands without gatekeepers. The Gambian diaspora played a powerful role in that country's transition away from autocracy, providing Gambians with access to information otherwise unavailable to them and helping to organize a united opposition.[80] As Nanjala Nyabola noted in *Digital Democracy, Analogue Politics*, Kenyans abroad—about half of whom are highly educated—regularly weigh in on developments at home. Some even mobilized abroad to protest the 2024 Finance Bill, marching to Kenyan embassies in Europe and North America in solidarity with domestic Kenyan protesters—and in so doing helped to draw even more international attention to the Gen Z grievances. Parts of the vast Nigerian diaspora mobilized abroad for #EndSARS and played a significant role in building online support for the Obi campaign, in some cases going so far as to post pictures of themselves online traveling home to vote. Senegal's diaspora joined in the recent protest movement, organizing demonstrations and pressure campaigns in France, Italy, the United Kingdom, Canada, and the United States. Professor Bamba Ndiaye has called the diaspora "the *sentinelle* [guardian] of Senegalese democracy."[81] Diaspora politics can be complicated and contentious, but there is no doubt that digital mobilizing has changed the game.[82]

The evidence that young Africans want to see transformational political change is undeniable, even as it manifests in different forms. Where opposition candidates who are seen as untainted by the status quo run in countries where some trust in the electoral system remains, change can come at the ballot box. In other instances, popular mobilization and protest outside of the electoral cycle gather more traction. But two questions loom over this broad hunger for reform. Can any change deliver dignity and opportunity on a scale commensurate with the region's demographic boom? This question, as yet unanswered, explains why developments in Senegal, Zambia, and now Kenya are watched so closely around the continent. While those experiments play out, the second question looms large. How will those threatened by change react?

Notes

1 Willow Berridge, Justin Lynch, Raga Makawi, and Alex de Waal, *Sudan's Unfinished Democracy: The Promise and Betrayal of a People's Revolution* (London: Hurst Publishers, 2022), 35.

2 "Senegal's Ousmane Sonko Given Two-month Suspended Term for Libel," *Al Jazeera*, March 30, 2023, https://www.aljazeera.com/news/2023/3/30/senegals-ousmane-sonko-given-2-month-suspended-term-for-libel.

3   Mamadou Abdoulaye Diallo, "AD711: At the Center of the Priorities of Young Senegalese: Management of the Economy, Insecurity, and Employment," *Afrobarometer Dispatch* 711, October 4, 2023, https://www.afrobarometer.org/publication/ad711-au-centre-des-priorites-des-jeunes-senegalais-la-gestion-de-leconomie-linsecurite-et-lemploi/.

4   Ngouda Dione, "Faye Sworn in as Senegal President, Cites 'profound desire for change,'" *Reuters*, April 2, 2024, https://www.reuters.com/world/africa/faye-sworn-senegal-president-cites-profound-desire-change-2024-04-02/.

5   Sarah Crowe and Diadie Ba, "Senegal Unveils 25-Year Economic and Social Development Plan," *Reuters*, October 14, 2024, https://www.reuters.com/world/africa/senegal-unveils-25-year-economic-social-development-plan-2024-10-14/.

6   Peter Lockwood, "Hustler Populism, Anti-Jubilee Backlash and Economic Injustice in Kenya's 2022 Elections," *African Affairs* 122, no. 487 (April 2023): 205–24, https://doi.org/10.1093/afraf/adad011.

7   Lockwood, "Hustler Populism," 215.

8   Dennis Lubanga, "Wapi Kazi?: Governors under Pressure as Unemployed Youths Who Back Their Bids Demand Jobs," *Tuko*, October 20, 2022, https://www.tuko.co.ke/politics/478671-wapi-kazi-governors-pressure-unemployed-youths-bids-demand-jobs/.

9   Rachel Savage and Marc Jones, "Kenya's Double-Digit Debt Costs Sign of the Tough Times," *Reuters*, February 15, 2024, https://www.reuters.com/business/finance/kenyas-double-digit-debt-costs-sign-tough-times-2024-02-13/.

10 Vitalis Kimutai, "Inside Government's Plan to Create 1m Overseas Jobs per Year," *The Nation*, August 8, 2023, https://nation.africa/kenya/news/government-plan-to-create-1m-overseas-jobs-per-year-4330086.

11 George Obulutsa and Hereward Holland, "Kenya's Opposition Holds Vigils for Slain and Injured Protesters," *Reuters*, July 26, 2023, https://www.reuters.com/world/africa/kenyas-opposition-holds-vigils-slain-injured-protesters-2023-07-26/.

12 Declan Walsh, "Kenya Stares into 'Abyss' as Soaring Prices and Feuding Leaders Bring Chaos," *New York Times*, July 20, 2023, https://www.nytimes.com/2023/07/20/world/africa/kenya-protests-tax-hikes.html.

13 Maverick Aoko (@AokoOtieno_), "The Anger is real," X post, July 12, 2023, https://twitter.com/AokoOtieno_/status/1679045216949469184.

14 Perpetua Etyang, "We Don't Have Jobs for You, Gachagua Tells Graduates," *The Star*, June 23, 2023, https://www.the-star.co.ke/news/2023-06-23-we-dont-have-jobs-for-you-gachagua-tells-graduates/.

15 Kenyans.co.ke (@Kenyans), "I don't want to sit here and lie that we have jobs for you," X post, June 23, 2023, https://twitter.com/Kenayns/status/1672212850234871811.

16 Lindwe Danflow, "Hustler Fund Rated Ruto's Greatest Achievement—Survey," *The Star*, July 13, 2023, https://www.the-star.co.ke/news/realtime/2023-07-13-hustler-fund-rated-rutos-greatest-achievement-survey/.

17 TL Elder (@mwabilimwagodi), "President Ruto is Going to Go Down as the Most Useless President of the Republic of Kenya," X post, November 5, 2023, https://twitter.com/mwabilimwagodi/status/1721094043973583038.

18 Kenyans.co.ke (@Kenyans), "70,000 Kenyans have lost their jobs from the period October 2022 to November 2023," X post, November 25, 2023, https://twitter.com/Keyans/status/1728282989447290972.

19 Dzuya Walter, "Boda Boda Riders Sue Gov't over Campaign Slogan, Say It Has Caused Them Psychological Trauma," *Citizen Digital*, January 4, 2024, https://www.citizen.digital/news/boda-boda-riders-sue-govt-over-campaign-slogan-say-it-has-caused-them-psychological-trauma-n334192.

20 Nanjala Nyabola, "Kenya: My Dress My Choice," *New African*, January 21, 2015, https://newafricanmagazine.com/9611/.

21 Lilys Njeru, "Why I Decided to Front Petition against Boda Boda Menace," *The Nation*, March 13, 2022, https://nation.africa/kenya/life-and-style/saturday-magazine/why-i-decided-to-front-petition-boda-boda-menace-3744774.

22 Irungu Houghton (Director of Amnesty International Kenya) in conversation with the author, Nairobi, August 2022.

23 Hon Gideon Kimaiyo (@GideonKimaiyo_), "I don't know how we created this activist country," X post, March 13, 2023, https://twitter.com/GideonKimaiyo_/status/1767786347887030513.

24 Job Mwaura, "Kenya Protests: Gen Z Shows the Power of Digital Activism—Driving Change from Screens to the Streets," *The Conversation*, June 22, 2024, https://theconversation.com/kenya-protests-gen-z-shows-the-power-of-digital-activism-driving-change-from-screens-to-the-streets-233065.

25 Muchiri Mike (@MuchiriiMike), "I want you guys to know that youth development expenditure has been cut by 42.86 percent to Sh100 million only," X post, June 28, 2024, https://x.com/MuchiriiMike/status/1806603482163454337.

26 Nendo Kenya, "The #Reject Revolution: When Tweets Take to the Streets. The Story of 25 Million Posts Powering Kenya's #RejectFinanceBill2024 protests," *Nendo*, July 8, 2024, https://www.nendo.co.ke/post/the-reject-revolution-kenyan-rejectfinancebill2024-protests.

27 Patrick Gathara, "Don't Let the Elders Steal Your Revolution," *The New Humanitarian*, July 10, 2024, https://www.thenewhumanitarian.org/opinion/2024/07/10/dont-let-elders-steal-your-revolution-kenya.

28 Marja Hinfelaar, Danielle Resnick, and Sishuwa Sishuwa, "Fragile Dominance? The Rise and Fall of Urban Strategies for Political Settlement Maintenance and Change in Zambia," in *Controlling the Capital: Political Dominance in the Urbanizing World*, ed. Tom Goodfellow and David Jackman (Oxford: Oxford University Press, 2023), 147, https://doi.org/10.1093/oso/9780192868329.003.0006.

29 Honore Banda, "Zambia's President Sata Raises Them Up to Let Them Down," *Africa Report*, October 1, 2021, https://www.theafricareport.com/6597/zambias-president-sata-raises-them-up-to-let-them-down/.

30 *Final Report: Republic of Zambia General Elections and Referendum* (Brussels: European Union, August 2016), https://www.eeas.europa.eu/sites/default/files/final_report_eu_eom_zambia.pdf.

31 Martin Kessler, "The Road to Zambia's 2020 Default," Finance for Development Lab, December 6, 2023, https://findevlab.org/the-road-to-zambias-2020-sovereign-debt-

default/#:~:text=On%2013th%20November%202020%2C%20Zambia,during%20the%20Covid%2D19%20pandemic.

32 Mutinta Himunyanga, "Watermelon Campaign: Can History Repeat Itself?" *Lusaka Times*, August 11, 2016, https://www.lusakatimes.com/2016/08/11/watermelon-campaign-can-history-repeat/.

33 Anonymous, "Of the Name Bally and HH," *Zambian Observer*, May 2, 2020, https://zambianobserver.com/of-the-name-bally-and-hh/.

34 Danielle Resnick, "How Zambia's Opposition Won," *Journal of Democracy* 33, no. 1 (January 2022): 77, https://www.journalofdemocracy.org/articles/how-zambias-opposition-won/.

35 Resnick, "How Zambia's Opposition Won."

36 "Police and DEC Investigates Display Sums of Cash on Social Media," *Lusaka Times*, March 5, 2021, https://www.lusakatimes.com/2021/03/05/police-and-dec-investigates-display-sums-of-cash-on-social-media/.

37 Hinfelaar, Resnick, and Sishuwa, "Fragile Dominance?"163.

38 Gabrielle Lynch and Elena Gadjanovaa, "Overcoming Incumbency Advantage: The Importance of Social Media on- and offline in Zambia's 2021 elections," *Journal of Eastern African Studies* 16, no. 4 (2022): 540, https://doi.org/10.1080/17531055.2023.2232241.

39 Resnick, "How Zambia's Opposition Won," 75.

40 *CCMG Verification Statement on the Accuracy of the Official 2021 Presidential Results* (Lusaka: Christian Churches Monitoring Group, August 16, 2021), https://ccmgzambia.org/ccmg-verification-statement-on-the-accuracy-of-the-official-2021-presidential-results/.

41 "Zambia Election: President Claims Vote Was Not Free and Fair," *BBC News*, August 14, 2021, https://www.bbc.com/news/world-africa-58215507.

42 Hakainde Hichilema, "Inauguration Speech by the President of the Republic of Zambia" (speech, Lusaka, August 24, 2021), Ministry of Commerce, Trade and Industry, https://www.mcti.gov.zm/wp-content/uploads/2023/02/President-Hakainde-Hichilema-Delivers-Inaugural-Speech.pdf.

43 Joseph Kalimbwe in conversation with the author, Lusaka, August 2022.

44 Fumba Chama ("Pilato") in conversation with the author, Lusaka, August 2022.

45 Josephine Appiah-Nyamekye Sanny, Shannon van Wyk-Khosa, and Joseph Asunka, "Africa's Youth: More Educated, Less Employed, Still Unheard in Policy and Development," *Afrobarometer Dispatch* No. 734, November 15, 2023, https://www.afrobarometer.org/wp-content/uploads/2023/11/AD734-PAP3-Africas-youth-More-educated-less-employed-still-unheard-Afrobarometer-18nov23.pdf.

46 Hakainde Hichilema (@HHichilema), "Two years ago, the people of #Zambia showcased the potency of our #democracy," X post, August 24, 2023, https://twitter.com/HHichilema/status/1694597622743343238.

47 Diggers.News (@DiggersOfNews), "We'll use drought to change Zambia forever—HH," X post, March 13, 2023, https://twitter.com/DiggersOfNews/status/1767778832214348054.

48. Boniface Dulani, Gildfred Boateng Asiamah, and Patrick Zindikirani, "Amid Rising Corruption, Most Africans Say They Risk Retaliation if They Speak Up," *Afrobarometer Dispatch* No. 743, December 6, 2023, https://www.afrobarometer.org/wp-content/uploads/2023/12/AD743-PAP5-Amid-rising-corruption-Africans-say-they-risk-retaliation-if-they-speak-up-Afrobarometer_3dec23.pdf.

49. Amnesty International, *"You have signed your death warrant": Torture and Other Ill Treatment in the Special Anti-Robbery Squad*. New York: Amnesty International, September 21, 2016, 5, https://www.amnesty.org/en/documents/afr44/4868/2016/en/.

50. Trish Lorenz, *Soro Soke: The Young Disruptors of an African Megacity* (Cambridge: Cambridge University Press, 2022), https://doi.org/10.1017/9781009211840.

51. Mayeni Jones, "SARS Ban: Nigeria Abolishes Loathed Federal Special Police Unit," *BBC news*, October 11, 2020, https://www.bbc.com/news/world-africa-54499497.

52. Prince Vincent-Anene, "#EndSARS PROTEST: How Nonviolent Movement Became Violent," Nonviolence Project at the University of Wisconsin, July 26, 2022, https://thenonviolenceproject.wisc.edu/2022/07/26/endsars-protest-how-nonviolent-movement-became-violent/.

53. Lorenz, *Soro Soke*.

54. Ben Ezeamalu, "Nigerian Army Killed Unarmed Protesters, Report Finds," *New York Times*, November 16, 2021, https://www.nytimes.com/2021/11/16/world/africa/nigeria-protest-report-massacare.html.

55. Lorenz, *Soro Soke*.

56. Maxwell Bone, "The Silence of the Obidients," *African Arguments*, February 9, 2024, https://africanarguments.org/2024/02/the-silence-of-the-obidients/.

57. Aanu Adeoye, "Peter Obi's 'Obidient' Movement Shakes up Nigerian Presidential Race," *Financial Times*, October 18, 2022, https://www.ft.com/content/92800e67-66a2-4eca-b5e5-009bf000c87a.

58. Nigerians, "#Towards2023 Peter Obi's social media movement probably being pushed by small number of people inside one room," Facebook video post, August 4, 2022, https://www.facebook.com/watch/?v=1525721417861728.

59. Kayode Oyero, "'It's My Turn Actually!' Tinubu Says in Acceptance Speech," Channels Television, March 1, 2023, https://www.channelstv.com/2023/03/01/its-my-turn-actually-tinubu-says-in-acceptance-speech/.

60. "Presidential Election—2023-02-25—Presidential," Nigeria Independent National Electoral Commission, accessed April 8, 2023, https://www.inecelectionresults.ng/pres/elections/63f8f25b594e164f8146a213?type=pres.

61. Amara Galileo, Raphael Mbaegbu, and Sunday Joseph Duntoye, "Nigerians Want Democracy, though Dissatisfaction Rises amid Worsening Economic Conditions," *Afrobarometer Dispatch* No. 606, February 21, 2023, https://www.afrobarometer.org/wp-content/uploads/2023/02/AD606-Nigerians-want-democracy%5ELJ-though-dissatisfaction-rises-in-worsening-economy-Afrobarometer-21feb23.pdf.

62. Mark Green, Derek Mitchell, and Daniel Twining, "Nigeria's Flawed Election Risks a Democratic Backslide," *Foreign Policy*, March 14, 2023, https://foreignpolicy.com/2023/03/14/nigeria-election-tunubu-democracy-irregularities-violence-inec/.

63 Ebenezer Obadare, "Peter Obi and a Dream Deferred," *Africa in Transition*, Council on Foreign Relations, March 22, 2023, https://www.cfr.org/blog/peter-obi-and-dream-deferred.

64 John Okoye (@JOHNOKO68305804), "If Obi lose hope dash out. Nigeria youth are eager for a new Nigeria," X repost, December 30, 2022, https://twitter.com/JOHNOKO68305804/status/1608975662618120194.

65 KWEKU THE HUSTLER, COMMANDER OF THE HEADLESS MOB (@Urchilla01), "I'm sorry, but I'm slowly getting to the point where I believe that a disintegration of Nigeria is the only solution," X post, January 25, 2023, https://twitter.com/IamUrchilla/status/1750422380139159895.

66 Larry Madowo, Bethlehem Feleke, and Fridah Okutoyi, "Many Talented Young Nigerians Are Leaving. Halting the Exodus Will Be a Task for the Next President," *CNN World*, February 27, 2023, https://www.cnn.com/2023/02/24/africa/nigeria-japa-exodus-trend-election-intl-cmd/index.html.

67 Ugonna-Ora Owoh, "The Word that Captures Nigerians' Feelings about the Future," *Foreign Policy*, August 12, 2023, https://foreignpolicy.com/2023/08/12/nigeria-japa-election-migration-tinubu-politics-economy/.

68 KIBUUKA BAMWEYANA (@aldrinewills), "Uganda forces of change have a lot to learn," X post, March 20, 2023, https://twitter.com/aldrinewills/status/1637720488905506816.

69 Linda Kasonde in conversation with the author in Lusaka, on August 9, 2022.

70 Amnesty International, "Uganda: Authorities Must Unconditionally Release Protestors Still Unlawfully Detained," June 25, 2024, https://www.amnesty.org/en/latest/news/2024/07/uganda-authorities-must-unconditionally-release-protestors-still-unlawfully-detained/.

71 Chris Kwaja and Matthew Edds-Reitman, "Nigeria at a Crossroads: Navigating Protests amid Elections," US Institute of Peace, October 1, 2024, https://www.usip.org/publications/2024/10/nigeria-crossroads-navigating-protests-amid-elections.

72 Chinedu Asadu, "Nigeria's Independence Anniversary Is Marked by Protests and Frustration over Economic Hardship," *AP News*, October 1, 2024, https://apnews.com/article/nigeria-independence-protests-tinubu-d321d54a7750e82b4391c27b28db68f2.

73 Sr_Comandante (@ManuchoComanda1), "População Senegalesa passa por cima da policia," X post, March 22, 2023, https://twitter.com/ManuchoComanda1/status/1638525548807827457.

74 Karen Allen, Jean le Roux, and Bonface Beti, *A Question of Influence? Case Study of Kenyan Elections in a Digital Age* (Pretoria: Institute for Security Studies, July 3, 2023), 6, https://issafrica.s3.amazonaws.com/site/uploads/EAR-49.pdf.

75 Bassirou Diomaye Faye (@DiomayeFaye), "To veterans, defense and security forces, I renew all recognition and confidence of the nation," X post, April 4, 2024, https://twitter.com/DiomayeFaye/status/1775829776705507707.

76 Africa Facts Zone (@AfricaFactsZone), "South Africa's ruling party, the ANC has failed to secure majority in the Parliament for the first time in 30 years," X post, June 1, 2024, https://x.com/AfricaFactsZone/status/1796874104567402857.

77 BBC News Africa (@BBCAfrica), "Zambia's Foreign Minister Stanley Kakubo resigns over cash-on-table video," X post, December 27, 2023, http://twitter.com/BBCAfrica/status/1740021595513495813.

78 Prof. J. Ole Kiyiapi (@JamesOleKiyiapi), "This is the attitude we NEED in Kenya," X post, October 10, 2023, https://twitter.com/JamesOleKiyapi/status/1711767077436928167.

79 Jeje Odea (@joshjeje2), "Road sign posts of the Zambian president reminding citizens that corruption is an enemy of development," X post, July 29, 2023, https://twitter.com/joshjeje2/status/1685265290295214080.

80 Amat Jeng, "Gambia's Democratic Transition: A Case Study of the Role of Political Elites in Democratic Transition" (Master's thesis, Uppsala University, 2019), https://www.diva-portal.org/smash/get/diva2:1388602/FULLTEXT01.pdf.

81 Borso Tall, "Protests and Pressure Force Senegal's Sall to Back Down—for Now," *World Politics Review*, February 20, 2024, https://www.worldpoliticsreview.com/senegal-elections-democracy-sall/.

82 For an excellent discussion of diaspora roles in African politics, see Terrence Lyons, "Diasporas and the Transnationalization of African Politics," *Oxford Research Encyclopedia of Politics*, June 25, 2019, accessed October 17, 2024, https://oxfordre.com/politics/view/10.1093/acrefore/9780190228637.001.0001/acrefore-9780190228637-e-696.

6

THE STATUS QUO STRIKES BACK

You want to disturb us? You are playing with fire, because we cannot allow you to disturb us.
  —PRESIDENT OF UGANDA YOWERI MUSEVENI, ADDRESSING THE NATION IN ADVANCE OF PLANNED ANTI-CORRUPTION PROTESTS ON JULY 20, 2024[1]

While young Africans learn from each other, so too do those in power who resist change in pursuit of regime survival. It's impossible not to notice populist authoritarians around the world taking a page from each other's books to stay in power and tamp down challengers, and African leaders are no exceptions. Several strategies can be employed to thwart the efforts of young Africans aiming to drive political transformation on the continent. Save for the digital innovations, these methods are not new, but some lend themselves particularly well to urban settings.

It starts with reinforcing cultural norms that emphasize respect for elders and view younger people as untested and unreliable. When I arrived in Botswana as the new US Ambassador in 2011, I was thirty-seven—too old to be a youth by the majority of definitions, but younger than most of my peers and predecessors. I was welcomed and treated with the courtesy that is a hallmark of Botswana's culture, but I could sense the discomfort of some of my interlocuters, particularly before they knew that I was married and had a child.

To be a "youth" in many African societies is to be waiting to assume the mantle of adulthood, which often requires sufficient income to secure housing and get married. Marc Sommers thoroughly laid out the socially constructed nature of the term in his book, *The Outcast Majority*, describing how youths confront the prospect of failing to achieve adulthood, leaving them marginalized and, in many cases, humiliated. He defines youth as "a young person with a tenuous social status and a hoped-for social transformation into adulthood. Which may not happen."[2]

For all the flowery speeches made about the leaders of the future, youth can be framed as an inferior status, and some senior leaders do not shy away from using this context to put young people in their place. On the flip side of sentiments celebrating the wisdom of elders are those dismissing the views of youth. Ugandan President Yoweri Museveni is perhaps the most blunt in this regard, having made it something of a tradition to insult young Ugandans in his annual speech marking International Youth Day, reveling in a culture that, historically at least, venerates elders. In 2020, he told his audience of young Ugandans to "Stop with the talking, talking, talking. You are impressing no one, especially me, because I am a former youth, I am here, you are talking to a former youth who started youth activities when I was 14."[3] Just two years later, he struck the same tone at the same event, admonishing the crowd to "stop really wasting our time because I really get tired when I come and hear people talking and lamenting . . . sit down because you are talking nothing."[4] Former Nigerian President Muhammadu Buhari suggested that young people in his country were lazy and uneducated, telling an audience in London that "more than 60% of the population is below 30, a lot of them haven't been to school and they are claiming that Nigeria is an oil producing country, therefore, they should sit and do nothing, and get housing, healthcare, education free."[5] It's not exactly empowering rhetoric.

Young people who engage in political action—particularly protest—are regularly dismissed with derogatory terms that belittle their agency or equate them with criminals, especially if they do not come from wealth. In Ethiopia, they have been called *adegegna bozene*, meaning dangerous vagrants.[6] In Sudan it is *shamasa*, "children of the sun," because they are found outside in the streets.[7] Terms like hoodlums, hooligans, and rabble-rousers are widely employed throughout the region. In 2020, Angolans who organized a march protesting the delay of local elections accused the ruling party of smearing them as "troublemakers, enemies of peace, vandals and frustrated."[8] The Zimbabwean government and its allies go as far as to label some youth activists on social media as "terrorists."[9] Former President Wade of Senegal accused youth activists of throwing "temper tantrums."[10] All of this delegitimatizing language does not just put young people in their place; it also makes their political agenda appear unpalatable. Research shows that for voters dissatisfied with a dominant party's performance, voting for an alternative requires perceiving that option as both effective and legitimate. In the absence of that perception, the dissatisfied elements of the electorate simply decline to vote at all.[11]

But reminding citizens where young people fall in traditional hierarchies and equating activism with criminality is only one approach. The powers that be can also tokenize, co-opt, divide, manipulate, instrumentalize, and intimidate young people to avoid succumbing to their demands for change.

Some governments aim to ease the pressure from their dissatisfied populations by arranging some youthful window dressing around their efforts, establishing formal structures intended to give the appearance of elevating young voices into the realm of state decision-making. The continent is rife with "youth councils," "youth representatives," "youth wings," and "youth ambassadors" that are cited approvingly by political elites—and sometimes by international donors. But these leadership roles for youth are often either devoid of real authority or are understood as spoils that elites dole out to loyalists. The Democratic Republic of the Congo even boasts an Orwellian-sounding Ministry of Youth and Patriotic Re-Awakening. Researchers examining formal youth-targeting strategies in Ethiopia, Mozambique, Uganda, and Zimbabwe, including youth councils and youth quotas, found such initiatives to be "part of the authoritarian rule book in all four countries."[12] It should come as no surprise that young people consistently indicate frustration with the tokenized nature of youth initiatives in the region.[13]

Co-Option

In societies awash in youth unemployment, ruling elites seeking to retain power can also strategically tap their resources to purchase the political support of young people. The economic vulnerability of many young Africans makes them ripe targets for cynical, short-term transactions that forestall political change.

Five months before Liberia's 2023 general elections, I spoke with young people in the capital, Monrovia, who consistently described just this sort of ephemeral, transactional relationship between youthful voters—by far the largest portion of the electorate—and candidates for political office. They talked about how election years present a one-off opportunity to extract material favors from the political class in exchange for votes, with little expectation for significant change. This episodic, profoundly unambitious model builds neither a sense of responsibility on the part of electoral victors, nor a sense of loyalty among voters. This may help explain why there appears to be little advantage to incumbency for legislators in Liberia, who are regularly limited by voters to a single term.[14] Political scientists have written about the dismal cycle produced by this brand of politics—wherein high turnover incentivizes office seekers to extract as much material gain as possible during their term, anticipating their access to power will be limited.[15]

Vote buying is by no means limited to Liberia, nor is it typically some kind of sub-rosa activity, despite being against local laws. During the most recent campaign season in Uganda, President Museveni personally carried parcels of cash to distribute to supporters.[16] In Nigeria, conventional wisdom holds that providing "stomach infrastructure" is the way to victory at the ballot box.[17] The focus on vote buying was so intense that many observers believe that the Central Bank of Nigeria moved to issue new currency in the lead-up to the election to render stockpiles of the old currency—perhaps intended to purchase votes—obsolete. In Zimbabwe, "'survival' underpins many decisions to demonstrate party support and uphold ZANU-PF dominance." A philosophy of *garawadya*, translating to "better to live having eaten" suggests that one should take whatever opportunity is available.[18] In Kenya, the Democratic Republic of the Congo, Benin, and even Botswana,[19] citizens, journalists, and researchers report that vote buying occurs. But research indicates that vote buying, ubiquitous as it might be, is rarely decisive when voters are assured of ballot secrecy. Voters might take incentives from multiple parties' candidates without the transaction affecting their voting intentions or behavior.[20]

Still, there are multiple, less-direct methods of co-opting young people. Favorable treatment when it comes to enforcing rules, implementing social programs, and accessing land in crowded urban spaces can be wielded as an important lever of power.[21] For example, the young drivers of motorcycles that function as inexpensive taxis in so many African cities, commonly known as boda-boda drivers, are especially susceptible to state inference. President Museveni sought to create a base of urban support, and to defang the opposition-led municipal government in Kampala, by frustrating efforts to regulate and tax the sector.[22] When that tactic proved insufficient to secure political elites' comfort, the ruling party turned to violent coercion, "terrorizing" and ultimately alienating drivers.[23]

Because so many urban dwellers are pushed into the informal economy for survival, they are particularly vulnerable to capricious enforcement of laws and regulations. Access to trade licenses, land, and even basic identification documents can be provided or withheld. Street vendors can either have their wares confiscated and be pushed out from high foot-traffic areas, or they can be permitted to work—depending on the will of the authorities. Squatters can be evicted from their spaces, left alone, or even given a pathway to legitimate land or home ownership. Generous sweeteners can have diminishing returns, however. Some research suggests that property-related co-option strategies in urban contexts have a limited shelf life. Once citizens gain access to land and even home ownership through support for dominant authorities, they are less easily manipulated.[24]

Employment and loan programs can similarly be targeted toward young people who support the regime; Uganda again provides multiple examples. In the run-up to Uganda's 2021 election, the ruling party created youth projects and youth groups wholesale, and then funneled cash to them. "No consistent criteria were used to select the beneficiaries, or determine how funds should be spent," and the organizations were not in the government's own official database for youth groups.[25] "Gifts" for youth are not limited to election season either; a particularly viral video circulated on social media in December 2023 showing a fertilizer giveaway at a belated National Youth Day celebration in Uganda. The event quickly devolved into a melee that prompted dismay among commenters.[26]

> The fertilizer can be distributed in a more dignified way . . . When we're respectful to our young people they'll be respectful to those around them as well.

> Make them poor and swimming poverty then pretend to help haha.

> General M7 imposed poverty is aimed at humiliation and dehumanizing Uganda.

Again, in addition to offending young people's sense of dignity, co-option does not necessarily buy loyalty. As a former chair of the Vendors' Association in an important Kampala market told researchers, the ruling party "thinks it is co-opting [vendors] but the truth is young people too have learnt to use the system to their advantage."[27]

In addition to enabling or prohibiting informal economic activities, the state can dangle formal job opportunities to those deemed supportive, and in countries where government is one of the largest employers, or where the links between government and the private sector are extremely close, this is a powerful form of co-option. Research in Zimbabwe found that many young Zimbabweans who participate in ruling-party activities are, privately, highly critical of the party and its leaders, but willing to be publicly supportive in exchange for access to jobs and benefits.[28] In fact, political scientists Lovise Aalen and Marjoke Oosterom have examined how Ethiopia, Mozambique, Uganda, and Zimbabwe use youth empowerment schemes as a form of patronage in service of regime interests. Their research found that an array of strategies ostensibly aimed at promoting youth employment and political participation were "open to abuse through ruling party patronage networks channeled to regime supporters."[29]

Ambitious young people in African cities often make reference to the importance of connections—be they personal, familial, tribal, or regional—to access dignified jobs. For example, in May 2023, a viral tweet asked, "Have you ever secured a job in Kenya solely based on merit, without any connections, networking, or bribery involved?" The responses made it clear that this was a hot topic.

> Not by a long shot—it's way harder because the number of qualified people searching for the same opportunities has increased while the opportunities haven't. There is however an aspect of pure luck that played a role back then and still does.

I have but sadly they haven't been great jobs. I think for plum positions you need connections. Sadly.

How would anyone think they have it easy surely?? Aren't you familiar with the staggering rate of unemployment in this country? What question is this.[30]

In Nigeria, the online discussion was similar after an influencer posted that Nigerians have less access to opportunity than Americans do, writing "If Google was a Nigerian creation, the staff would be the children of the rich, middle class, and connected."

You are 100% correct about this . . . good jobs in Nigeria are often reserved to well heeled families and it shouldn't always be.

This truth applies to almost every African nation, what can we do to change the status quo of the current problem?[31]

Indeed, in December 2023, the Ugandan State Minister of Finance was lambasted on social media for giving a graduation speech encouraging youth to "hunt for jobs instead of waiting on connections."

She thinks we're not hunting. Bambi.

Our economy is a connection-driven economy, not a competence driven economy!!

I guess they could just kneel down and beg instead, amirite?![32]

Divide and Conquer

While polling might show a great deal of solidarity among young people in terms of their top concerns and priorities, complex identities can be exploited to divide youth movements. Ethnicity, religion, and language can all be exploited to pit young people against each other. In part because youth are the majority of the politically enfranchised population in many countries, it can be easier to segment the electorate by these other categories, leaving generational solidarity an afterthought.

In Nigeria's most recent elections, the more the upstart Nigerian presidential candidate Peter Obi's campaign was associated with the aspirations of his Igbo ethnic group, or with Nigeria's Christian population, the less it resonated with youth from other Nigerian ethnic and religious constituencies. In urban melting pots where ethnicity is less salient, Obi thrived—but the electoral map shows that he was not able to turn out the youth vote in large parts of the Hausa and Fulani Muslim north. The religious and ethnic fault lines in Nigeria had as much or more to do with the 2003 electoral outcome as the disparities in campaign war chests and on-the-ground organizing muscle.[33]

Socioeconomic status is another dividing line that is particularly powerful in urban settings. Professionalized civil society leaders—whose voices are easiest to find in digital spaces as well as conference rooms and public debates, and whose offices are often found behind guarded gates—can easily be understood as "other" by poorer youths with less formal education, and vice versa. As Lisa Mueller insightfully notes in her work on contemporary African protests, more secure, middle-class civil society leaders may be motivated by a desire to protect political and civil rights while the masses they mobilize have more material concerns. The cooperation can fray quickly. In the context of mass mobilization and agitation for change, "popular protest can frighten the elite into building those walls between themselves and the poor even higher."[34] Other scholars go even further, suggesting that opposition to the governing status quo expressed by civil society elites is safer, and more likely to be tolerated, than that expressed by poorer urban dwellers.[35]

Foot Soldiers

In some instances, young people are instrumentalized by the state to violently protect the status quo. State authorities have moved to enlist them in paramilitary movements to actively and violently repress fellow young people organizing in the opposition, and the catalog of pro-government militias on the continent is vast.[36] For example, Togo's Faure Gnassingbé mobilized young militiamen alongside formal security personnel to quash the Faure Must Go movement that mobilized massive and largely youthful demonstrations in 2017 and 2018.[37] Uganda's "Arrow Boys" were formed to fight a local insurgency, but then redirected to help "manage voting" during multiple election cycles, having outlasted the insurgent threat that ostensibly required their formation. Zimbabwe's "green bombers," who have intimidated and terrorized their fellow citizens since 2001, were trained by the National Youth Service to act as ruling-party enforcers, with the "service" curriculum including topics like interrogation techniques. The program was discontinued after several years, but two years before the 2023 election, Zimbabwe's cabinet approved a revival. The new National Youth Training Program was an initiative of the Ministry of Youth, Sports, Art, and Recreation, notably in consultation with the Ministry of Defense and War Veterans. In addition to fearing a return of the violence associated with the earlier program, young Zimbabweans worried that participation might become a requirement for job-seekers in the country.[38]

The last point is important, because these efforts are attuned to youth's desire for livelihoods and, by offering young people a modicum of power and authority over others, they can provide a means of survival and even, in some cases, a kind of dignity. Unfortunately, they also help to establish violence as a feature of political competition in more competitive democratic contexts. In Zambia's context of tight political competition, most major political parties have some history with violent youth wings, and during the 2021 elections, journalists reported on violent clashes between youthful partisans.[39] In a combination of dividing and instrumentalizing approaches, Kenya hosts multiple youth gangs that are regularly mobilized by politicians at election time, the most infamous being the Mungiki.[40] A group with origins stretching back decades, Mungiki, which is legally banned in Kenya, today comprises largely poor young men from the Kikuyu ethnic group.[41] Its Kikuyu roots have helped politicians maintain the social divides that can prevent cohesive mass movements that challenge the status quo. Like many instrumentalized groups, Mungiki does not exist only to serve political elites—it operates as an extortion racket[42] and has in some instances gotten involved in social service delivery where the state is absent. For a period of time, it even had its own registered political party, enabling it to play a more active role in Kenya's ever-shifting landscape of political coalitions.[43]

Threats

Repression is often dressed up in law, an approach that has a deterrent effect in addition to providing an avenue for quickly silencing and delegitimizing voices demanding change. Examples are rife. In the run-up to elections in 2023, Zimbabwe enacted a law popularly known as the "Patriotic Bill," which criminalized speech that harms "the national interests of Zimbabwe." Of course, in a country long dominated by one political party, that means that criticism of government can be deemed against the law. In Senegal, just weeks after major demonstrations protesting the arrest of an opposition leader, legislators approved legal reforms that would make "seriously disturbing public order" akin to acts of terrorism.[44]

Insulting the head of state can also land citizens in jail, making attempts to hold leaders accountable for government failures a dicey proposition. In 2023, a popular Angolan social media figure, Ana da Silva Miguel (known as Neth Nahara online) was convicted and sentenced to prison time for committing an "outrage against the state" for recording a TikTok video in which she criticized the president for the government's disorganization and failure to deliver social services.[45] Similar laws are on the books in Cameroon, the Democratic Republic of the Congo, and Cote d'Ivoire.

A legitimate need to regulate cyberspace also provides new opportunities for repression. Kenya's Information and Communication Act made "misuse of a communications device" a crime, language so sweeping that it was repealed as unconstitutional in 2018. But its successor, the Cybercrimes Act, still criminalizes the sharing of "false, misleading, or fictious data," wording that Freedom House called "ripe for abuse by public officials looking to silence critical reporting online."[46] In 2023, Uganda's Constitutional Court eventually stepped in to nullify a particularly egregious portion of the country's Computer Misuse Act, which criminalized any digital missive that "disturbs the peace, quiet or right of privacy of any person with no purpose of legitimate communication."[47] The law had been used to prosecute journalists and government critics, and portions of it remain in force, including provisions that criminalize "misuse of social media" such as sending or sharing unsolicited information or "malicious information."[48]

Finally, there is always state violence. Research has found that governments are more likely to engage in repression when faced with a large proportion of youth in their population.[49] The 2022 Ibrahim Index of African Governance found that excessive force against majority youth protesters was on the rise, counting forty-six such instances across the continent in 2012, but 248 by 2022.[50] From the Lekki Toll Gate shooting in Nigeria to the 2023 Goma massacre in the Democratic Republic of the Congo,[51] numerous African states have used lethal force in response to unarmed protests.

New Tactics for Old Regimes

Reliance on digital media and online organizing also exposes youth movements to digital surveillance and manipulation from foreign and domestic sources. Following the Arab Spring, several African governments stepped up their capacity to monitor, manipulate, and stifle online discourse.

On and offline, increased surveillance can also limit the capacity of dissatisfied youth to effectively organize and challenge authorities. Studies show significant state expenditures on surveillance technologies. Governments "are using mobile phone spyware, internet interception devices, social media monitoring and biometric identity systems. Artificial intelligence for facial recognition and car number plate recognition is another digital surveillance technology in their growing toolkit."[52] From Rwanda, an autocracy where surveillance is ubiquitous in citizens' lives,[53] to Zambia, a democracy that has deployed smart-city technology from China and interception technology from Israel,[54] authorities are collecting information about their populations on a massive scale. It is difficult to imagine that public awareness of these practices does not influence citizens' decisions about what to say and with whom to associate.

In addition to keeping tabs on citizens, governments censor specific content, or shut down the internet entirely. Ethiopia, the Gambia, Ghana, Kenya, Nigeria, Rwanda, and Sudan have all used state authority to censor digital content.[55] As noted in Map 6.1, internet shutdowns have been employed in more than half of the region. Moreover, as Jimmy Kainja has noted, "there is another form of shutdown that should be considered, and that is the reluctance of governments across the African continent to improve connectivity."[56] This reluctance could help to explain the gulf between stated aspirations to digitize economies with limited state investment in connectivity (as opposed to large investments in surveillance). But censorship, throttling, and shutdowns cost struggling African economies over $1.7 billion in 2023,[57] and only reinforce a sense of antagonism between citizens and the state.

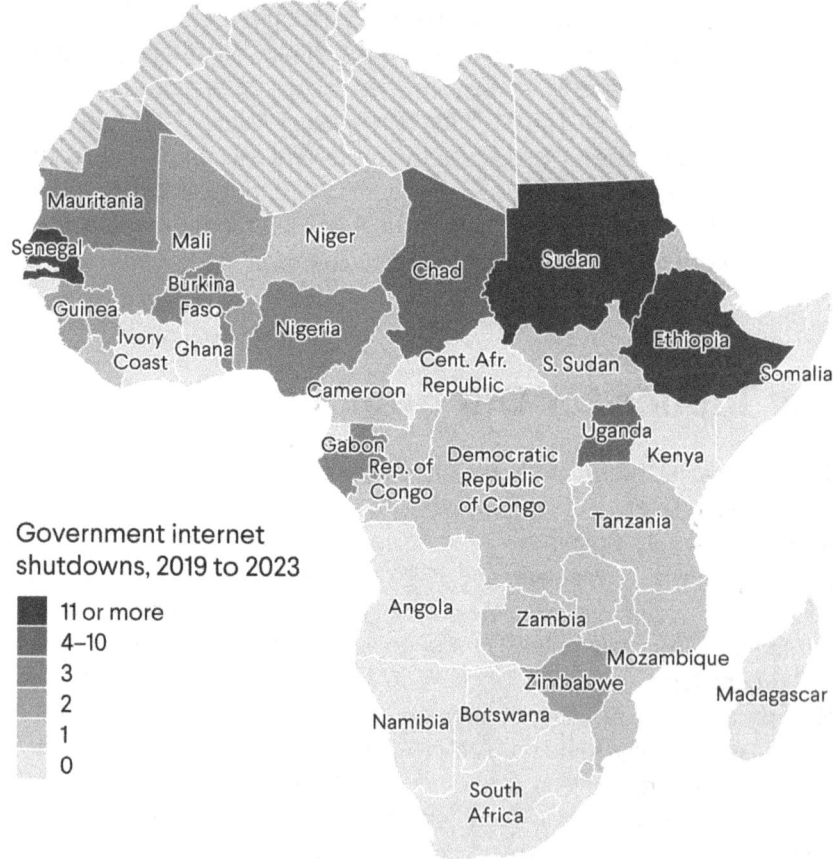

Map 6.1 Most African Countries Have Imposed Internet Shutdowns
(Note: Only includes government-imposed internet shutdowns). *Credit: Will Merrow, Council on Foreign Relations, Sources: KeepItOn Database of Internet Shutdowns; Cloudflare Outage Monitor*

THE STATUS QUO STRIKES BACK

Ugandans, for example, are keenly aware of their government's attempt to limit their digital discourse, particularly after the government's attempts to control "rumor mongering" with a social media tax from 2018 to 2021, which required citizens to pay a daily tax in order to access social media platforms; followed by the 12 percent internet data tax; and the 2021 Facebook ban.[58] But they also boast some of the liveliest social and political commentary on the internet. Social media users have contributed to a series of tongue-in-cheek "exhibitions" to expose what they see as governance failures, from the Kampala "pothole" exhibition, featuring photos of spectacular roadway damage, to the "health" exhibition, which included images of security forces manhandling striking medical interns.[59] In April 2023, Ugandans speculated that the government might block access to Twitter as they did to Facebook due to the many "exhibition" hashtags.

> Government will just block twitter in Uganda . . . these hashtags are giving officials headache.
>
> If they can't do anything then let them resign and let those who can come
>
> No breathing space
>
> Let them do what ever, like flowing water, we shall get another outlet
>
> If they do heeeeeee they will continue up to Google Maps . . . as the last social platform alive[60]

A thorough discussion of the burgeoning arsenal of digital manipulation techniques, from astroturfing to deep fakes, is beyond the scope of this book. But one does not need to be an expert on artificial intelligence or manipulating social media algorithms to see that digital space in many African countries is hotly contested territory. According to Freedom House, Angola, Ethiopia, Ghana, Kenya, Nigeria, Sudan, the Gambia, Uganda, and Zimbabwe have all deployed state-backed commentators to manipulate online discussions in their favor.[61] Generative AI has been used in several countries, including Nigeria, to smear opponents. In January 2024, the BBC exposed a network of almost two hundred fake social media accounts on X and Facebook that used photographs of real people (including a very surprised American health consultant) to create fake account profiles, which posted fervent support of the Ugandan government while threatening its critics.[62] Another block of coordinated, pro-Ugandan government accounts was identified by Meta in 2021, and similar groups have been uncovered that aimed to boost support for the Angolan government in 2022.[63]

It's important to note that young Africans are not just the targets of digital manipulation; they are also implementors of it. Just as young people eager for work can be mobilized into militia members, so too can young people be instrumentalized for digital repression. In 2018, Uhuru Kenyatta's Presidential Strategic Communications Unit employed Kenyan superusers and influences to manage his reputation,[64] foreshadowing the way the 2022 campaign would involve the monetizing of social networks, bankrolled by political elites.[65] This didn't happen surreptitiously: university students were actively recruited on campus to participate in influence campaigns associated with the 2022 election, a cycle that comprised the use of deep fakes aimed at dividing Kenyans, discrediting electoral institutions, voter suppression, and promoting fictional endorsements.[66]

The list goes on. In January 2023, the BBC reported on how Nigerian politicians promised government contracts, offered political appointments, and secretly paid social media influencers as much as $43,000 in exchange for spreading disinformation about political opponents.[67] Cameroon's government launched a group of "social media patriots" to promote "the adoption of good behavior, good attitudes, and the promotion of harmonious living together." Only those with significant existing social media followings were invited to apply.[68]

In their study of modern dictatorships, Sergei Guriev and Daniel Treisman have written about how "huge effort then goes into discrediting the challenger, distorting his record, blocking his communications, and priming the public with negative emotional associations, all while trying to avoid raising his public profile by, for instance, saying his name."[69] But similar tactics are increasingly employed in states that are not governed by dictators. In Kenya's last election cycle, the country's twelve million regular users of social media were bombarded by disinformation and misinformation about leading candidates for office. Meanwhile, the targets of concerted online smear campaigns were not just political opponents, but influential, independent voices as well. In June 2022, the Kenyan website *The Elephant* published the results of its investigations into fake hashtag movements and bots that aim to undermine civil society, claiming, "Our investigations have uncovered how such malicious, coordinated, inauthentic attacks that seek to silence members of civil society, muddy their reputations and stifle the reach of their messaging, is a growing problem."[70]

The amount of money and effort the political status quo devotes to minimizing the political power of youth is telling. Elites are outnumbered and face real challenges in finding sufficient resources to meet political demands or, failing that, finance co-option, manipulation, and repression. Many are turning to external actors—either as sources of support or scapegoats for popular anger—to ease the pressure.

Notes

1. Uganda Broadcasting Corporation, "Live: Museveni Addresses Nation on Matters of National Interest," YouTube video, July 20, 2024, https://www.youtube.com/watch?v=dYyNSruz4Mg.
2. Marc Sommers, *The Outcast Majority: War, Development, and Youth in Africa* (Athens: University of Georgia Press, 2015), 14.
3. "President Museveni's 2020 International Youth Day Address," NTV Uganda, YouTube video, 49:31, August 12, 2020, https://www.youtube.com/watch?v=B3Qohqjvz8M.
4. Tobbias Jolly Owiny, "Go to the Farm and Dig, Museveni Tells Youth," *Daily Monitor*, August 28, 2022, https://www.monitor.co.ug/uganda/news/national/go-to-the-farm-and-dig-museveni-tells-youth-3928728.
5. Samuel Ogundipe, "Buhari Criticises Nigerian Youth as Lazy, Uneducated," *Premium Times*, April 19, 2018, https://www.premiumtimesng.com/news/headlines/265484-buhari-criticises-nigerian-youth-as-lazy-uneducated.html?tztc=1.
6. Asanake Kefale, Mohammed Dejen, and Lovise Aalen, "Neglect, Control and Co-optation: Major Features of Ethiopian Youth Policy since 1991," *CMI Working Paper* 2021, 3, Christian Michelsen Institute for Science and Intellectual Freedom, https://www.cmi.no/publications/7829-neglect-control-and-co-optation-major-features-of-ethiopian-youth-policy-since-1991.
7. Willow Berridge, Justin Lynch, Raga Makawi, and Alex de Waal, *Sudan's Unfinished Democracy: The Promise and Betrayal of a People's Revolution* (London: Hurst Publishers, 2022), 162.
8. "Organizers of the November 11 march reject violence and manipulation," *Ver Angola*, November 6, 2020, https://www.verangola.net/va/en/112020/Society/22675/Organizers-of-the-November-11-march-reject-violence-and-manipulation.htm.
9. Jeffrey Moyo, "Zimbabwean Regime Shifts Oppression to Social Media," *Anadolu Agency*, February 16, 2021, https://www.aa.com.tr/en/africa/zimbabwean-regime-shifts-oppression-to-social-media/2146273.
10. Tim Judah, "The Pop Star and the President," *Foreign Policy*, February 1, 2012, https://foreignpolicy.com/2012/02/01/the-pop-star-and-the-president/.
11. Collette Schultz-Herzenberg and Robert Britt Mattes, "It Takes Two to Toyi-Toyi: One Party Dominance and Opposition Party Failure in South Africa's 2019 National Election," *Democratization* 30, no. 7, July 11, 2023, https://doi.org/10.1080/13510347.2023.2228710.
12. Lovise Aalen and Marjoke Oosterom, "Young Africans Could Disrupt Authoritarian States but They Don't—Here's Why," *The Conversation*, January 7, 2024, https://theconversation.com/young-africans-could-disrupt-authoritarian-states-but-they-dont-heres-why-218179.
13. *Walking the Walk: Prioritizing Youth Political and Civic Engagement in Renewing Democracy* (Baltimore, MD: Democracy Moves, Johns Hopkins Stavros Niarchos Foundation SNF Agora Institute, December 5, 2023), https://static1.

squarespace.com/static/5fd023409ea96b5f982e6c63/t/61af57ec288f4528f5c ab584/1638881741797/Walking+the+Walk.

14   Henry Karmo, "Liberia: Senate Pro Tempore Hopes the 2023 Turnover in the Senate Would Be Better than Previous Results," *Front Page Africa*, January 17, 2023, https://frontpageafricaonline.com/news/liberia-senate-pro-tempore-hopes-the-2023-turnover-in-the-senate-would-be-better-than-previous-results/.

15   See for example, Jeremy Bowles and Benjamin Marx, "Turnover and Accountability in Africa's Parliaments," *SSRN*, November 23, 2023, https://papers.ssrn.com/sol3/papers.cfm?abstract_id=4642554.

16   Nansozi K. Muwanga, Paul I. Mukwaya, and Tom Goodfellow, "Carrot, Stick, and Statute: Elite Strategies and Contested Dominance in Kampala," in *Controlling the Capital: Political Dominance in the Urbanizing World*, ed. Tom Goodfellow and David Jackman (Oxford: Oxford University Press, 2023), 71.

17   Ayisha Osori, "Nigeria's elections have bigger problems than vote trading," *Al Jazeera*, February 17, 2023, https://www.aljazeera.com/opinions/2023/2/17/nigerias-elections-have-bigger-problems-than-vote-trading.

18   JoAnn McGregor and Kudzai Chatiza, "Geographies of Urban Dominance: The Politics of Harare's Periphery," in *Controlling the Capital: Political Dominance in the Urbanizing World*, ed. Tom Goodfellow and David Jackman (Oxford: Oxford University Press, 2023).

19   Tsaone Basimanebotlhe, "Saleable Voters Defend Vote Buying," *Mmegi Online*, February 2, 2024, https://www.mmegi.bw/news/saleable-voters-defend-vote-buying/news.

20   Jenny Guardado and Leonard Wantchekon, "Do Electoral Handouts Affect Voting Behavior?" *Afrobarometer Working Paper* no. 171, March 2017, https://www.afrobarometer.org/wp-content/uploads/2022/02/afropaperno171_electoral_handouts_and_voting_behavior.pdf.

21   Authors refer to these practices as "coercive distribution": Tom Goodfellow and David Jackman, "Introduction," in *Controlling the Capital: Political Dominance in the Urbanizing World* (Oxford: Oxford University Press, 2023), 12.

22   Tom Goodfellow, "Taming the 'Rogue' Sector: Studying State Effectiveness in Africa through Informal Transport Politics," *Comparative Politics* 47, no. 2 (January 2015): 127–47, https://doi.org/10.5129/001041515814224462.

23   Muwanga, Mukwaya, and Goodfellow, "Carrot, Stick, and Statute," 76.

24   McGregor and Chatiza, "Geographies of Urban Dominance."

25   Muwanga, Mukwaya, and Goodfellow, "Carrot, Stick, and Statute," 71.

26   Daily Monitor (@DailyMonitor), "WATCH: Police officers filmed trying to restrain a group of youth," X post, December 7, 2023, https://twitter.com/DailyMonitor/status/1732812494240895470.

27   Muwanga, Mukwaya, and Goodfellow, "Carrot, Stick, and Statute," 73–4.

28   Marjoke Oosterom and Simbarashe Gukurume, "The Risk of Authoritarian Renewal in Zimbabwe: Understanding ZANU-PF Youth," *CMI Brief* 2023, no.1, Christian Michelsen Institute for Science and Intellectual Freedom, https://www.cmi.no/

29. Aalen and Oosterom, "Young Africans Could Disrupt Authoritarian States."
30. Gina Kungu (@Gina_Kungu), "Have you ever secured a job in Kenya solely based on merit?" X post, May 9, 2023, https://twitter.com/Gina_Kungu/status/1655877236447223810.
31. Kalu Aja (@FinPlanKaluAja1), "I have lived in America and Nigeria," X post, October 24, 2023, https://twitter.com/FinPlanKaluAja1/status/1716915734302036053.
32. Daily Monitor (@DailyMonitor), "Hunt for jobs instead of waiting on connections," X post, December 9, 2023, https://twitter.com/DailyMonitor/status/1733497089089216800.
33. Ebenezer Obadare, "A Religious War," *Africa in Transition*, Council on Foreign Relations, April 11, 2023, https://www.cfr.org/blog/religious-war.
34. Adam Branch and Zachariah Mampilly, *Africa Uprising: Popular Protest and Political Change* (London: Bloomsbury Publishing, 2015), 75.
35. See Branch and Mampilly, *Africa Uprising*, particularly chapter 4.
36. See the work of Sabine Carey, who has led a research team compiling data on pro-government militias; Sabine Carey, Neil J. Mitchell, and Katrin Paula, "The Life, Death and Diversity of Pro-Government Militias: The Fully Revised Pro-Government Militias Database Version 2.0," *Research and Politics* 9, no. 1 (2022), https://journals.sagepub.com/doi/10.1177/20531680211062772.
37. "Party Militias—A Threat to Security and Military Professionalism," *Africa Center for Strategic Studies*, November 2, 2021, https://africacenter.org/spotlight/party-militias-threat-security-military-professionalism/.
38. Muneinazvo Kujeke, "Zimbabwe's Notorious Youth Service Revived ahead of Election Season," Institute for Security Studies Africa, June 21, 2021, https://issafrica.org/iss-today/zimbabwes-notorious-youth-service-revived-ahead-of-election-season.
39. Kabale Ignatius Mukunto, "Electoral Violence and Young Party Cadres in Zambia," *Journal of African Elections* 18, no. 1 (July 2019), https://www.eisa.org/storage/2023/05/2019-journal-of-african-elections-v18n1-electoral-violence-young-party-cadres-zambia-eisa.pdf.
40. Bodil Folke Frederiksen, "Mungiki, Kenya's Violent Youth Gang, Serves Many Purposes: How Identity, Politics, and Crime Keep it Alive," *The Conversation*, February 11, 2024, https://theconversation.com/mungiki-kenyas-violent-youth-gang-serves-many-purposes-how-identity-politics-and-crime-keep-it-alive-221791.
41. Victor Abuso, "Kenya: Fear of Resurgence of Banned Mungiki Sect as Hundreds Arrested," *The Africa Report*, January 3, 2024, https://www.theafricareport.com/331983/kenya-fears-of-resurgence-of-banned-mungiki-sect-as-hundreds-arrested/.
42. Mercy Mwai, "Mungiki Gang on the Prowl, Claim Central Leaders," *People Daily Kenya*, November 23, 2023, https://www.pd.co.ke/news/mungiki-gang-on-the-prowl-claim-central-leaders-211431/.

43 For a useful, though somewhat dated, discussion of Mungiki, see Jacob Rasmussen, "Mungiki as Youth Movement: Revolution, Gender and Generational Politics in Nairobi, Kenya," *YOUNG* 18, no. 3 (2010): 301–19, https://journals.sagepub.com/doi/10.1177/110330881001800304.

44 "Senegal: New Counterterror Laws Threaten Rights," *Human Rights Watch*, July 5, 2021, https://www.hrw.org/news/2021/07/05/senegal-new-counterterror-laws-threaten-rights.

45 "Angola: TikToker Jailed for Criticizing the President: Ana da Silva Miguel (also known as Neth Nahara)," *Amnesty International*, December 15, 2023, https://www.amnesty.org/en/documents/afr12/7535/2023/en/.

46 Freedom House, "Kenya: Cybercrimes Law Restricts Media Freedom," Freedom House press release, May 15, 2018, https://freedomhouse.org/article/kenya-cybercrimes-law-restricts-media-freedom.

47 Elias Biryabarema, "Uganda Court Quashes Part of Law Used against Government Critics," *Reuters*, January 10, 2023, https://www.reuters.com/world/africa/uganda-court-quashes-part-law-used-against-government-critics-2023-01-10/.

48 Hanibal Goitom, "Uganda: Computer Misuse (Amendment) Act Enacted," *Global Legal Monitor*, Law Library of Congress, January 6, 2023, https://www.loc.gov/item/global-legal-monitor/2023-01-05/uganda-computer-misuse-amendment-act-enacted.

49 Ragnhild Nordas and Christian Davenport, "Fight the Youth: Youth Bulges and State Repression," *American Journal of Political Science* 57, no. 4 (October 2013): 926–40, https://www.jstor.org/stable/23496665?seq=2.

50 Mo Ibrahim Foundation, *2022 Ibrahim Index of African Governance—Index Report* (London: Mo Ibrahim Foundation, January 2023), https://assets.iiag.online/2022/2022-Index-Report.pdf.

51 Richard Moncrieff and Onesphore Sematumba, "Massacre in Goma Clouds DR Congo's Elections and UN Mission's Future," *International Crisis Group*, September 15, 2023, https://www.crisisgroup.org/africa/great-lakes/democratic-republic-congo/massacre-goma-clouds-dr-congos-elections-and-un.

52 Tony Roberts, "Some African Governments Are Spending Millions to Spy on Their Citizens—Stifling Debate and Damaging Democracy," *The Conversation*, November 1, 2023, https://theconversation.com/some-african-governments-are-spending-millions-to-spy-on-their-citizens-stifling-debate-and-damaging-democracy-215554.

53 Louis Gitinywa, "Authoritarianism and Digital Surveillance: Has the Internet Become a New Battleground for Monitoring Public Dissent in Rwanda?" *Media Defence*, January 16, 2023, https://www.mediadefence.org/news/authoritarianism-and-digital-surveillance-rwanda/.

54 Sam Phiri and Kiss Abraham, *Mapping the Supply of Surveillance Technologies to Africa Zambia Country Report* (Brighton: Institute of Development Studies, 2023), 121–35, https://opendocs.ids.ac.uk/opendocs/bitstream/handle/20.500.12413/18120/ADRN_Surveillance_Supply_Chain_Report_Zambia_Country_Report.pdf?sequence=7&isAllowed=y.

55 Adrian Shahbaz, Allie Funk, Jennifer Brody, et al., "Freedom on the Net 2023: The Repressive Power of Artificial Intelligence," *Freedom House*, 2023, https://

freedomhouse.org/sites/default/files/2023-10/Freedom-on-the-net-2023-DigitalBooklet.pdf.

56. Jimmy Kainja, "Access Denied: How Limited Internet Connectivity Erodes Democracy," *Democracy in Africa*, March 2023, https://democracyinafrica.org/access-denied-how-limited-internet-connectivity-erodes-democracy/.

57. Samuel Woodhams and Simon Migliano, "Government Internet Shutdowns Have Cost $53 Billion since 2019," *TOP10VPN*, March 8, 2024, https://www.top10vpn.com/research/cost-of-internet-shutdowns/.

58. Daniel Mwesigwa, "Uganda Abandons Social Media Tax but Slaps New Levy on Internet Data," *CIPESA*, July 1, 2021, https://cipesa.org/2021/07/uganda-abandons-social-media-tax-but-slaps-new-levy-on-internet-data/#:~:text=Introduced%20on%20July%201%2C%202018,Facebook%2C%20Twitter%2C%20and%20WhatsApp.

59. Gloria Irankunda and Faith Amongin, "Ugandans Yearn for More Online 'exhibitions,'" *Daily Monitor*, June 26, 2023, https://www.monitor.co.ug/uganda/news/national/ugandans-yearn-for-more-online-exhibitions–4283892.

60. The Allan County (@AllanSseky), "Government will just block twitter in Uganda," X post, April 24, 2023, https://twitter.com/AllanSseky/status/1650450535332425729.

61. Shahbaz, Funk, Brody, et al., "Freedom on the Net 2023."

62. Marco Silva, "Ugandan Internet Propaganda Network Exposed by the BBC," *BBC Verify*, January 20, 2024, https://www.bbc.com/news/world-africa-67803493.

63. Shahbaz, Funk, Brody, et al., "Freedom on the Net 2023."

64. Nanjala Nyabola, *Digital Democracy, Analogue Politics: How the Internet Era is Transforming Politics in Kenya* (London: Bloomsbury Publishers, 2018).

65. Karen Allen, Jean le Roux, and Bonface Beti, *A Question of Influence? Case Study of Kenyan Elections in a Digital Age* (Pretoria: Institute for Security Studies Africa, July 3, 2023), https://issafrica.org/research/east-africa-report/a-question-of-influence-case-study-of-kenyan-elections-in-a-digital-age.

66. Allen, le Roux, and Beti, *A Question of Influence?*

67. Chiagozie Nwonwu, Fauziyya Tukur, and Yemisi Oyedepo, "Nigeria Elections 2023: How Influencers Are Secretly Paid by Political Parties," *BBC Global Disinformation Team*, January 17, 2023, https://www.bbc.com/news/world-africa-63719505.

68. Paul Reinhard Wandji, "Cameroon: Government to Recruit 1,000 Social Media Experts to Combat Hate Speech," *Journal du Cameroun*, January 18, 2023, https://www.en.journalducameroun.com/cameroon-government-to-recruit-1000-social-media-experts-to-combat-hate-speech/.

69. Sergei Guriev and Daniel Treisman, *Spin Dictators: The Changing Face of Tyranny in the 21st Century* (Princeton, NJ: Princeton University Press, 2022), 81.

70. Odanga Madung, "How Twitter's Negligence is Harming Kenya's Democracy," *The Elephant*, July 1, 2022, https://theelephant.info/op-eds/2022/07/01/how-twitters-neglicgence-is-harming-kenyas-democracy/.

7
THE OUTSIDERS

The world is changing. And we need to start re-imagining Africa's place in it.

—EDWARD PAICE[1]

In 2023, Afrobarometer's polling showed that on average across thirty-four countries, positive perceptions of the influence of the United States and China were equal, with about half of citizens believing these external powers to be a force for good.[2] For both countries, this represented a significant decline in popularity. There could be many explanations—a significant slowdown in Chinese financing flows to the continent, concerns about debt burdens, frustrations with the economic hangover from the COVID crisis combined with geopolitical tensions in Europe that affected the cost of living in Africa, and worsening climatic conditions caused by major economies' emissions. But it could also be the case that the dissatisfaction many young Africans feel about authorities is bleeding over from the domestic to the international. When external powers are closely associated with the status quo, they are easily vilified.

That tendency is heightened by African awareness of their rich natural resources and of the historical injustice in the way those resources have been exploited. In a recent survey of eighteen-to-twenty-four-year-olds in fifteen African countries* conducted by the Ichikowitz Family Foundation, 62 percent of respondents agreed with the statement "foreign companies have been allowed to take advantage of my country's resources without sufficiently benefitting locals."[3] This serves as the backdrop for the global scramble to secure critical minerals to fuel the green economy of the future. It's a context ripe for suspicion and recrimination.

I've long been struck by the persistence of suspicions that the United States is behind this or that development on the continent and conspiracies that see

---

*Sample polled Angola, Congo-Brazzaville, Democratic Republic of Congo, Ethiopia, Gabon, Ghana, Kenya, Malawi, Mozambique, Nigeria, Rwanda, South Africa, Sudan, Uganda, and Zambia.

agents of Washington pulling strings to generate conflict or misery for some imagined American gain. The contrast between the constant struggle others and I have waged to get Africa-related issues on the agenda in Washington and the notion that the developments unfolding across the continent are part of some master plan is always disorienting.

For example, in June 2023 commenters speculated that the United States was behind a horrifying terrorist attack at a school in Uganda due to Washington's disapproval of Uganda's anti-LGBTQ laws.[4] Likewise, in 2022 social media users from around the region responded to a straightforward post from "Africa Facts Zone" that announced a new oil find in Angola by warning of US intervention.

> USA about to enforce democracy and the rule of law in Angola.

> Numerous NGOs, whose objective is to "deepen democracy," will be mushrooming soon in that country.

> Shhhhhhh, the western oligarchs are reading this.[5]

Similar comments followed an announcement that rare earth minerals were found in Kenya.[6]

Of course, there are real historical reasons for suspicion of the United States—and almost any other outside power—on the continent. Any US policymaker who has ever gotten an earful from South African officials about US support for the apartheid regime, or Congolese interlocutors about the fate of Patrice Lumumba, is regularly reminded of this fact. But in the era of volatility, it's more than the long shadow of history that creates mistrust. The economic, military, and cultural power of the United States—its very strength in the international system—make the country a prime target for resentment. The powers that be are failing young African populations. It's an easy jump from recognizing that structural forces seem to be stacked against young Africans to concluding that this is the intention of the chief architect and most powerful actor in the international system. This is one reason why US hand-wringing about the fate of the rules-based international order raises hackles on the African continent. It's not an order that most Africans would rush to defend.

The tsunami of anti-French sentiment washing over West and Central Africa is an object lesson in this regard. Resentment of France in francophone Africa is not new; it has certainly been apparent to me since my first trip to Cameroon in the mid-1990s. Any honest history of French involvement in its former colonies during the Cold War era is replete with reasons why: France's strategy to retain influence in the region involved shadowy elite deals and military interventions. But while the excesses of French policy peaked several decades ago, anger at France has exploded in intensity in the present. Generational and political change is at the heart of this paradox. As Michael Shurkin aptly noted, France "took for granted the support of West Africans and Sahelians, perhaps because their contacts were limited to those among African countries' Francophile elites. Unfortunately, those elites are losing influence and power. They also failed to do more to engage with francophone African public opinion."[7]

That youthful public has been unequivocal in their desire to see France "*degage*" or get out. The most visible symbols of France come in for the most criticism, from the currency in use in West and Central Africa, known as the CFA franc[†] (which is pegged to the Euro) to the French military presence in the region.[8] Reforms to the CFA used in West Africa have eliminated the controversial requirement that half of the region's foreign exchange reserves be held in the French Treasury; French forces have left Burkina Faso, Mali, and Niger, though they remain in Gabon, Djibouti, Senegal, and Cote d'Ivoire.[9] But these changes are unlikely to quell the anger directed at Paris. Young protesters railing against the status quo in their countries have targeted French embassies and French businesses. This surge of anger has been helped along by social media and a concerted Russian campaign that has accelerated and taken advantage of—but did not create—the sentiment.

A Little Respect

Complaints about Western "lecturing" and "scolding" are ubiquitous in the region, made worse by the obvious power differential between aid donors and recipients, the inconsistencies baked into foreign policy that tries to pursue national interests and champion democratic values simultaneously, the domestic foibles and failures of Western states that call into question any purported moral authority, and a global media context in which racist and anachronistic assumptions about African societies persist (and are regularly skewered by young Africans online). Add the brutal legacy of colonialism, and resentment is the unsurprising result.

That resentment can also be politically useful. In 2023, Congolese President Felix Tshisekedi scored political points domestically by scolding French President Emmanuel Macron publicly for a "paternalistic tone" and called for France and the West to be more respectful of African partners. Video of the incident went viral and was widely applauded online.

> African leaders are finally standing up to the bullying & patronizing tactics of the Western imperialists!! The multipolar world order is going to be quite interesting indeed.

[†]CFA stands for *Communauté financière africaine* or *Coopération financière en Afrique centrale*. It is used in Benin, Burkina Faso, Cameroon, Central African Republic, Chad, Equatorial Guinea, Gabon, Guinea-Bissau, Cote d'Ivoire, Mali, Niger, Republic of the Congo, Senegal, and Togo.

Africa is so done with France and GB.

Very good. High time they understand we are not their kid nations.[10]

It could not have worked out better for Tshisekedi, who was less than a year out from facing voters in his reelection campaign. He was able to position himself as a man unafraid to stand up to the powerful West—a position further solidified by his insistence that the UN peacekeeping mission in the DRC withdraw. But a Beijing-based internet company seized on the moment and embellished it further, posting to social media the false claim that Macron said that Africa should be "handed over to France" during the interaction with Tshisekedi.[11] It's just one example of how easily African actors and other major powers can cast anti-Western sentiment to advance their own political interests.

Russia, too, amplifies these types of moments, associating Moscow with African equities simply by reposting them. The Russian Embassy in Kenya retweeted a video of President Ruto addressing President Macron about reforms of the global economic governance system, summarizing Ruto's points with zeal.[12] "President Ruto to the West: 1. We no longer want IMF and the World Bank. 2. We need a new financial . . . organization of equals. 3. Things are not going forward, they are going backwards. You are not hearing us." Russia offers no plausible alternative to the international financial institutional architecture but positions itself as an ally simply by amplifying criticism.

China and Russia both claim to be more respectful partners than Western actors. Authoritarian narratives would seem a poor fit for messages about respect for societies, but the jiu-jitsu is managed by elevating a specific understanding of sovereignty as the *sine qua non* of respectful international relations. As Joseph Siegle wrote, "by focusing on the autonomy of the state rather than the individual, these arguments shrewdly portray ruling parties as the defenders (and interpreters) of their nations' freedom from foreign interference."[13] Thus Russia, the source of mercenaries who have massacred African civilians with impunity in the Sahel,[14] positions itself as a shining example of respecting Africa. So too does China, whose President Xi told African heads of state in 2024 that the "Western approach" to modernization "has inflicted immense suffering" on Chinese and African peoples alike, and that together, China and Africa would "redress the historical injustices of the modernization process."[15] In this telling, the profound power differential between China and Africa is irrelevant, as is the fact that China has been happy to keep the details of financing agreements with political elites secret, even when African citizens will be on the hook for repayment, while trumpeting its "noninterference" as a respectful posture.

These narratives also suggest that democracy was imposed on unwilling societies by Western powers, and because so many African states have pseudo-democracies in which elections occur, but citizens have no real ability to hold leaders accountable, authoritarians' line of attack is directed at an already weakened brand. The linkage between unsatisfactory governance, so-called democracy, and the West has taken root among some. It's not just paid influencers and bots doing the bidding of authoritarian powers that amplify this link; so do some very frustrated Africans. Consider comments from Cameroonians after the coup in Niger:

> It is sad explaining the issue of Paul Biya and Cameroon, and one sad thing is that Cameroon is in a civil war right now, but these agents of the west called African leaders are not talking about it. Tomorrow the imperialist France & America will come and talk about democracy in Africa.
>
> THE AGENT OF THE WESTERN DEMOCRACY PAUL BIYA ALWAYS SELLING COLLECTIVE INTERESTS OF HIS CITIZENS TO REMAIN IN POWER EXPOSED.[16]

The notion that African leaders in general, and Paul Biya in particular, are "agents" of a unified West that uses them for its own purposes seems bizarre to many in the Western world. But from the perspective of citizens who have been treated contemptuously by leaders who are solicitous to foreign heads of state that command significant resources, the idea can make some sense.

If the United States and Europe are awkwardly positioned for the era of volatility, other major powers are capitalizing on the moment. China and Russia have seized on widespread dissatisfaction with the status quo to cast themselves as champions of an alternative order. China, already the region's largest trading partner and a source of much-needed infrastructure investment, has long offered itself up as an exemplar of authoritarian development, its economic transformation proof of what can be accomplished if one forgoes civil liberties and submits to state control. The contrast with multiparty democracy is explicit and intentional.

At the societal level, China has invested heavily in messaging campaigns across Africa, spotlighting positive developments and linking them to strong China-Africa ties.[17] Chinese news agency Xinhua has more bureaus in Africa than any other news agency.[18] China Radio International's Facebook pages in Hausa and Swahili have more than a million followers apiece.[19] The China Global Television Network (CGTN) recruits high-profile African hosts and validators to reinforce Chinese narratives, and Chinese firms have used equity investments in African media houses to gain more editorial control.[20] Over sixty Confucius Institutes at African universities seek to create new affinities not just for Chinese culture, but for its governing principles as well.[21]

Meanwhile at the state level, China offers methods to bolster regime security by enhancing central government surveillance and control, from facial recognition software to networked "safe cities" cameras. Of course, China is not alone in exporting cyberespionage and surveillance technology—so too do Israeli, Bulgarian, and British firms.[22] Many of the technologies governments have used to block signals (often to jam cellular connectivity) were initially purchased as antiterrorism or VIP protection tools, raising questions about the role that external actors who prioritize security issues play in creating an environment for repression.[23] As Africa trends toward volatility, the methods which enable the state to contain demands for change may become even more significant.

Russia, too, characterizes itself as a leader in building an alternative global order. As President Putin told African leaders at the 2023 Russia-Africa Summit, "the era of hegemony of one or several countries is receding into the past, albeit not without resistance on the part of those who got used to their own uniqueness and monopoly in global affairs."[24] Russian Foreign Minister Sergey Lavrov was even more pointed in a message he delivered to the "Russia-Africa: What's Next?" youth forum in October 2022. "We are united by the rejection of the so-called 'rules-based order' that the former colonial powers are imposing on the world," he asserted.[25]

This rhetoric is accompanied by overt and covert messaging and disinformation campaigns. Moscow has used multiple media outlets like RT, Sputnik, and the Cameroon-based Afrique Media to reach African audiences and has cultivated and bankrolled numerous African influencers and "activists."[26] Russia has also helped to create fake civil society organizations to give the impression of a grassroots groundswell of support. In Uganda alone, viewers of the Ugandan Broadcasting Corporation are shown several hours of RT content daily, which hardly seems a celebration of Ugandan sovereignty.

Both China and Russia, as founding members of the BRICS group, seek to gain African support for reducing global dependence on the US dollar and reforming international institutions. The BRICS expansion in 2023 added Ethiopia and Egypt to the African roster alongside South Africa; reportedly many more African countries are hoping to be included in future expansions.

But it may not be so easy to ride the wave of sentiment in favor of change over the long term. The notion of Russia and China as change agents sits uncomfortably beside both countries' efforts to help African governments maintain their power. Today, Russia seems ascendent in Africa, having emerged from its post-Soviet era of neglect (for many years Russia's significance was largely as an arms exporter and little more) to pursue a low-cost, high-return strategy of using information operations to thwart Western interests, sow suspicion of democratic governance and international institutions, and trade security assistance to ruling elites in exchange for access to lucrative resources. It's certainly gained some traction; the Bennett Institute for Public Policy at Cambridge University found that 68 percent of citizens in francophone Africa had positive views of Russia.[27] But

THE OUTSIDERS

Russia, with its value proposition rooted in ensuring regime survival, is bound to have trouble too. While there will be a steady supply of floundering governments looking for a life preserver as they prove unable to meet popular demands for jobs, services, and security, Russia's strategy of presenting itself as a heroic savior in support of change only works once. Ultimately, Russia will find itself in the business of protecting the unpopular status quo.

China has a related problem. The dominant party model is integral to the Chinese brand, making resistance to change and political experimentation part of their value proposition. The Chinese Communist Party (CCP) has deep historic ties to several African political parties, like those that have controlled Tanzania and Zimbabwe since independence. China even trains African political parties' officials with CCP instructors at the Mwalimu Julius Nyerere Leadership School that it funds in Tanzania, where the ruling parties of South Africa, Namibia, Angola, Zimbabwe, Mozambique, and the host nation work on strategies to maintain power, improve ideological discipline, and resist an imagined Western regime change agenda.[28] Change is what African societies are seeking, but at China's political training center on the continent, change is a threat that is, by definition, driven by neo-imperialist agendas.[29]

Political volatility means that if external powers are closely associated with domestic authorities, those powers' stock will wax and wane with popular satisfaction. When the Patriotic Front (PF) took power in Zambia in 2011, it did so in part by accusing the previous government of selling out the country to China. But the PF ended up doubling down on the relationship with Beijing, including opaque financing deals that left the country even more indebted than the Zambian public initially realized.[30] Now, the PF and other opposition parties claim that President Hichilema's government is too close to the West, particularly to the United States, and urge their social media followers to "save" Zambia from Western imperialism.[31] That message may have limited resonance while Hichilema remains popular—recent polling shows that Zambian views of the United States and Chinese influence are largely similar[32]—but as Zambians' patience with their leadership wanes, frustration with the UPND may lead to greater anti-US sentiment.

It's also important not to underestimate African societies and their awareness of complicated relationships and attempts to manipulate them. In Kenya, young people profess admiration for China's development model but also mobilize to reject secrecy around Chinese financing for public infrastructure. In Senegal, online commenters call out Russian-backed influencers.[33] Africans are well aware of the manipulation of their information environment, and more than 75 percent of Kenyans, South Africans, and Nigerians surveyed have expressed concern about misinformation.[34]

The Way Ahead

I've been watching these dynamics unfold across Africa and working to understand them because I believe they are profoundly important factors shaping the global future. There can be no reforming of international institutions and norms without Africans helping to establish those rules, and no meeting global challenges like transitioning to a green economy without Africans contributing to solutions. But I am also a creature of my own context, an American who spent many years working for the US government, who is deeply familiar with the lens through which the US government perceives African states and societies. The combination of my interests and my experience has led me to conclude that US policymakers are ill equipped for the era of volatility. It's not just that we have no good answers to the question of how to help create jobs at a scale and pace to match Africa's growth. It's that the way we do business is particularly ill-suited to engaging a region in flux. Understanding how ardently young Africans crave new political narratives, new leaders, and new directions should inform US policy and its framing.

This point was driven home to me when a thoughtful, longtime Africa-watcher with deep US government experience reached out in the wake of Mozambique's contentious 2024 elections. He felt caught off guard by the emergence of a new, "third force" on Mozambique's political scene that had been dominated by two parties since independence. Our exchange helped me realize that, as a policy community, we keep thinking that the way it's been is the way it will always be, which makes no sense in societies that are changing so rapidly and profoundly. Experience and expertise are important, but they can also steep decision-makers in paradigms that are growing more obsolete by the day and render them insensitive to chronic issues that are urgent from the perspective of young African citizens.

Partnering with Societies, Not Just Governments

Too often, the United States has viewed Africa as a venue for competition with other major powers, oversimplifying African states' foreign policy as joining one "team" or another. The Biden administration took great pains to assert that it is not demanding that African countries choose between the West and China or Russia—but the frequency with which they emphasize this point often read like a case of protesting too much.

It makes sense that African governments want as wide a range of potential partners as possible, so that they may choose the most beneficial pairings on an à la carte basis. But while foreign countries may make easy targets for resentment, ultimately external powers will play, at best, a supporting role in whatever new story young, urban, and connected Africans create about the nature of the state in their societies. Successfully working with African states in the future will require understanding those stories, which means diplomats need to listen more closely when young Africans articulate their vision for the next chapter. That would require staffing embassies in Africa properly—itself an uphill climb[35]—and reaching out beyond the usual elite circles to understand the perspectives of struggling, urban young adults. It would also mean devoting more energy to working with a wide network of partners outside of central governing authorities and large development contractors. Identifying the voices of social authority in faith, business, and cultural communities that can help to provide continuity to relations will be essential when there is a great deal of churn at the top. The United States, with our pluralistic society, is blessed with multiple points of contact between the components of our civil society and those of different African states, and our government should do more to harness those disparate contacts to better understand our African partners. But broadening our networks and presence and listening with more care will accomplish little unless those efforts are linked to thoughtful, future-oriented action.

That does not mean racing to emulate the strategies of other external actors. Consider the US Africa Summit the United States hosted in 2022, only the second time such a summit was held. This required a massive logistical effort on the part of the United States, but other than imposing deadlines for deliverables from our own bureaucracy, it did not fundamentally advance US interests. Moreover, African resentment has been growing around these types of "Africa plus one" convenings, which are hosted by China, Russia, Japan, South Korea, Saudi Arabia, and Indonesia, among others. It's not just African leaders who are tired of being summoned to global capitals en masse for often shallow engagements that fail to differentiate among different countries' needs; it's also African publics for whom these gatherings can seem like remote distractions from pressing issues. The place to engage African leadership as a whole is at the African Union headquarters in Addis Ababa, not Washington, DC.

The temptation to compete with others for the favor of African leaders must be resisted. Ultimately, states pursuing geostrategic competition between governance models, such as liberal democratic states versus authoritarian development states, may find Africa slippery ground, as societies veer from one experiment to another in a quest for governance that can meet the tremendous challenges of the demographic moment. This could advantage states that take a purely transactional, rather than ideological view of diplomatic relationships in

Africa. Gulf states, already extremely active in the Horn of Africa as investors, suppliers of arms, and facilitators of financial flows, may find their transactional approach appreciated by successive, seemingly ideologically opposed, governments. On the other hand, they may find that young Africans online increasingly work to hold them accountable for the entities they support.

Perhaps the most basic lesson US policymakers need to draw is the importance of not over-personalizing bilateral relationships, or overinvesting in any specific government. As protests against Macky Sall heated up in Senegal, many online linked their frustrations to France and the United States because of their perceived support for Sall.

"Elites sold to foreign interests" Senegal is on fire and escapes the control of Paris "We are fed up with France," "France gets out": the submission of President Macky Sall to ECOWAS, in Paris—and therefore in Washington, the real power—set fire to the powder.[36]

France is scared of losing Senegal as well

France pushed the elections to clean their profile and come back to the table to vote[37]

After Kenya's Gen Z uprising of 2024, widespread anger with Ruto and his heavy-handed response to the protests was also targeted at the US Ambassador to Kenya, Meg Whitman. Once the results of the US presidential election became clear, Kenyans began a massive online campaign urging Washington to #RecallMegWhitman, accompanied by photos of her looking chummy with President Ruto.[38]

Guilt by association flows in both directions. The United States can be tarnished by appearing close to an unpopular leader, and leaders can suffer from a clumsy American embrace. In the eyes of policymakers in Washington, DC throughout the Biden administration, President Ruto of Kenya was a vitally important partner. Kenya is an island of order and hub of innovation in an increasingly tumultuous subregion of the continent. The US-Kenyan partnership is deep and multifaceted, encompassing security cooperation, increased trade ties, public health, and development work. Even better, Ruto, despite a checkered history, emerged as a champion of African equities, speaking out on the injustices of climate change experienced by Africans but created elsewhere, and calling for change to the international financial institutions. Here, it would seem, is a partner with whom we could work closely to reform the rules-based order.

Ruto's calls for change in the way the international system works are appreciated on the ground, but they are also taken with several grains of salt, because while calling for reform, he has had to work with the system as it is, squeezing the tax base to hit IMF revenue targets. One social media commentator memorably described the Kenyan president as "Pan-African in the streets but Bretton Woods in the sheets."[39]

In fact, America's warm embrace of Ruto is, at best, a double-edged sword for him at home. Gestures meant to signal support aren't always met with enthusiasm. Online commenters found media reports of President Ruto's enthusiastic announcement of his state visit invitation to Washington a reason for skepticism.

> Where are those who shouted loudly about Sovereignty, ooh, sijui independence etc? Your favourite puppet, oops, president is excited, oh.
>
> Misplaced priorities, a whole president getting excited for a mere state visit which won't benefit hustlers in any way
>
> Can someone fact check the bit about no African president being invited to the White House in the last 20 years? Plus does endorsement by the US govt. mean so much to us? Many dictators have held talks with the US president. That doesn't whitewash their sins.[40]

Yet, illustrating how African politics are not dominated by major power rivalries, Kenyan skepticism about the West doesn't necessarily equate to enthusiasm for rivals like China. When news broke of a multiyear Chinese hacking campaign to gain access to Kenyan government agencies, including the National Intelligence Service, the reaction on social media reflected an across-the-board cynicism about external powers.[41]

> Western nations and now China are known to legally or illegally access dev. countries' data. This data then forms the basis of their economic and diplomatic policies for such nations. The quest for markets for their products is still on & Africa is the target.
>
> The moment I knew that our Traffic control systems are powered by Huawei I knew we are finished as a country.
>
> So these people have any respect for our country?[42]

Adjusting Priorities

Too often, US efforts to engage African partners miss the mark in responding to the most urgent concerns of youthful populations. For many years, the vast majority—roughly 70 percent—of US foreign assistance in Africa was spent on health programs, and particularly on combating HIV.[43] This work was important and lifesaving, but it did not speak to the most urgent priorities of African societies as identified in poll after poll. Most young Africans do not have a memory of the worst days of the AIDS crisis on the continent. But they are acutely aware of their needs for job opportunities and government that provides safety rather than inspiring fear. US officials making speeches about our decades-long investment in fighting AIDS and young Africans demanding dignified jobs are talking past each other.

The US-Zambia relationship is a case in point. For years, the vast majority of US assistance to Zambia is focused on combating HIV. But Zambians rarely discuss this help online. Instead, they are preoccupied with the state of the economy and the urgent need for jobs. The parade of high-level US officials visiting Lusaka since President Hichilema was elected had few concrete outcomes for Zambians other than worsened traffic. The online discourse is skeptical.

> The level of interest USA has shown in Zambia it's questionable.

> What has become of sudden interest to the Americans now? never have those people (Americans) look out for the interests of others.

> The visit won't yield anything positive just like your foreign trips your excellence. What should we expect as a country

> It's all geopolitics, Mr. President, and the winner will never be Zambia. US never fights in anyone's corner, they only create new corners for themselves in your country.[44]

The drawn-out nature of Zambia's debt restructuring, which Hichilema called "an indictment" of the international system,[45] made the optics particularly dicey. Americans kept showing up to talk about how much they support Zambia, but the most powerful nation in the world couldn't seem to deliver on efforts to get their debt deal over the finish line. It did not matter that China was Zambia's largest bilateral creditor. The US embrace looked empty—or worse.

Aside from illustrating that the issue of unsustainable debt must be addressed in a more holistic way, among the lessons that the United States should draw is that we need new, more flexible tools that can help willing and accountable partners deliver quick wins while longer-term strategies—like the Lobito corridor investments that should ultimately attract more investments and drive job creation in Angola, the Democratic Republic of Congo, and Zambia—take root. Development policy and commercial diplomacy should prioritize job creation, the continent's most obvious need that is an afterthought, at best, in US policy.

Policymakers also need to recognize that Africans aren't just paying attention to US policies in their countries, they are also watching the totality of world events, and are keenly aware that the West's response to conflict in Ukraine, or terrorist attacks in Israel, looks dramatically different from the attention given to the devastating war in Sudan, or attacks on civilians in the DRC.

Millions and millions of dead, but they are neither Ukrainian nor Israeli nor Palestinian. The world doesn't care and even the so-called African organizations don't care I sincerely think so, many African leaders deserve life in prison.[46]

The lesson is, if you wanna kill people & get away with it, no media noise, kill Africans, everyone who has killed millions of Africans is a hero, no sanction, no condemnation, no apology, life goes on.[47]

Somehow the world's largest displacement crisis—which in 2024 was in Sudan—or the sites of that largest number of lethal terrorist attacks on earth—which for several years running have occurred in the Sahel—don't seem urgent to major powers. The tragic desperation of young Africans who risk, and often lose, their lives trying to make their way to Europe (or increasingly, to the United States),[48] provoke a great deal of discussion about enforcing borders and far less about how to generate more opportunity at the source. Although most African migration is intraregional, and less than a third of African migrants live in Europe, the discourse around African migration in Europe is increasingly panicked.[49] In multiple instances, Europe has funded authorities with horrifying human rights records and histories of mistreating migrants to "control" migration before it reaches European shores.[50] The fact that climate change is driving unusual migratory flows, while African states contributed almost nothing to the world's carbon emissions, only makes the situation worse. Combined with the dismissive disdain too often experienced by Africans abroad, or in the consular lines at Western embassies, the message transmitted constantly undervalues young African lives.

Change will require moving Africa out of the periphery of US foreign policy thinking. It is still the case that serious foreign policy professionals with global portfolios and responsibilities know very little about the African continent, and struggle to grasp how US interests suffer when we treat African issues as third-tier priorities, or fall back on old, lazy paradigms to guide policy.

Stability versus Dynamism

Take, for example, our very understanding of "stability."‡ Of course, disorder is costly; it can entail violence and suffering, create unpredictability that repels investment, make it impossible to manage dangerous crises, create opportunities

---

‡Parts of this discussion of stability originally appeared in the *American Ambassador's Review*, Michelle Gavin, "Rethinking Stability in Africa," *American Ambassadors Live!*, Council of American Ambassadors, November 3, 2021, https://www.americanambassadorslive.org/post/rethinking-stability-in-africa.

for terrorists and criminal groups, and often spills across borders. The urgent needs of young Africans cannot be met in such a context, nor can international cooperation deliver much in the way of progress.

But far too often, the pursuit of "stability" in principle has translated to support for an existing order and political status quo in practice, regardless of how repressive or how brittle that order becomes. Policy in Chad offers a good example. The United States spent years investing in a close relationship with the late President Idriss Déby and considered him a close partner in combating terrorism and promoting "regional stability," despite his government's record of beating peaceful protesters, torturing dissidents, holding sham elections, blurring the lines between civil and military authority, and running the government as a family business. When Déby was killed in 2021, the unconstitutional installation of his son at the head of government only confirmed that the weight of Chad's formal laws paled in comparison to the vested interests of a small clique. In turn, Washington's tepid response—policymakers declined to acknowledge that a coup d'etat had occurred—made it clear that in the case of Chad, the United States preferred to continue working with a known quantity.

The notion that change would necessarily threaten US interests, or usher in an unreliable or incompetent new partner, locks the United States into increasingly uncomfortable relationships. Such partnerships make a mockery of our claims to champion democracy and transparency and create bountiful opportunities for adversaries to vilify the United States as the arbiter and defender of fundamentally unjust status quo. It also confuses consistency for stability. Ignoring the growing rifts between the governing and governed until they boil over often leaves the United States to confront the instability and insecurity it had feared, while bearing the burden of historical association with a detested regime.

Kenya's Gen Z protesters have helped to point toward a constructive way forward, by focusing much of their ire on corruption and impunity. Fighting those poisons will be a consistent priority even as leaders come and go, and will be crucial for the success of society as a whole, not just a particular government. The job-creation challenge will persist, but that doesn't mean that political developments will race to the bottom. Afrobarometer's polling shows that support for democracy can be resilient in the face of poverty, but diminishes substantially in a context of corruption, poor quality elections, and an absence of accountability.[51] Additionally, new thinking on how to make the most of democratic openings[52] even in fragile states also provides some guideposts for the future, emphasizing the importance of inclusivity and high-level engagement. The road ahead is complex, but it will include real opportunities alongside the perils.

An important start is to step up efforts to help African states combat corruption and recoup illicit financial flows, centering accountable governance and transparency in our efforts rather than democracy. This support will not be taken up by all parties, but the United States should find ways to offer it whether power is held constitutionally or has been seized by force. It's entirely possible that some junta leaders on the continent believe their own rhetoric, and feel duty-bound to clean up what they, and many others, perceived to be a predatory, self-serving state. Thorny questions about how recovered funds should be returned are not reasons to shy away from these efforts. Continued support, where possible, for independent, professional journalism is another critical governance effort. Subsidizing training for forensic accountants, procurement officers, and compliance professionals—and finding ways to talk about this work without putting those people at risk, is another prong. Of course, all of this assumes that the United States remains interested in fighting corruption, improving transparency, and respecting free and independent at home. Broadly, aligning the United States with the popular demand for government that focuses state resources on the needs of the population is an effort the United States is unlikely to regret even as political volatility persists.

Given the scale and pace of demographic and resulting social change across Africa, it makes sense that African politics today would regularly feature transfers of power and ongoing rounds of structural reforms to modernize institutions and respond to the massive social change underway across African states. In fact, popular protests were on the rise throughout the region until the COVID-19 disruptions.[53] This does not have to translate to a landscape of chaos. Done right, power transfers and civil demonstrations prevent disorder and mitigate the causes of conflict by accommodating popular demands, bolstering consensus around the rules that define civic life, and strengthen the connective tissue between the governing and the governed. African experiments could point to innovations that struggling democracies, including the United States, might try.

The political future in the region will not look like the recent past. The worst thing the United States or others could do would be to express alarm at this prospect or continue to be shocked by change. A close second would be to treat the region as a backwater, showing interest in its natural resources but total disdain for the aspirations of its growing population. Acknowledging that African popular demands will be difficult for any government to satisfy does not equate to Afro-pessimism—it's Afro-realism. In places where governing institutions have been compromised or eroded by decades of personalized rule, political turnovers will be difficult to translate into better governance quickly. External powers may be able to help underperforming leaders hold on for longer than they would otherwise, but the demand signals from African publics will be undeniable. Young, urban, connected societies are demanding change, and they are likely to keep it up for some time. Powers that purport to believe in government that responds to popular will need to get comfortable with new faces and new ideas.

Notes

1. Declan Walsh, "The World is Becoming More African," *New York Times*, October 28, 2023, https://www.nytimes.com/interactive/2023/10/28/world/africa/africa-youth-population.html.
2. Cobus van Staden, "New Afrobarometer Poling Shows Both China and the U.S. Losing Popularity in Africa," China Global South Project, April 27, 2023, https://chinaglobalsouth.com/analysis/new-afrobarometer-polling-shows-both-china-and-the-u-s-losing-popularity-in-africa/.
3. Ichikowitz Family Foundation, *African Youth Survey 2022* (Johannesburg: IFF, June 2022), 68, https://ichikowitzfoundation.com/storage/ays/ays2022.pdf.
4. See comments, Larry Madowo (@LarryMadowo), "DEVELOPING: At least 26 people were killed at a school in Kasese in western Uganda by armed rebels," X post, June 17, 2023, https://twitter.com/LarryMadowo/status/1669953653279543298.
5. Africa Facts Zone (@AfricaFactsZone), "Angola, Africa's second largest oil producer has discovered a new oil bloc," X post, January 12, 2023, https://twitter.com/AfricaFactsZone/status/1613507687479746561.
6. Africa Archives (@Africa_Archives), "Kenya has announced that it has found large deposits of a rare mineral," X post, January 27, 2023, https://twitter.com/Africa_Archives/status/1751303575878132174.
7. Michael Shurkin, "Anti-French Sentiment in Africa: An American Perspective," *La Revue Internationale et Stratégique* 1, no. 133 (2024): 163–71, https://www.cairn.info/revue-internationale-et-strategique-2024-1-page-163.htm?contenu=article#pa23.
8. Alain Antil, Thierry Vircoulon, and Francois Giovalucchi, "Themes, Actors and Functions of Anti-French Discourse in French-speaking Africa," *IFRI Studies*, Institut Français des Relations Internationales, June 14, 2023, https://www.ifri.org/fr/publications/etudes-de-lifri/thematiques-acteurs-fonctions-discours-anti-francais-afrique.
9. Shola Lawal, "Au revoir, Sahel: Did 2023 Crush France's Influence in Africa?" *Al Jazeera*, December 31, 2023, https://www.aljazeera.com/news/2023/12/31/au-revoir-sahel-did-2023-crush-frances-influence-in-africa.
10. DD Geopolitics (@DD_Geopolitics), "Macron gets slapped by the President of the Democratic Republic of Congo," X post, March 5, 2023, https://twitter.com/DD_Geopolitics/status/1632546619290955778.
11. Tommy Wang, "False Posts Misrepresent Tense Exchange between France's Macron and DR Congo's Tshisekedi," AFP Fact Check, March 27, 2023, https://factcheck.afp.com/doc.afp.com.33BQ7JJ.
12. Russian Embassy in Kenya (@russembkenya), "President Ruto to the West," X post, June 28, 2023, https://twitter.com/russembkenya/status/1673916634489311233.
13. Joseph Siegle, *Winning the Battle of Ideas: Exposing Global Authoritarian Narratives and Revitalizing Democratic Principles* (Washington DC: National Endowment for Democracy, February 2024), 6, https://www.ned.org/wp-content/uploads/2024/02/NED_FORUM-Authoritarianism-Narratives.pdf.

14 "Mali: Army, Wagner Group Atrocities against Civilians," Human Rights Watch, March 28, 2024, https://www.hrw.org/news/2024/03/28/mali-army-wagner-group-atrocities-against-civilians.

15 *Xinhua*, "Full Text: Keynote Address by Chinese President Xi Jinping at Opening Ceremony of 2024 FOCAC Summit," September 5, 2024, https://english.www.gov.cn/news/202409/05/content_WS66d964bdc6d0868f4e8eaa07.html.

16 Dr. David Matsanga (@MatsangaDr), "Another one loading . . . Waah Africa?" X post, August 8, 2023, https://twitter.com/MatsangaDr/status/1688844568928636928.

17 Joshua Eisenman, "China Is Tweaking Its Propaganda for African Audiences," *Foreign Policy*, March 16, 2023, https://foreignpolicy.com/2023/03/16/china-propaganda-africa-soft-power/.

18 Joshua Eisenman, *China's Media Propaganda in Africa: A Strategic Assessment* (Washington, DC: US Institute of Peace, March 2023), https://www.usip.org/sites/default/files/2023-03/sr_516-china_media_propaganda_africa.pdf.

19 Sarah Cook, "Beijing's Global Media Influence 2022: Authoritarian Expansion and the Power of Democratic Resilience," *Freedom House*, September 8, 2022, https://freedomhouse.org/report/beijing-global-mediainfluence/2022/authoritarian-expansion-power-democratic-resilience.

20 Eisenman, *China's Media Propaganda in Africa*.

21 Kate Bartlett, "As West Shuts China's Confucius Institutes, More Open in Africa," *Voice of America*, November 16, 2022, https://www.voanews.com/a/as-west-shuts-china-confucius-institutes-more-open-in-africa/6837437.html.

22 Bulelani Jili, "The Spread of Surveillance Technology in Africa Stirs Security Concerns," Africa Center for Strategic Studies, December 11, 2020, https://africacenter.org/spotlight/surveillance-technology-in-africa-security-concerns/.

23 Marisa Lourenço, "Signal Interrupted: When State Security Goes Rogue," *Democracy in Africa*, April 4, 2023, https://democracyinafrica.org/signal-jamming-when-state-security-goes-rogue/.

24 "Putin Woos African Leaders at a Summit in Russia with Promises of Expanding Trade and Other Ties," *AP News*, July 28, 2023, https://apnews.com/article/russia-africa-summit-putin-food-grain-00408e40403c3c30f89371a474bb4f9d.

25 "Video Message from the Minister of Foreign Affairs of the Russia Federation S. V. Lavrov to the Participants of the Second International Youth Forum 'Russia-Africa: What Next?' Moscow, October 24, 2022," Ministry of Foreign Affairs of the Russia Federation, October 24, 2022, https://www.mid.ru/ru/foreign_policy/news/1834826/?lang=en&ysclid=l9mze27pw8172677184.

26 U.S. Department of State Global Engagement Center, *Yevgeniy Prigozhin's Africa-Wide Disinformation Campaign*, November 4, 2022, https://www.state.gov/disarming-disinformation/yevgeniy-prigozhins-africa-wide-disinformation-campaign/.

27 Han Isha, Xavier Romero-Vidal, and Roberto Foa, "Is the World Dividing in Two? How People across the Globe View China, Russia, and the United States," Bennett Institute for Public Policy at Cambridge University, November 27, 2022, https://www.bennettinstitute.cam.ac.uk/blog/world-dividing-in-two/.

28 Paul Nantulya, "China's First Political School in Africa," Africa Center for Strategic Studies, November 7, 2023, https://africacenter.org/spotlight/china-first-political-school-africa/.

29 Peter Fabricius, "When 'democracy' Becomes 'regime change,'" Institute for Security Studies, December 15, 2017, https://issafrica.org/iss-today/when-democracy-becomes-regime-change.

30 Helen Reid and Chris Mfula, "Zambia's Chinese Debt Nearly Twice Official Estimate, Study Finds," *Reuters*, September 28, 2021, https://www.reuters.com/world/africa/zambias-chinese-debt-nearly-twice-official-estimate-study-finds-2021-09-28/.

31 Cynthia Kamwengo, "Social Media Debates on Zambia's Evolving Relations with the West and East," *Megatrends Afrika*, German Institute for International and Security Affairs, February 2024, https://www.swp-berlin.org/assets/afrika/publications/policybrief/MTA_Policy_Brief_Kamwengo_Zambia_and_Social_Media_final.pdf.

32 Edward Chibwili, "Perceptions of China's Influence on Zambia Remain Positive, though on the Decline," *Afrobarometer Dispatch* No. 759, January 19, 2024, https://www.afrobarometer.org/wp-content/uploads/2024/01/AD759-Zambians-perceptions-of-Chinese-influence-positive-but-declining-Afrobarometer-19jan24.pdf.

33 See responses to Nathalie Yamb's post on Senegal's 2024 elections, Nathalie Yamb (@Nath_Yamb), "Opposants emprisonnés, candidats éliminés, conseil constitutionnel et DGE aux orders," X post, January 9, 2024, https://twitter.com/Nath_Yamb/status/1744705880786866374.

34 Nic Newman, Richard Fletcher, Anne Schulz, et al., *Reuters Institute Digital News Report 2021: 10th Edition* (Oxford: Reuters Institute for the Study of Journalism, June 2021), https://reutersinstitute.politics.ox.ac.uk/sites/default/files/2021-06/Digital_News_Report_2021_FINAL.pdf.

35 Robbie Gramer and Amy Mackinnon, "U.S. Embassies in Africa Are Chronically Short-Staffed," *Foreign Policy*, July 22, 2022, https://foreignpolicy.com/2022/07/22/africa-embassies-short-staffed-us-sahel-china-russia/.

36 A__Samedi (@_samedi_), "'Elites vendues aux intérêts des étrangers': le Sénégal s'embrase et échappe au contrôle de Paris," X post, August 9, 2023. https://twitter.com/_samedi_/status/1689354431572119552.

37 lemonde063, "#politics #courdetatconstitutionnelesenegal," comments on TikTok video, February 4, 2024, https://www.tiktok.com/@lemonde063/video/7331740651853221128?q=senegal&t=1707491934776.

38 I am Chege (@James041), "We are all pushing the #RecallMegWhitman," X post, November 6, 2024, https://twitter.com/_James041/status/1854076358046912523.

39 (Comment since deleted) William Samoei Ruto, PhD (@WilliamsRuto), "Addressing youth on climate change and financing at the Champs de Mars, Paris, France," X post, June 23, 2023, https://twitter.com/WilliamsRuto/status/1672119927564644353.

40 Citizen TV Kenya (@citizentvkenya), "President William Ruto: I have just come from a meeting with the Ambassador of the US." X post, February 25, 2024, https://twitter.com/citizentvkenya/status/1761775674702876942.

41 Aaron Ross, James Pearson, and Christopher Bing, "Exclusive: Chinese Hackers Attacked Kenyan Government as Debt Strains Grew," *Reuters*, May 24, 2023,

https://www.reuters.com/world/africa/chinese-hackers-attacked-kenyan-government-debt-strains-grew-2023-05-24/.

42 Paul Olind (@OlindPaul), "China ran a 3 year hacking campaign targeting Kenyan government agencies including a server exclusively used by NIS," X post, May 24, 2023, https://twitter.com/OlindPaul/status/1661253901981720576.

43 Tomas F. Husted, Alexis Arieff, Lauren Ploch Blanchard, and Nicolas Cook, "U.S. Assistance for Sub-Saharan Africa: An Overview," Congressional Research Service, November 7, 2023, https://sgp.fas.org/crs/row/R46368.pdf.

44 Hakainde Hichilema (@HHichilema), "Looking forward to welcoming the USA second family," X post, March 14, 2023, https://twitter.com/HHichilema/status/1635603348014415874.

45 Joseph Cotterill and Alec Russell, "Zambia Says $13bn Debt Stand-off is 'indictment' of Global System," *Financial Times*, March 20, 2024, https://www.ft.com/content/c528daac-fd80-490e-aee1-29a18154f79b.

46 Damien Oc (@thiernobalde85), "Des milliones et des millions des morts," comment on X post, October 21, 2023, https://twitter.com/thiernobalde85/status/1715691116559733021.

47 PSAF (@Mlotha_ka_Nhlek), "The lesson is, if you wanna kill people & get away with it," comment on X post, October 9, 2023, https://twitter.com/Mlotha_ka_Nhlek/status/1711283176780259808.

48 Miriam Jordan, "African Migration to the U.S. Soars as Europe Cracks Down," *New York Times*, January 5, 2024, https://www.nytimes.com/2024/01/05/us/africa-migrants-us-border.html.

49 *Africa and Europe: Facts and Figures on African Migrations* (London: Mo Ibrahim Foundation, February 2022), https://mo.ibrahim.foundation/our-research/data-stories/aef-african-migrations.

50 Jerome Tubiana, "Europe Is Making Sudan's Refugee Crisis Worse," *Foreign Policy*, January 8, 2024, https://foreignpolicy.com/2024/01/08/sudan-darfur-refugee-crisis-eu-migration/#:~:text=The%20EU%20was%20then%20accused,as%20Hemeti%E2%80%94repeatedly%20bragged%20that.

51 *Afrobarometer*, "African Insights 2024: Democracy at Risk—the People's Perspective," Flagship report, July 17, 2024, https://www.afrobarometer.org/wp-content/uploads/2024/05/Afrobarometer_FlagshipReport2024_English.pdf.

52 Brittany Gleixner-Hayat, "U.S. Support for Democratic Openings in Conflict-Affected Countries: Lessons from Ethiopia and Sudan," *Carnegie Endowment for International Peace*, October 2, 2024, https://carnegieendowment.org/research/2024/10/us-democracy-assistance-sudan-ethiopia?lang=en.

53 Zoe Marks, Erica Chenoweth, and Jide Okeke, "Why People Power is Rising in Africa," *Foreign Affairs*, April 25, 2019, https://www.foreignaffairs.com/articles/africa/2019-04-25/people-power-rising-africa.

POSTSCRIPT

I had largely finished this manuscript by the middle of 2024. Since then, the United States government and US foreign policy have been reshaped, sometimes dramatically, by the second administration of President Donald J. Trump. In a matter of weeks, a host of tools that policymakers had used to engage Africans and African states were eliminated as the Agency for International Development was dismantled, the Millennium Challenge Corporation shut down, Voice of America's journalists fired, and the National Endowment for Democracy defunded. Foreign students became targets of suspicion—particularly if they expressed solidarity with Palestinians, a very common sentiment throughout Africa—and visas ever more difficult to obtain. Travelers from Chad, the Republic of Congo, Equatorial Guinea, Eritrea, Somalia, and Sudan were banned from the United States, and those from more than twenty additional African countries are being threatened with similar action.

Administration officials made it clear that they would prioritize deal-making and transactional arrangements rather than democratic principles or human rights issues. South Africa proved to be an exception to this rule, as the Trump administration amplified false narratives about a campaign of genocide aimed at white South Africans, going so far as to fast-track the resettlement of white South African families in the United States even as other, fully vetted and cleared refugees who had waited for years and were days away from resettling in America suddenly found the doors to the United States slammed shut.

I wrote this book to call attention to the dynamism in African politics, the importance of taking public opinions—which for Africa means youthful opinions—seriously, and the hazards of relying on elite relationships. The current United States government is unlikely to heed that call, despite the rather obvious realities that a focus on white grievance is not a winning public diplomacy strategy on the continent, and uncertainty doesn't provide the best context for deal-making. Politics matter, and "winning" transactions may prove ephemeral.

Nonetheless, some of the Trump administration's early steps—or at least their statements—might resonate with young Africans. The early emphasis on commercial diplomacy is welcome, as job-creating investment is desperately wanted and needed (although the confusing tariff rates unveiled on April 2, 2025, do not bode well for trade relations). The demolition of old foreign assistance models comes with real costs, but also the benefit of abolishing old donor-recipient power dynamics that bred resentment in the region. Certainly, there is a large and receptive audience for an end to moral posturing and a focus on action rather than rhetoric.

I argue for more diplomatic attention to African societies—not just governments. But in this moment, cuts to the foreign service and skepticism about the value of the US diplomatic footprint in the region preclude that kind of deeper networking weaving. The abolition of a separate Africa Directorate at the National Security Council indicates that the United States has no intention of emulating China, Russia, or the Gulf States in making Africa a strategic priority. The comparative advantage the United States might have had in the region over competitors—a willingness to align with forces fighting corruption—may no longer exist. The administration issued new guidelines for enforcement of the Foreign Corrupt Practices Act that suggest disinterest in corrupt acts that do not disadvantage US business, and the president himself engaged in behaviors that would have been considered egregious examples of self-dealing and conflict of interest only a few short years ago.

Yet it's also the case that the ingredients for better mutual understanding and stronger relationships remain potent, and in some cases more prominent than before, as the US government comes to more closely resemble governments in the region. The United States now has an aging leader who enjoys publicly flirting with the idea of a third term. The professional civil service is being hollowed out and government and political loyalty, rather than integrity or expertise, is the most important criterion for office. Ostentatious displays of wealth are merged with performative displays of power, a combination deeply familiar to many African societies. Those perceived as allies of the ruling party receive pardons for their crimes, reinforcing the idea that there is one set of rules for those "on the team" and a different set for everyone else. Displays of military might and heavily armed law enforcement are meant to instill fear widely and discourage dissent. Perhaps the coming era of US–African relations will involve more mutual learning and deeper societal connections, as communities on both sides of the Atlantic try to find a new basis for trust in governing institutions.

Regardless of what is happening in the United States, young Africans, emboldened by their demographic strength and the urgency of their needs, will continue their efforts to reshape their societies and the world. They will not dwell on signals coming from Washington. It's up to the United States to find pathways to relevant partnership, or to simply accept being left behind.

—Michelle Gavin
June 2025

BIBLIOGRAPHY

A__Samedi (@_samedi_). "'Elites vendues aux intérêts des étrangers': le Sénégal s'embrase et échappe au contrôle de Paris." X post, August 9, 2023. https://twitter.com/_samedi_/status/1689354431572119552.

Aalen, Lovise, and Marjorie Oosterom. "Young Africans Could Disrupt Authoritarian States but They Don't—Here's Why." *The Conversation*, January 7, 2024. https://theconversation.com/young-africans-could-disrupt-authoritarian-states-but-they-dont-heres-why-218179.

Abuso, Victor. "Kenya: Fear of Resurgence of Banned Mungiki Sect as Hundreds Arrested." *The Africa Report*, January 3, 2024. https://www.theafricareport.com/331983/kenya-fears-of-resurgence-of-banned-mungiki-sect-as-hundreds-arrested/.

Adebayo, Bukola. "Uganda Court Upholds Law that Could Allow Yoweri Museveni to be President for Life." *CNN*, July 27, 2018. https://www.cnn.com/2018/07/27/africa/uganda-presidential-age-limit/index.html.

Adeoye, Aanu. "Peter Obi's 'Obidient' Movement Shakes Up Nigerian Presidential Race." *Financial Times*, October 18, 2022. https://www.ft.com/content/92800e67-66a2-4eca-b5e5-009bf000c87a.

ADF Magazine. "Growing Family Dynasties Undermine Accountability, Encourage Corruption." Last modified December 28, 2022. https://adf-magazine.com/2022/12/growing-family-dynasties-undermine-accountability-encourage-corruption/.

Adika, Newton. "Social Media Usage Trends in Africa: GeoPoll Report." *GeoPoll*, September 6, 2023. https://www.geopoll.com/blog/social-media-usage-trends-in-africa-geopoll-report/.

Africa Archives (@Africa_Archives). "Kenya has announced that it has found large deposits of a rare mineral." X post, January 27, 2023. https://twitter.com/Africa_Archives/status/1751303575878132174.

Africa Center for Strategic Studies. "Mali Catastrophe Accelerating under Junta Rule." July 10, 2023. https://africacenter.org/spotlight/mali-catastrophe-accelerating-under-junta-rule/.

Africa Center for Strategic Studies. "Party Militias—A Threat to Security and Military Professionalism." November 2, 2021. https://africacenter.org/spotlight/party-militias-threat-security-military-professionalism/.

Africa Center for Strategic Studies. "Term Limit Evasions and Coups in Africa: Two Sides of the Same Coin." October 24, 2023. https://africacenter.org/spotlight/term-limit-evasions-coups-africa-same-coin/.

Africa Confidential. "Merci, Papa." April 29, 2005. https://www.africa-confidential.com/article-preview/id/1481/Merci%2c_Papa.

BIBLIOGRAPHY

Africa Facts Zone (@AfricaFactsZone). "South Africa's ruling party, the ANC has failed to secure majority in the Parliament for the first time in 30 years." X post, June 1, 2024. https://x.com/AfricaFactsZone/status/1796874104567402857.

African Development Bank. *Africa's Macroeconomic Performance and Outlook January 2024*. Abidjan: African Development Bank, 2024. https://www.afdb.org/en/documents/africas-macroeconomic-performance-and-outlook-january-2024.

African Development Bank. "Africa's Population Explosion is a Ticking Time Bomb—African Development Bank Governors." African Development Bank, March 7, 2018. https://www.afdb.org/en/news-and-events/africas-population-explosion-is-a-ticking-timebomb-african-development-bank-governors-17900.

African Development Bank. "Particularly Exposed to Climate Shocks, African Cities are Turning to Adaptation and Resilience." November 14, 2022. https://www.afdb.org/en/news-and-events/particularly-exposed-climate-shocks-african-cities-are-turning-adaptation-and-resilience-56462.

Africanews. "Malians Celebrate Return of Interim PM." September 28, 2022. https://www.africanews.com/2022/09/28/malians-celebrate-return-of-interim-pm/.

Africanews. "South Africa: Ramaphosa Launches First Campaign Rally for 2024 Elections." Last modified September 4, 2023. https://www.africanews.com/2023/09/04/south-africa-ramaphosa-launches-first-campaign-rally-for-2024-elections/.

Africanews with AP. "Gabon's Opposition Leader Claims Coup is a 'Family Affair.'" September 1, 2023. https://www.africanews.com/2023/09/01/gabons-opposition-leader-claims-coup-is-a-family-affair/.

The Africa Report. "Zimbabwe: Apathy Derails Young Prospective Voters." April 7, 2023. https://www.theafricareport.com/298317/zimbabwe-apathy-derails-young-prospective-voters/.

African Media Agency. "Corruption Is the Most Common Story Africa's Youth Hear about the Continent." November 20, 2021. https://africanmediaagency.com/corruption-is-the-most-common-story-africas-youth-hear-about-the-continent/.

African Union. "African Charter on Democracy, Elections and Governance." January 30, 2007. https://au.int/sites/default/files/treaties/36384-treaty-african-charter-on-democracy-and-governance.pdf.

African Union. "African Youth Charter." July 2, 2006. https://au.int/sites/default/files/treaties/7789-treaty-0033_-_african_youth_charter_e.pdf.

Afrobarometer. "African Insights 2024: Democracy at Risk—the People's Perspective." Flagship report, July 17, 2024. https://www.afrobarometer.org/wp-content/uploads/2024/05/Afrobarometer_FlagshipReport2024_English.pdf.

Afrobarometer. "Afrobarometer Data Show Worrying Trends for Democracy in Africa, Prof. Gyimah-Boadi Warns." News release, June 16, 2023. https://www.afrobarometer.org/wp-content/uploads/2023/06/News-release-Afrobarometer-data-show-worrying-trends-for-democracy-in-Africa-bh-16june23.pdf.

Afrobarometer. "Summary of Results: Afrobarometer Round 9 Survey in Kenya, 2022." August 16, 2022, 1–85. https://www.afrobarometer.org/wp-content/uploads/2022/08/KEN-_-AB-R9_-Summary-of-Results-16aug22.pdf.

Afrobarometer. "Young Zimbabweans Less Likely than their Elders to Cast their Ballots on Election Day, New Afrobarometer Survey Shows." August 22, 2023. https://www.afrobarometer.org/wp-content/uploads/2023/08/News_release-Young-Zimbabweans-less-likely-to-vote-Afrobarometer-22aug23.pdf.

BIBLIOGRAPHY

Afrobarometer Network. "Africans Want More Democracy, but their Leaders Still Aren't Listening." *Afrobarometer Policy Paper* No. 85, January 2023, 1–44. https://www.afrobarometer.org/wp-content/uploads/2023/01/PP85-PAP20-Africans-want-more-democracy-but-leaders-arent-listening-Afrobarometer-Pan-Africa-Profile-17jan23.pdf.

Aikeins, Enoch Randy. "Corruption in Africa Deepens the Wounds of COVID-19." Institute for Security Studies, May 19, 2022. https://issafrica.org/iss-today/corruption-in-africa-deepens-the-wounds-of-covid-19.

Aja, Kalu (@FinPlanKaluAja1). "I have lived in America and Nigeria." X post, October 24, 2023. https://twitter.com/FinPlanKaluAja1/status/1716915734302036053.

Akinniyi, Toyin. "Interview: How Can Nigeria Build Trust in Public Institutions?" *Luminate*, August 7, 2023. https://www.luminategroup.com/posts/story/interview-how-can-nigeria-build-trust-in-public-institutions.

Akua, Nalova. "Central Africa's Dinosaur Regimes and the Art of Coup-proofing." *African Arguments*, November 27, 2023. https://africanarguments.org/2023/11/central-africas-dinosaur-regimes-and-the-art-of-coup-proofing/.

Al Jazeera English. "Ali Bongo's 'make noise' Plea Turns into Meme." YouTube video, 1:25, September 4, 2023. https://www.youtube.com/watch?v=K5Bv1IVRZMc.

Al Jazeera. "Gabon Election: Jean Ping Lays Claim to Presidency Win." August 29, 2016. https://www.aljazeera.com/news/2016/8/29/gabon-election-jean-ping-lays-claim-to-presidency-win.

Al Jazeera. "Guinea's Suppression of Protests Stokes Anger against Military." May 25, 2023. https://www.aljazeera.com/news/2023/5/25/guineas-suppression-of-protests-stokes-anger-against-military.

Al Jazeera. "In Pictures: Many Guineans Celebrate as Soldiers Seize Power." September 6, 2021. https://www.aljazeera.com/gallery/2021/9/6/many-guineans-celebrate-as-soldiers-seize-power.

Al Jazeera. "Mali President Resigns after Military Mutiny: Live Updates." August 10, 2020. https://www.aljazeera.com/news/2020/8/19/mali-president-resigns-after-military-mutiny-live-updates.

Al Jazeera. "Senegal's Ousmane Sonko Given Two-month Suspended Term for Libel." March 30, 2023. https://www.aljazeera.com/news/2023/3/30/senegals-ousmane-sonko-given-2-month-suspended-term-for-libel.

The Allan County (@AllanSseky). "Government will just block twitter in Uganda." X post, April 24, 2023. https://twitter.com/AllanSseky/status/1650450535332425729.

Allen, Karen, Jean le Roux, and Bonface Beti. *A Question of Influence? Case Study of Kenyan Elections in a Digital Age*. Pretoria: Institute for Security Studies, July 3, 2023. https://issafrica.s3.amazonaws.com/site/uploads/EAR-49.pdf.

Allison, Simon. "Chapter 10: Reinventing the Newspaper for the WhatsApp Age." In *WhatsApp and Everyday Life in West Africa*, edited by Idayat Hassan and Jamie Hitchen. London: Bloomsbury Publishing, 2022.

Al Mouahidi, Khalid. "Gabon: Noureddin Bongo Valentin Appointed to a Strategic Position in the Ruling Party." *MedaFrica*, March 11, 2022. https://medafricatimes.com/date/2022/03.

Amnesty International. "Angola: TikToker Jailed for Criticizing the President: Ana da Silva Miguel (also known as Neth Nahara)." December 15, 2023. https://www.amnesty.org/en/documents/afr12/7535/2023/en/.

Amnesty International. "Togo: Free Participation in Election Process is Made Impossible." Amnesty International public statement, April 20, 2005. https://www.amnesty.org/en/wp-content/uploads/2021/08/afr570102005en.pdf.

BIBLIOGRAPHY

Amnesty International. "Uganda: Authorities Must Unconditionally Release Protestors Still Unlawfully Detained." June 25, 2024. https://www.amnesty.org/en/latest/news/2024/07/uganda-authorities-must-unconditionally-release-protestors-still-unlawfully-detained/.

Amnesty International. "'You Have Signed Your Death Warrant': Torture and Other Ill Treatment in the Special Anti-Robbery Squad." New York, September 21, 2016. https://www.amnesty.org/en/documents/afr44/4868/2016/en/.

Anami, Luke. "Kenya Election: Lowest Turnout in 15 Years as Youth Stay Away." *The East African*, August 14, 2022. https://www.theeastafrican.co.ke/tea/news/east-africa/lowest-turnout-in-15-years-as-youth-stay-away-3913984.

André, James. "Alpha Conde Declared Winner in Guinea Presidential Run-off." *France24*, last modified November 16, 2010. https://www.france24.com/en/20101115-guinea-alpha-conde-wins-presidential-vote-electoral-commission-diallo-politics-africa-cnei.

Angonoticias. "'O MPLA não tem medo' da destituição." July 27, 2023. https://www.angonoticias.com/Artigos/item/74438/o-mpla-nao-tem-medo-da-destitucao.

Anku, Amaka, and Tochi Eni-Kalu. "Africa's Slums Aren't Harbingers of Anarchy—They're Engines of Democracy." *Foreign Affairs*, December 16, 2019. https://www.foreignaffairs.com/africa/africas-slums-arent-harbingers-anarchy-theyre-engines-democracy.

Anonymous. "Of the Name Bally and HH." *Zambian Observer*, May 2, 2020. https://zambianobserver.com/of-the-name-bally-and-hh/.

Antil, Alain, Thierry Vircoulon, and Francois Giovalucchi. "Themes, Actors and Functions of anti-French Discourse in French-speaking Africa." IFRI Studies, Institut Français des Relations Internationales, June 14, 2023. https://www.ifri.org/fr/publications/etudes-de-lifri/thematiques-acteurs-fonctions-discours-anti-francais-afrique.

Antunes Gomes, Catarina, and Cesaltina Abreu. "Angola: 'Much Effort was Put into Excluding People from the Electoral Process.'" *CIVICUS*, September 12, 2022. https://www.civicus.org/index.php/media-resources/news/interviews/6024-angola-much-effort-was-put-into-excluding-people-from-the-electoral-process.

AP News. "Putin Woos African Leaders at a Summit in Russia with Promises of Expanding Trade and Other Ties." July 28, 2023. https://apnews.com/article/russia-africa-summit-putin-food-grain-00408e40403c3c30f89371a474bb4f9d.

Arieff, Alexis, and Lauren Ploch Blanchard. "'An Epidemic of Coups' in Africa? Issues for Congress." *Congressional Research Service*, February 11, 2022. https://crsreports.congress.gov/product/pdf/IN/IN11854.

Armed Conflict Location and Event Data Project. "ACLED 2021: The Year in Review." March 8, 2022. https://acleddata.com/2022/03/08/2021-year-in-review/#conclusion.

Asadu, Chinedu. "Nigeria's Independence Anniversary is Marked by Protests and Frustration over Economic Hardship." *AP News*, October 1, 2024. https://apnews.com/article/nigeria-independence-protests-tinubu-d321d54a7750e82b4391c27b28db68f2.

Associated Press. "Tens of Thousands Protest in Mali amid Growing Opposition to Keita Presidency." *New York Times*, last modified August 19, 2020. https://www.nytimes.com/2020/06/19/world/africa/mali-protests-keita.html.

Atabong, Amindeh Blaise. "Cameroon President's 90th Birthday Marked by Cocktail of Woes." *Reuters*, February 13, 2023. https://www.reuters.com/world/africa/cameroon-presidents-90th-birthday-marked-by-cocktail-woes-2023-02-13/.

Atuhaire, Patience. "Uganda's Yoweri Museveni: How an ex-Rebel Has Stayed in Power for 35 Years." *BBC News*, May 10, 2021. https://www.bbc.com/news/world-africa-55550932.

Azelton, Aaron, Bret Barrowman, and Lisa Reppell. "Raising Their Voices: How Effective are Pro-Youth Laws and Policies?" *Consortium for Elections and Political Process Strengthening* (2019), 1–112. https://www.iri.org/wp-content/uploads/legacy/iri.org/iri_proyouth-report_.pdf.

Baddorf, Zack. "Rwanda President's Lopsided Re-election Is Seen as a Sign of Oppression." *New York Times*, August 6, 2017. https://www.nytimes.com/2017/08/06/world/africa/rwanda-elections-paul-kagame.html.

Banda, Honore. "Zambia's President Sata Raises Them up to Let Them Down." *Africa Report*, October 1, 2021. https://www.theafricareport.com/6597/zambias-president-sata-raises-them-up-to-let-them-down/.

Bartlett, Kate. "As West Shuts China's Confucius Institutes, More Open in Africa." *Voice of America*, November 16, 2022. https://www.voanews.com/a/as-west-shuts-china-confucius-institutes-more-open-in-africa/6837437.html.

Basimanebotlhe, Tsaone. "Saleable Voters Defend Vote Buying." *Mmegi Online*, February 2, 2024. https://www.mmegi.bw/news/saleable-voters-defend-vote-buying/news.

Bassirou Diomaye Faye (@DiomayeFaye). "To veterans, defense and security forces, I renew all recognition and confidence of the nation." X post, April 4, 2024. https://twitter.com/DiomayeFaye/status/1775829776705507707.

BBC News. "Equatorial Guinea Vice President's Superyacht and Homes Seized in South Africa." February 13, 2023. https://www.bbc.com/news/world-africa-64627695.

BBC News. "Mali Coup: Thousands Take to Bamako Streets to Celebrate." August 21, 2020. https://www.bbc.com/news/world-africa-53868236.

BBC News. "Muhammadu Buhari: Twitter Deletes Nigerian Leader's 'civil war' Post." June 2, 2021. https://www.bbc.com/news/world-africa-57336571.

BBC News. "Zambia Election: President Claims Vote Was Not Free and Fair." August 14, 2021. https://www.bbc.com/news/world-africa-58215507.

Bearak, Max. "How Africa Will Become the Center of the World's Urban Future." *Washington Post*, November 19, 2021. https://www.washingtonpost.com/world/interactive/2021/africa-cities/.

Bernard, Pauline. "The Politics of the Luweero Skulls: The Making of Memorial Heritage and Post-Revolutionary State Legitimacy over the Luweero Mass Graves in Uganda." *Journal of Eastern African Studies* 11, no. 1 (2017): 188–209. https://doi.org/10.1080/17531055.2017.1288959.

Berridge, Willow, Justin Lynch, Raga Makawi, and Alex de Waal. *Sudan's Unfinished Democracy: The Promise and Betrayal of a People's Revolution*. London: Hurst Publishers, 2022.

Biryabarema, Elias. "Uganda Court Quashes Part of Law Used against Government Critics." *Reuters*, January 10, 2023. https://www.reuters.com/world/africa/uganda-court-quashes-part-law-used-against-government-critics-2023-01-10/.

Blanshe, Musinguzi. "Uganda: Between Muhoozi and Rwabwogo, Who Will Succeed Museveni?" *Africa Report*, September 9, 2024. https://www.theafricareport.com/360778/uganda-between-muhoozi-and-rwabwogo-who-will-succeed-museveni/.

Boakye, Bridget. "Social Media Futures: How to Change the African Narrative." Tony Blair Institute for Global Change, April 19, 2021. https://www.institute.global/insights/tech-and-digitalisation/social-media-futures-how-change-african-narrative.

Boateng Asiamah, Gildfred, Ousmane Djiby Sambou, and Sadhiska Bhoojedhur. "AD486: Africans Say Governments Aren't Doing Enough to Help Youth."

BIBLIOGRAPHY

Afrobarometer, November 4, 2021. https://www.afrobarometer.org/publication/ad486-africans-say-governments-arent-doing-enough-help-youth/.

Bone, Maxwell. "The Silence of the Obidients." *African Arguments*, February 9, 2024. https://africanarguments.org/2024/02/the-silence-of-the-obidients/.

Bonkoungou, Mathieu, and Nadoun Coulibaly. "Kabore Wins Burkina Faso Presidential Election." *Reuters*, last modified November 30, 2015. https://www.reuters.com/article/us-burkina-election/kabore-wins-burkina-faso-presidential-election-idUSKBN0TJ0QT20151201/.

Bowles, Jeremy, and Benjamin Marx. "Turnover and Accountability in Africa's Parliaments." *SSRN*, November 23, 2023. https://papers.ssrn.com/sol3/papers.cfm?abstract_id=4642554.

Branch, Adam, and Zachariah Mampilly. *Africa Uprising: Popular Protest and Political Change*. London: Bloomsbury Publishing, 2015, 75.

Business Ghana. "President Launches National Youth Policy for Next Decade." August 15, 2022. http://www.businessghana.com/site/news/General/268623/President-launches-National-Youth-Policy-for-next-decade.

Bwire, Job. "I'm tired of Waiting, I'll Stand for Presidency in 2026 – Muhoozi." *The Monitor*, March 16, 2023. https://www.monitor.co.ug/uganda/news/national/i-m-tired-of-waiting-i-ll-stand-for-presidency-in-2026-muhoozi-4160712.

Camara, Mouhamed. "Guinée: Un challenge inspiré de la photo de Alpha Condé fait sensation sur les réseaux sociaux (photos)." *Sene.News*, last modified September 10, 2021. https://www.senenews.com/senenews-people/insolites-buzz/guinee-un-challenge-inspire-de-la-photo-de-alpha-conde-fait-sensation-sur-les-reseaux-sociaux-photos_367791.html.

Campbell, John. *Nigeria: Dancing on the Brink*. Lanham, MD: Rowman & Littlefield, 2013.

Carey, Sabine, Neil J. Mitchell, and Katrin Paula. "The Life, Death and Diversity of Pro-Government Militias: The Fully Revised Pro-Government Militias Database Version 2.0." *Research and Politics* 9, no. 1 (2022), https://journals.sagepub.com/doi/10.1177/20531680211062772.

Centre for Affordable Housing Finance in Africa. *2023 Yearbook: Housing Finance in Africa*. Johannesburg: Centre for Affordable Housing Finance in Africa, 2023. https://housingfinanceafrica.org/app/uploads/2023/10/2023-CAHF-Yb_Compressed-14.11.2023.pdf.

César Chiyaya (@cesarchiyaya). "Dia da #PAZ." Twitter post, April 3, 2020. https://twitter.com/mr_chiyaya/status/1642997019298996225.

César Chiyaya (@cesarchiyaya). "O BP do MPLA escreveu o comunicado com o caps lock ligado?" X post, July 21, 2023. https://twitter.com/cesarchiyaya/status/1682360855965446147.

Cheeseman, Nic, Karuti Kanyinga, and Gabrielle Lynch, eds. *The Oxford Handbook of Kenyan Politics*. Oxford: Oxford University Press, 2020.

Cheeseman, Nic, and Brian Klaas. *How to Rig an Election*. New Haven, CT: Yale University Press, 2018.

Chevrier, Jeremy. *Exploring the Connections between Poverty, Lack of Economic Opportunity, and Violent Extremism in sub-Saharan Africa*. Washington, DC: USAID Center for Resilience, November 2017. https://pdf.usaid.gov/pdf_docs/PA00WQ7X.pdf.

Chibwili, Edward. "Perceptions of China's Influence on Zambia Remain Positive, though on the Decline." *Afrobarometer Dispatch* No. 759, January 19, 2024. https://www.

afrobarometer.org/wp-content/uploads/2024/01/AD759-Zambians-perceptions-of-Chinese-influence-positive-but-declining-Afrobarometer-19jan24.pdf.

Chinono, Hopewell (@daddyhope). "For the first time in the history of post colonial Zimbabwe, ZANUPF has no election manifesto, it has nothing to sell at all." X post, July 24, 2023. http://twitter.com/daddyhope/status/1683377840551501824.

Chitanga, Gideon H. "Global Broadcast Media is Still Relying on Stereotypical Narratives about Africa." *Africa No Filter*, 2022. https://africanofilter.org/documents/Gideon-H-Chitanga_Global-broadcast-media.pdf.

Christian Churches Monitoring Group. *CCMG Verification Statement on the Accuracy of the Official 2021 Presidential Results*. Lusaka, August 16, 2021. https://ccmgzambia.org/ccmg-verification-statement-on-the-accuracy-of-the-official-2021-presidential-results/.

Cincotta, Richard. "Demographic Security Comes of Age." *Environmental Change and Security Program Report* 10 (Wilson Center, 2004). https://www.wilsoncenter.org/publication/demographic-security-comes-age?collection=14103.

Cincotta, Richard. "Predicting the Rise and Demise of Liberal Democracy: How Well Did We Do?" *New Security Beat*, August 17, 2021. https://www.newsecuritybeat.org/2021/08/predicting-rise-demise-liberal-democracy/.

CIPESA, "Despots and Disruptions: Five Dimensions of Internet Shutdowns in Africa." February 2019, 1–13. https://cipesa.org/wp-content/files/briefs/report/Despots-And-Disruptions_March-20.pdf.

Citizen TV Kenya (@citizentvkenya). "President William Ruto: I have just come from a meeting with the Ambassador of the US." X post, February 25, 2024. https://twitter.com/citizentvkenya/status/1761775674702876942.

Civicus Lens. "Angola: The Democratic Transition That Never Was." September 13, 2022. https://lens.civicus.org/angola-the-democratic-transition-that-never-was/.

Cline Center for Advanced Social Research. "Frequency of Coup Events from 1945 to 2023, by Country." University of Illinois, accessed April 2, 2024. https://clinecenter.illinois.edu/project/research-themes/democracy-and-development/coup-detat-project/freq-table.

The Community Court of Justice of ECOWAS. "The Registered Trustees of the Socio-Economic Rights and Accountability Project (SERAP) v. Federal Republic of Nigeria." Judgement no. ECW/CCJ/JUD/08/21, April 26, 2021. http://www.courtecowas.org/wp-content/uploads/2021/08/JUD-ECW-CCJ-JUD-08-21-Registered-Trustees-of-the-Socio-Economic-Accountability-Projet-SERAP-vs.-FED.-REP.-of-NIGERIA-26_04_21.pdf.

Cook, Sarah. "Beijing's Global Media Influence 2022: Authoritarian Expansion and the Power of Democratic Resilience." *Freedom House*, September 8, 2022. https://freedomhouse.org/report/beijing-global-mediainfluence/2022/authoritarian-expansion-power-democratic-resilience.

Cotterill, Joseph, and Alec Russell. "Zambia Says $13bn Debt Stand-off is 'indictment' of Global System." *Financial Times*, March 20, 2024. https://www.ft.com/content/c528daac-fd80-490e-aee1-29a18154f79b.

Crowe, Sarah, and Diadie Ba. "Senegal Unveils 25-year Economic and Social Development Plan." *Reuters*, October 14, 2024. https://www.reuters.com/world/africa/senegal-unveils-25-year-economic-social-development-plan-2024-10-14/.

Dahir, Abdi Latif. "Uganda Blocks Facebook ahead of Contentious Election." *New York Times*, January 13, 2021. https://www.nytimes.com/2021/01/13/world/africa/uganda-facebook-ban-elections.html.

BIBLIOGRAPHY

Daily Monitor (@DailyMonitor). "Facebook are arrogant. They are being used to attack us." X post, December 23, 2022. https://twitter.com/DailyMonitor/status/1606242894112620544.

Daily Monitor (@DailyMonitor). "Hunt for jobs instead of waiting on connections." X post, December 9, 2023. https://twitter.com/DailyMonitor/status/1733497089089216800.

Danflow, Lindwe. "Hustler Fund Rated Ruto's Greatest Achievement – Survey." *The Star*, July 13, 2023. https://www.the-star.co.ke/news/realtime/2023-07-13-hustler-fund-rated-rutos-greatest-achievement-survey/.

DD Geopolitics (@DD_Geopolitics). "Macron Gets Slapped by the President of the Democratic Republic of Congo." X post, March 5, 2023. https://twitter.com/DD_Geopolitics/status/1632546619290955778.

Democracy Moves. *Walking the Walk: Prioritizing Youth Political and Civic Engagement in Renewing Democracy*. Baltimore, MD: Johns Hopkins Stavros Niarchos Foundation SNF, Agora Institute, December 5, 2023. https://static1.squarespace.com/static/5fd023409ea96b5f982e6c63/t/61af57ec288f4528f5cab584/1638881741797/Walking+the+Walk.

Deng, Francis M. "Ethnicity: An African Predicament." *Brookings*, June 1, 1997. https://www.brookings.edu/articles/ethnicity-an-african-predicament/.

Diallo, Mamadou Abdoulaye. "AD711: At the Center of the Priorities of Young Senegalese: Management of the Economy, Insecurity, and Employment." *Afrobarometer Dispatch* 711, October 4, 2023. https://www.afrobarometer.org/publication/ad711-au-centre-des-priorites-des-jeunes-senegalais-la-gestion-de-leconomie-linsecurite-et-lemploi/.

Diggers.News (@DiggersOfNews). "We'll use drought to change Zambia forever—HH." X post, March 13, 2023. https://twitter.com/DiggersOfNews/status/1767778832214348054.

Dione, Ngouda. "Faye Sworn in as Senegal President, Cites 'profound desire for change.'" *Reuters*, April 2, 2024. https://www.reuters.com/world/africa/faye-sworn-senegal-president-cites-profound-desire-change-2024-04-02/.

Di Placido, Dani. "'Boy Math' and 'Girl Math' Meme, Explained." *Forbes*, September 29, 2023. https://www.forbes.com/sites/danidiplacido/2023/09/29/boy-math-and-girl-math-meme-explained/?sh=3262c94568b1.

Dizolele, Mvemba Phezo. "Bobi Wine on Youth Movements and Liberation." Center for Strategic and International Studies, August 24, 2023. https://www.csis.org/podcasts/africa/bobi-wine-youth-movements-and-liberation.

Dobbs, Kirstie Lynn. "Fact or Fluff? The Impact of Youth Quotas on the Electoral Behaviour and Attitudes of Young People." *Journal of Representative Democracy* 58, no. 4 (2022): 501–24. https://doi.org/10.1080/00344893.2021.1984286.

Dryding, Dominique. "Are South Africans Giving up on Democracy?" *Afrobarometer*, July 14, 2020. https://www.afrobarometer.org/wp-content/uploads/2022/02/ab_r7_dispatchno372_are_south_africans_giving_up_on_democracy.pdf.

Duerksen, Mark. "Disinformation Drilling into Africa's Information Ecosystems." Africa Center for Strategic Studies, February 8, 2023. https://africacenter.org/experts/disinformation-drilling-africa-information-ecosystems/.

Dulani, Boniface Gildfred Boateng Asiamah, and Patrick Zindikirani. "Amid Rising Corruption, Most Africans Say They Risk Retaliation if They Speak Up." *Afrobarometer Dispatch* No. 743, December 6, 2023, 1–25. https://www.afrobarometer.org/wp-content/uploads/2023/12/AD743-PAP5-Amid-rising-corruption-Africans-say-they-risk-retaliation-if-they-speak-up-Afrobarometer_3dec23.pdf.

Duntoye, Sunday Joseph, and Raphael Mbaegbu. "Young Nigerians Prioritise Security, Jobs, the Economy for Government Action." *Afrobarometer Dispatch* No. 708, September 2023, 1–11. https://www.afrobarometer.org/wp-content/uploads/2023/09/AD708-Young-Nigerians-prioritise-security%5ELLLJ-jobs%5ELLLJ-economy-for-govt-action-Afrobarometer-29sep23.pdf.

Ebeku, Kaniye S. A. "The Succession of Faure Gnassingbe to the Togolese Presidency: An International Law Perspective." *Current African Issues* 30 (2005): 1–33. https://www.diva-portal.org/smash/get/diva2:240415/FULLTEXT02.pdf.

The Economist. "The New Scramble for Africa." March 7, 2019. https://www.economist.com/leaders/2019/03/07/the-new-scramble-for-africa.

The Economist. "Where Will the Next Coup Be in Africa?" October 9, 2023. https://www.economist.com/graphic-detail/2023/10/09/where-will-the-next-coup-be-in-africa.

Eisenman, Joshua. "China Is Tweaking Its Propaganda for African Audiences." *Foreign Policy*, March 16, 2023. https://foreignpolicy.com/2023/03/16/china-propaganda-africa-soft-power/.

Eisenman, Joshua. *China's Media Propaganda in Africa: A Strategic Assessment*. Washington, DC: US Institute of Peace, March 2023. https://www.usip.org/sites/default/files/2023-03/sr_516-china_media_propaganda_africa.pdf.

The Elephant. "A Memoir of the Bush War and the Press in Uganda – Review." June 20, 2019. https://www.theelephant.info/analysis/2019/06/20/combatants-a-memoir-of-the-bush-war-and-the-press-in-uganda-review/.

Esau, Iain. "Moralising Museveni Chastises Uganda's Youth and Berates European NGOs." *Upstream*, last modified February 11, 2022. https://www.upstreamonline.com/politics/moralising-museveni-chastises-ugandas-youth-and-berates-european-ngos/2-1-1164192.

Etyang, Perpetua. "We Don't Have Jobs for You, Gachagua Tells Graduates." *The Star*, June 23, 2023. https://www.the-star.co.ke/news/2023-06-23-we-dont-have-jobs-for-you-gachagua-tells-graduates/.

European Union Election Observation Mission. *Final Report: Republic of Zambia General Elections and Referendum*. Brussels: European Union, August 2016. https://www.eeas.europa.eu/sites/default/files/final_report_eu_eom_zambia.pdf.

Ezeamalu, Ben. "Nigerian Army Killed Unarmed Protesters, Report Finds." *New York Times*, November 16, 2021. https://www.nytimes.com/2021/11/16/world/africa/nigeria-protest-report-massacare.html.

Fabricius, Peter. "UNITA Shakes the Foundations of MPLA Rule in Angola." Institute for Security Studies, September 2, 2022. https://issafrica.org/iss-today/unita-shakes-the-foundations-of-mpla-rule-in-angola.

Fabricius, Peter. "When 'democracy' Becomes 'regime change.'" Institute for Security Studies, December 15, 2017. https://issafrica.org/iss-today/when-democracy-becomes-regime-change.

Felton, Jamy. "Increasingly Non-Partisan, South Africans Willing to Trade Elections for Security, Housing, Jobs." *Afrobarometer*, October 30, 2018. https://www.afrobarometer.org/wp-content/uploads/2022/02/ab_r7_dispatchno248_south_africa_elections1.pdf.

Foa, R. S., A. Klassen, D. Wenger, A. Rand, and M. Slade. *Youth and Satisfaction with Democracy: Reversing the Democratic Disconnect?* Cambridge: Centre for the Future of Democracy, October 2020. https://www.bennettinstitute.cam.ac.uk/wp-content/uploads/2022/06/Youth_and_Satisfaction_with_Democracy-lite.pdf.

BIBLIOGRAPHY

Foreign Policy Editors. "Mugabe's Promise: A Transcript of the Late Leader's Address to the Nation on March 4, 1980." *Foreign Policy*, September 6, 2019. https://foreignpolicy.com/2019/09/06/mugabes-promise/.

France 24. "Nigeria's Twitter Ban Unlawful: W. African Court." July 14, 2022. https://www.france24.com/en/live-news/20220714-nigeria-s-twitter-ban-unlawful-w-african-court.

Frederiksen, Bodil Folke. "Mungiki, Kenya's Violent Youth Gang, Serves Many Purposes: How Identity, Politics, and Crime Keep it Alive." *The Conversation*, February 11, 2024. https://theconversation.com/mungiki-kenyas-violent-youth-gang-serves-many-purposes-how-identity-politics-and-crime-keep-it-alive-221791.

Freedom House. "Angola." *Freedom in the World 2023: Marking 50 Years in the Struggle for Democracy*, accessed March 19, 2024. https://freedomhouse.org/country/angola/freedom-world/2023.

Freedom House. "Kenya: Cybercrimes Law Restricts Media Freedom." Freedom House press release, May 15, 2018. https://freedomhouse.org/article/kenya-cybercrimes-law-restricts-media-freedom.

Freedom House. "Togo." *Freedom in the World 2020: A Leaderless Struggle for Democracy*. Accessed February 27, 2024. https://freedomhouse.org/country/togo/freedom-world/2020.

Frère, Marie-Soleil, and Pierre Englebert. "Briefing: Burkina Faso—The Fall of Blaise Compaoré." *African Affairs* 114, no. 455 (2015): 295–307. https://doi.org/10.1093/afraf/adv010.

Gahene, Ambrose. "Use of Facebook Still Illegal Says Uganda Communications Commission." CIO Africa, March 5, 2022. https://cioafrica.co/use-of-facebook-still-illegal-says-uganda-communications-commission/.

Galileo, Amara, Raphael Mbaegbu, and Sunday Joseph Duntoye. "Nigerians Want Democracy, though Dissatisfaction Rises amid Worsening Economic Conditions." *Afrobarometer Dispatch* No. 606, February 2023, 1–14. https://www.afrobarometer.org/wp-content/uploads/2023/02/AD606-Nigerians-want-democracy%5ELLLJ-though-dissatisfaction-rises-in-worsening-economy-Afrobarometer-22feb23.pdf.

Gandhi, Dhruv. "Figures of the Week: Public Spending on Education in Africa." Brookings, February 13, 2020. https://www.brookings.edu/articles/figures-of-the-week-public-spending-on-education-in-africa/.

Gardner, Tom. *The Abiy Project: God, Power, and War in the New Ethiopia*. London: Hurst Publishers, 2024.

Gathara, Patrick. "Don't Let the Elders Steal Your Revolution." *The New Humanitarian*, July 10, 2024. https://www.thenewhumanitarian.org/opinion/2024/07/10/dont-let-elders-steal-your-revolution-kenya.

Gavin, Michelle. "America's Failure of Imagination in Sudan." *Foreign Affairs*, February 4, 2022. https://www.foreignaffairs.com/articles/sudan/2022-02-04/america-sudan-bashir-military-coup.

Gavin, Michelle. "A Dispiriting UNGA." *Africa in Transition*, Council on Foreign Relations, September 27, 2023. https://www.cfr.org/blog/dispiriting-unga.

Gavin, Michelle. "Rethinking Stability in Africa." *American Ambassadors Live!* Council of American Ambassadors, November 3, 2021. https://www.americanambassadorslive.org/post/rethinking-stability-in-africa.

Gavin, Michelle. "The Roots of Burkina Faso's Crisis." *Africa in Transition*, Council on Foreign Relations, November 19, 2019. https://www.cfr.org/blog/roots-burkina-fasos-crisis.

Githongo, John. "An Election about Nothing." *Africa Is a Country*, May 18, 2022. https://africasacountry.com/2022/03/an-election-about-nothing.

Gitinywa, Louis. "Authoritarianism and Digital Surveillance: Has the Internet Become a New Battleground for Monitoring Public Dissent in Rwanda?" *Media Defence*, January 16, 2023. https://www.mediadefence.org/news/authoritarianism-and-digital-surveillance-rwanda/.

Gleixner-Hayat, Brittany. "U.S. Support for Democratic Openings in Conflict-Affected Countries: Lessons from Ethiopia and Sudan." *Carnegie Endowment for International Peace*, October 2, 2024. https://carnegieendowment.org/research/2024/10/us-democracy-assistance-sudan-ethiopia?lang=en.

Global Organized Crime Index. "Nigeria." Accessed March 19, 2024. https://ocindex.net/country/nigeria.

Godwin, Peter. *The Fear: Robert Mugabe and the Martyrdom of Zimbabwe*. New York: Hachette Book Group, 2011.

Goitom, Hanibal. "Uganda: Computer Misuse (Amendment) Act Enacted." *Global Legal Monitor*, Law Library of Congress, January 6, 2023. https://www.loc.gov/item/global-legal-monitor/2023-01-05/uganda-computer-misuse-amendment-act-enacted.

Goodfellow, Tom. "Taming the 'Rogue' Sector: Studying State Effectiveness in Africa through Informal Transport Politics." *Comparative Politics* 47, no. 2 (January 2015): 127–47, https://doi.org/10.5129/001041515814224462.

Goodfellow, Tom, and David Jackman. "Introduction." In *Controlling the Capital: Political Dominance in the Urbanizing World*. Oxford: Oxford University Press, 2023, 12.

Gramer, Robbie, and Amy Mackinnon. "U.S. Embassies in Africa Are Chronically Short-Staffed." *Foreign Policy*, July 22, 2022. https://foreignpolicy.com/2022/07/22/africa-embassies-short-staffed-us-sahel-china-russia/.

Green, Mark, Derek Mitchell, and Daniel Twining. "Nigeria's Flawed Election Risks a Democratic Backslide." *Foreign Policy*, March 14, 2023. https://foreignpolicy.com/2023/03/14/nigeria-election-tunubu-democracy-irregularities-violence-inec/.

GSMA Intelligence. "The Mobile Economy Sub-Saharan Africa 2023." GSMA, October 17, 2023. https://www.gsma.com/solutions-and-impact/connectivity-for-good/mobile-economy/sub-saharan-africa/.

Guardado, Jenny, and Leonard Wantchekon. "Do Electoral Handouts Affect Voting Behavior?" *Afrobarometer Working Paper* no. 171, March 2017. https://www.afrobarometer.org/wp-content/uploads/2022/02/afropaperno171_electoral_handouts_and_voting_behavior.pdf.

Guriev, Sergei, and Daniel Treisman. *Spin Dictators: The Changing Face of Tyranny in the 21st Century*. Princeton, NJ: Princeton University Press, 2022.

Gygli, Savina, Florian Haelg, Niklas Potrafke, and Jan-Egbert Sturm. "The KOF Globalisation Index—Revisited." *Review of International Organizations* 14, no. 3 (2019), 543–74. https://doi.org/10.1007/s11558-019-09344-2.

Hamasi, Linnet. "Political Parties, Democracy, and the 2022 Kenyan Elections." *Kujenga Amani*, August 5, 2022. https://kujenga-amani.ssrc.org/2022/08/05/political-parties-democracy-and-the-2022-kenyan-elections/.

Harding, Robin. *Rural Democracy: Elections and Development in Africa*. Oxford: Oxford University Press, 2020.

Hassan, Idayat, and Jamie Hitchen. *WhatsApp and Everyday Life in West Africa*. London: Bloomsbury Publishing, 2022.

Hassan, Idayat, and Alex Vines. "Nigeria: Trust and Turnout Define 2023 Elections." Chatham House, March 31, 2023. https://www.chathamhouse.org/2023/03/nigeria-trust-and-turnout-define-2023-elections.

Hichilema, Hakainde. "Inauguration Speech by the President of the Republic of Zambia." Speech, Lusaka, August 24, 2021, Ministry of Commerce, Trade and Industry. https://www.mcti.gov.zm/wp-content/uploads/2023/02/President-Hakainde-Hichilema-Delivers-Inaugural-Speech.pdf.

Hichilema, Hakainde (@HHichilema). "Two years ago, the people of #Zambia showcased the potency of our #democracy." X post, August 24, 2023. https://twitter.com/HHichilema/status/1694597622743343238.

Himunyanga, Mutinta. "Watermelon Campaign: Can History Repeat Itself?" *Lusaka Times*, August 11, 2016. https://www.lusakatimes.com/2016/08/11/watermelon-campaign-can-history-repeat/.

Hinfelaar, Marja, Danielle Resnick, and Sishuwa Sishuwa. "Fragile Dominance? The Rise and Fall of Urban Strategies for Political Settlement Maintenance and Change in Zambia." In *Controlling the Capital: Political Dominance in the Urbanizing World*, edited by Tom Goodfellow and David Jackman. Oxford: Oxford University Press, 2023, 147. https://doi.org/10.1093/oso/9780192868329.003.0006.

Hinshaw, Drew, and Joe Parkinson. "Can't Find Cameroon's President? Try Geneva's Intercontinental Hotel." *Wall Street Journal*, November 4, 2018. https://www.wsj.com/articles/where-does-the-lion-sleep-tonight-genevas-intercontinental-hotel-1541368940.

Hoffman, Leena Koni, and Raj Navanit Patel. "Vote-Selling Behaviour and Democratic Dissatisfaction in Nigeria." Chatham House, July 2022. https://www.chathamhouse.org/sites/default/files/2022-07/2022-07-28-vote-selling-nigeria-hoffmann-patel.pdf.

Honwana, Alcinda M. *The Time of Youth: Work, Social Change, and Politics in Africa*. Boulder, CO: Kumarian Press, 2012.

Human Rights Watch. "Chad: Pre-Election Crackdown on Opponents." April 8, 2021. https://www.hrw.org/news/2021/04/08/chad-pre-election-crackdown-opponents.

Human Rights Watch. "Guinea: Government Dissolves Opposition Coalition." August 11, 2022. https://www.hrw.org/news/2022/08/11/guinea-government-dissolves-opposition-coalition.

Human Rights Watch. "Mali: Army, Wagner Group Atrocities against Civilians." March 28, 2024. https://www.hrw.org/news/2024/03/28/mali-army-wagner-group-atrocities-against-civilians.

Human Rights Watch. "Mali: Security Forces Use Excessive Force at Protests." August 12, 2020. https://www.hrw.org/news/2020/08/12/mali-security-forces-use-excessive-force-protests.

Human Rights Watch. "Senegal: New Counterterror Laws Threaten Rights." July 5, 2021. https://www.hrw.org/news/2021/07/05/senegal-new-counterterror-laws-threaten-rights.

Husted, Tomas F., Alexis Arieff, Lauren Ploch Blanchard, and Nicolas Cook. "U.S. Assistance for Sub-Saharan Africa: An Overview." Congressional Research Service, November 7, 2023. https://sgp.fas.org/crs/row/R46368.pdf.

I am Chege (@James041). "We are all pushing the #RecallMegWhitman." X post, November 6, 2024. https://twitter.com/_James041/status/1854076358046912523.

Ichikowitz Family Foundation. *African Youth Survey 2022*. Johannesburg: IFF, June 2022. https://ichikowitzfoundation.com/storage/ays/ays2022.pdf.

Inglehart, Ronald. "The Silent Revolution in Europe: Intergenerational Change in Post-Industrial Societies." *American Political Science Association* 65, no. 4 (December 1971): 991–1017. https://doi.org/10.2307/1953494.

International Association of Genocide Scholars. "Resolution on State Repression in Zimbabwe." June 7, 2005. https://genocidescholars.org/wp-content/uploads/2019/04/IAGS-RESOLUTION-ON-ZIMBABWE-7-June-2005.pdf.

International Election Observation Mission. "IRI Preliminary Statement of the 2024 Mozambique General and Provincial Assembly Elections." International Republican Institute, October 11, 2024. https://www.iri.org/resources/iri-releases-preliminary-statement-on-mozambiques-general-election-o-iri-divulga-declaracao-preliminar-sobre-as-eleicoes-gerais-de-mocambique/.

International Telecommunications Union. "Eritrea: Universal and Meaningful Connectivity." Last updated 2023. https://datahub.itu.int/dashboards/umc/?e=ERI.

International Telecommunications Union. "Mobile-Cellular Telephone Subscriptions per 100 Inhabitants, by Region, 2023." ITU Facts and Figures 2023, accessed April 1, 2024. https://www.itu.int/itu-d/reports/statistics/2023/10/10/ff23-subscriptions/.

Interparliamentary Union. "Data on Age: Global and Regional Averages." Updated March 2023. https://data.ipu.org/age-brackets-aggregate?month=3&year=2023.

Irankunda, Gloria, and Faith Amongin. "Ugandans Yearn for More Online 'exhibitions.'" *Daily Monitor*, June 26, 2023. https://www.monitor.co.ug/uganda/news/national/ugandans-yearn-for-more-online-exhibitions–4283892.

Isbell, Thomas. "WP196: Keeping Tabs? Perceptions of Relative Deprivation and Political Trust in Africa." *Afrobarometer Working Paper* 196, February 21, 2023. https://www.afrobarometer.org/publication/wp196-keeping-tabs-perceptions-of-relative-deprivation-and-political-trust-in-africa/.

Isha, Han, Xavier Romero-Vidal, and Roberto Foa. "Is the World Dividing in Two? How People across the Globe View China, Russia, and the United States." Bennett Institute for Public Policy at Cambridge University, November 27, 2022. https://www.bennettinstitute.cam.ac.uk/blog/world-dividing-in-two/.

Jeng, Amat. "Gambia's Democratic Transition: A Case Study of the Role of Political Elites in Democratic Transition." Master's thesis, Uppsala University, 2019. https://www.diva-portal.org/smash/get/diva2:1388602/FULLTEXT01.pdf.

Jett, Dennis. "Mozambique is a Failed State. The West Isn't Helping It." *Foreign Policy*, March 7, 2020. https://foreignpolicy.com/2020/03/07/mozambique-is-a-failed-state-the-west-isnt-helping-it/.

Jili, Bulelani. "The Spread of Surveillance Technology in Africa Stirs Security Concerns." Africa Center for Strategic Studies, December 11, 2020. https://africacenter.org/spotlight/surveillance-technology-in-africa-security-concerns/.

Jones, Mayeni. "SARS Ban: Nigeria Abolishes Loathed Federal Special Police Unit." *BBC News*, October 11, 2020. https://www.bbc.com/news/world-africa-54499497.

Jordan, Miriam. "African Migration to the U.S. Soars as Europe Cracks Down." *New York Times*, January 5, 2024. https://www.nytimes.com/2024/01/05/us/africa-migrants-us-border.html.

Judah, Tim. "The Pop Star and the President." *Foreign Policy*, February 1, 2012. https://foreignpolicy.com/2012/02/01/the-pop-star-and-the-president/.

Kainja, Jimmy. "Access Denied: How Limited Internet Connectivity Erodes Democracy." *Democracy in Africa*, March 2023. https://democracyinafrica.org/access-denied-how-limited-internet-connectivity-erodes-democracy/.

BIBLIOGRAPHY

Kakooza, Bart. "Museveni Swearing Ceremony 1986." YouTube video, 36:07, May 23, 2023. https://www.youtube.com/watch?v=ygFtVOe7C2o.

Kamwengo, Cynthia. "Social Media Debates on Zambia's Evolving Relations with the West and East." Megatrends Afrika, German Institute for International and Security Affairs, February 2024. https://www.swp-berlin.org/assets/afrika/publications/policybrief/MTA_Policy_Brief_Kamwengo_Zambia_and_Social_Media_final.pdf.

Kaplan, Robert D. "Anarchy Unbound: The New Scramble for Africa." *New Statesman*, August 16, 2023. https://www.newstatesman.com/long-reads/2023/08/anarchy-unbound-scramble-africa-niger-robert-kaplan

Kaplan, Robert D. "The Coming Anarchy." *The Atlantic*, February 1994. https://www.theatlantic.com/magazine/archive/1994/02/the-coming-anarchy/304670/.

Karmo, Henry. "Liberia: Senate Pro Tempore Hopes the 2023 Turnover in the Senate Would Be Better than Previous Results." *Front Page Africa*, January 17, 2023. https://frontpageafricaonline.com/news/liberia-senate-pro-tempore-hopes-the-2023-turnover-in-the-senate-would-be-better-than-previous-results/.

Kefale, Asanake, Mohammed Dejen, and Lovise Aalen. "Neglect, Control and Co-optation: Major Features of Ethiopian Youth Policy since 1991." *CMI Working Paper 2021: 3*, Christian Michelsen Institute for Science and Intellectual Freedom. https://www.cmi.no/publications/7829-neglect-control-and-co-optation-major-features-of-ethiopian-youth-policy-since-1991.

Kenyan Facts (@KResearcher). "African dictators looking at this and wondering why a 'young man' like Biden would willingly not want to continue being president." X post, July 21, 2024. https://x.com/KResearcher/status/1815084790980190403.

Kenyans.co.ke (@Kenyans). "I don't want to sit here and lie that we have jobs for you." X post, June 23, 2023. https://twitter.com/Kenayns/status/1672212850234871811.

Kenyans.co.ke (@Kenyans). "70,000 Kenyans have lost their jobs from the period October 2022 to November 2023." X post, November 25, 2023. https://twitter.com/Keyans/status/1728282989447290972.

Kessler, Martin. "The Road to Zambia's 2020 Default." Finance for Development Lab, December 6, 2023. https://findevlab.org/the-road-to-zambias-2020-sovereign-debt-default/#:~:text=On%2013th%20November%202020%2C%20Zambia,during%20the%20Covid%2D19%20pandemic.

Keulder, Christiaan, and Robert Mattes. "Why are Africans Dissatisfied with Democracy? Think Corruption." *Afrobarometer*, November 25, 2021. https://www.afrobarometer.org/articles/why-are-africans-dissatisfied-democracy-think-corruption/.

Kgosi (@Kgosi__sa). "Best selling book." TikTok, May 15, 2024. https://www.tiktok.com/@kgosi__sa/video/7369319210910043398?lang=en.

Kibirige, Francis. "Summary of Results: Afrobarometer Round 9 Survey in Uganda, 2022." *Afrobarometer*, 2023. https://www.afrobarometer.org/publication/uganda-round-9-summary-of-results/.

KIBUUKA Bamweyana (@aldrinewills). "Uganda forces of change have a lot to learn." X post, March 20, 2023. https://twitter.com/aldrinewills/status/1637720488905506816.

Kimaiyo, Hon Gideon (@GideonKimaiyo_). "I don't know how we created this activist country." X post, March 13, 2023. https://twitter.com/GideonKimaiyo_/status/1767786347887030513.

Kimotho, Maureen. "More Men than Women Use Social Media: Report." *NTV*, February 21, 2023. https://ntvkenya.co.ke/news/more-men-than-women-use-social-media-report/.

Kimutai, Vitalis. "Inside Government's Plan to Create 1m Overseas Jobs per Year." *The Nation*, August 8, 2023. https://nation.africa/kenya/news/government-plan-to-create-1m-overseas-jobs-per-year-4330086.

Kindzeka, Moki Edwin. "Cameroon President Celebrates 89th Birthday." *VOA News*, February 14, 2022. https://www.voanews.com/a/cameroon-president-celebrates-89th-birthday/6440796.html.

Kipkemoi, Felix. "Kagame's Son Ian Joins Presidential Security Team." *The Star*, January 18, 2023. https://www.the-star.co.ke/news/realtime/2023-01-18-kagames-son-ian-joins-presidential-security-team/.

Kiyiapi, Prof. J. Ole (@JamesOleKiyiapi). "This is the attitude we NEED in Kenya." X post, October 10, 2023. https://twitter.com/JamesOleKiyapi/status/1711767077436928167.

Knight, Tessa. "Ethiopian Diaspora Groups Organize Click-to-Tweet Tigray Campaigns amid Information Scarcity." DFR Lab via *Medium*, April 23, 2021. https://medium.com/dfrlab/ethiopian-diaspora-groups-organize-click-to-tweet-tigray-campaigns-amid-information-scarcity-7e8d7ed73e2f.

Kujeke, Muneinazvo. "Zimbabwe's Notorious Youth Service Revived ahead of Election Season." Institute for Security Studies, June 21, 2021. https://issafrica.org/iss-today/zimbabwes-notorious-youth-service-revived-ahead-of-election-season.

Kunambura, Andrew. "Zimbabwe: Harare Circus Rages On, Capital Run by Two Mayors." *allAfrica*. https://allafrica.com/stories/202206040079.html.

Kungu, Gina (@Gina_Kungu). "Have you ever secured a job in Kenya solely based on merit?" X post, May 9, 2023. https://twitter.com/Gina_Kungu/status/1655877236447223810.

Kuyoro, Mayowa, Acha Leke, Olivia White, et al., "Reimagining Economic Growth in Africa: Turning Diversity into Opportunity." McKinsey Global Institute, June 5, 2023. https://www.mckinsey.com/mgi/our-research/reimagining-economic-growth-in-africa-turning-diversity-into-opportunity.

Kwaja, Chris, and Matthew Edds-Reitman. "Nigeria at a Crossroads: Navigating Protests amid Elections." US Institute of Peace, October 1, 2024. https://www.usip.org/publications/2024/10/nigeria-crossroads-navigating-protests-amid-elections.

Lawal, Shola. "Au revoir, Sahel: Did 2023 Crush France's Influence in Africa?" *Al Jazeera*, December 31, 2023. https://www.aljazeera.com/news/2023/12/31/au-revoir-sahel-did-2023-crush-frances-influence-in-africa.

Le Monde with AFP. "Guinea Capital Brought to Standstill by General Strike against Junta." *Le Monde*, February 26, 2024. https://www.lemonde.fr/en/international/article/2024/02/26/guinea-capital-brought-to-standstill-by-general-strike-against-junta_6560870_4.html.

Lemonde063. "#politics #courdetatconstitutionnelesenegal." Comments on TikTok video, February 4, 2024, https://www.tiktok.com/@lemonde063/video/7331740651853221128?q=senegal&t=1707491934776.

Levitsky, Steven, and Lucan A. Way, *Competitive Authoritarianism: Hybrid Regimes after the Cold War*. Cambridge: Cambridge University Press, 2010.

Lockwood, Peter. "Hustler Populism, Anti-Jubilee Backlash and Economic Injustice in Kenya's 2022 Elections." *African Affairs* 122, no. 487 (April 2023): 205–24. https://doi.org/10.1093/afraf/adad011.

Lopes, Marina. "Mozambique Mayor Puts Fear in Frelimo." *Reuters*, last modified September 20, 2012. https://www.reuters.com/article/us-mozambique-politics/mozambique-mayor-puts-fear-in-frelimo-idUSBRE88J0ST20120920.

BIBLIOGRAPHY

Lorenz, Trish. *Soro Soke: The Young Disruptors of an African Megacity*. Cambridge: Cambridge University Press, 2022. https://doi.org/10.1017/9781009211840.

Lourenço, Marisa. "Signal Interrupted: When State Security Goes Rogue." *Democracy in Africa*, April 4, 2023. https://democracyinafrica.org/signal-jamming-when-state-security-goes-rogue/.

Lubanga, Dennis. "Wapi Kazi?: Governors under Pressure as Unemployed Youths Who Back Their Bids Demand Jobs." *Tuko*, October 20, 2022. https://www.tuko.co.ke/politics/478671-wapi-kazi-governors-pressure-unemployed-youths-bids-demand-jobs/.

Lubwama, Siraje, and Sadab Kitatta Kaaya. "Museveni Blasts Ministers over Bobi Wine." *The Observer*, May 8, 2019. https://observer.ug/news/headlines/60629-museveni-blasts-ministers-over-bobi-wine.

Lumumba, Patrice. "Speech at the Opening of the All-African Conference in Leopoldville." Speech, Leopoldville, August 25, 1960, Patrice Lumumba Archive. https://www.marxists.org/subject/africa/lumumba/1960/08/25.htm.

Lusaka Times. "Police and DEC Investigates Display Sums of Cash on Social Media." March 5, 2021. https://www.lusakatimes.com/2021/03/05/police-and-dec-investigates-display-sums-of-cash-on-social-media/.

Lynch, Gabrielle, and Elena Gadjanovaa. "Overcoming Incumbency Advantage: The Importance of Social Media on- and offline in Zambia's 2021 Elections." *Journal of Eastern African Studies* 16, no. 4 (2022): 540. https://doi.org/10.1080/17531055.2023.2232241.

Lyons, Terrence. "Diasporas and the Transnationalization of African Politics." *Oxford Research Encyclopedia of Politics*. June 25, 2019. Accessed October 17, 2024. https://oxfordre.com/politics/view/10.1093/acrefore/9780190228637.001.0001/acrefore-9780190228637-e-696.

Maclean, Ruth. "He's Energized Nigeria's Young Voters. Will They Turn Out for Him?" *New York Times*, February 18, 2023. https://www.nytimes.com/2023/02/18/world/africa/nigeria-election-youth-obi.html.

Madowo, Larry (@LarryMadowo). "DEVELOPING: At least 26 people were killed at a school in Kasese in western Uganda by armed rebels." X post, June 17, 2023. https://twitter.com/LarryMadowo/status/1669953653279543298.

Madowo, Larry, Bethlehem Feleke, and Fridah Okutoyi. "Many Talented Young Nigerians are Leaving. Halting the Exodus will be a Task for the Next President." *CNN World*, February 27, 2023. https://www.cnn.com/2023/02/24/africa/nigeria-japa-exodus-trend-election-intl-cmd/index.html.

Madung, Odanga. "How Twitter's Negligence is Harming Kenya's Democracy." *The Elephant*, July 1, 2022. https://theelephant.info/op-eds/2022/07/01/how-twitters-neglicgence-is-harming-kenyas-democracy/.

Makokha, Kwamchetsi. "Saba Saba and the Evolution of Citizen Power." *The Elephant*, July 7, 2020. https://www.theelephant.info/features/2020/07/07/saba-saba-and-the-evolution-of-citizen-power/.

Malephane, Libuseng. "Digital Divide: Who in Africa is Connected and Who is Not." *Afrobarometer Dispatch* No. 582, December 14, 2022. https://www.afrobarometer.org/wp-content/uploads/2022/12/AD582-PAP18-Digital-divide-Who-in-Africa-is-connected-and-who-is-not-Afrobarometer-Pan-Africa-Profile-14dec22.pdf.

Maringa, George. "Election 2022 to Feature Highest Number of Registered Voters, Polling Stations in Kenya's History." *The Standard*. https://www.standardmedia.co.ke/national/article/2001448421/election-2022-to-feature-highest-number-of-registered-voters-polling-stations-in-kenyas-history.

Marks, Zoe, Erica Chenoweth, and Jide Okeke. "Why People Power is Rising in Africa." *Foreign Affairs*, April 25, 2019. https://www.foreignaffairs.com/articles/africa/2019-04-25/people-power-rising-africa.

Matiashe, Farai Shawn. "Zimbabwe: With its Two-Thirds Majority, how far Will ZANU-PF Go?" *The Africa Report*, February 15, 2024. https://www.theafricareport.com/336371/zimbabwe-with-its-two-thirds-majority-how-far-will-zanu-pf-go/.

Matsanga, Dr. David (@MatsangaDr). "Another one loading . . . Waah Africa?" X post, August 8, 2023. https://twitter.com/MatsangaDr/status/1688844568928636928.

Mattes, Robert. "Democracy in Africa: Demand, Supply, and the 'dissatisfied democrat.'" *Afrobarometer Policy Paper* No. 54, February 2019, 1–30. https://www.afrobarometer.org/wp-content/uploads/migrated/files/publications/Policy%20papers/ab_r7_policypaperno54_africans_views_of_democracy1.pdf.

Matty Jaw, Sait. "WhatsApp, Youth and Politics in the Gambia: An Analysis of 'Democratic Gambia.'" In *WhatsApp and Everyday Life in West Africa*, edited by Idayat Hassan and Jamie Hitchen. London: Zed Books, 2022.

Maverick Aoko (@AokoOtieno_). "The anger is real." X post, July 12, 2023. https://twitter.com/AokoOtieno_/status/1679045216949469184.

Maystadt, Jean-François, and Muhammad-Kabir Salihu. "National or Political Cake? The Political Economy of Intergovernmental Transfers in Nigeria." *Journal of Economic Geography* 19, no. 5 (September 2019): 1119–42. https://doi.org/10.1093/jeg/lby032.

McAllister, Bradley. "Rwanda Voters Approve Constitutional Referendum to Extend Presidential Term Limit." *The Jurist*, December 19, 2015. https://www.jurist.org/news/2015/12/rwandans-vote-in-favor-of-extending-presidential-term-limit/.

McBain, Will. "TikTok Wins over Africa's Youth." *African Business*, October 11, 2021. https://african.business/2021/10/finance-services/tiktok-wins-over-africas-youth.

M'Cormack-Hale, Fredline, and Mavis Zupork Dome. "AD551: Support for Elections Weakens among Africans: Many See Them as Ineffective in Holding Leaders Accountable." *Afrobarometer Dispatch* no. 551, September 16, 2022. https://www.afrobarometer.org/publication/ad551-support-for-elections-weakens-among-africans-many-see-them-as-ineffective-in-holding-leaders-accountable/.

McGregor, JoAnn, and Kudzai Chatiza. "Geographies of Urban Dominance: The Politics of Harare's Periphery." In *Controlling the Capital: Political Dominance in the Urbanizing World*, edited by Tom Goodfellow and David Jackman. Oxford: Oxford University Press, 2023.

Melly, Paul. "Africa's Political Dynasties: How Presidents Groom Their Sons for Power." *BBC News*, May 29, 2021. https://www.bbc.com/news/world-africa-57176712.

Mersie, Ayenat. "Eritrean President Sidesteps Questions about Troops in Ethiopia." *Reuters*, last modified February 9, 2023. https://www.reuters.com/world/africa/eritrea-president-says-rights-violations-by-eritrean-troops-ethiopia-fantasy-2023-02-09/.

Middle Eastern Media Research Institute. "Interim President of Burkina Faso Traore Speaking at Russia-Africa Summit: Russia Is Part of the Family for Africa." *Special Dispatch* no. 10742. https://www.memri.org/reports/interim-president-burkina-faso-traore-speaking-russia-africa-summit-russia-part-family.

Mimault, Anne, and Thiam Ndiaga. "Burkina Faso Crowd Celebrates West Africa's Latest Coup." *Reuters*, January 25, 2022. https://www.reuters.com/world/africa/burkina-faso-crowd-celebrates-west-africas-latest-coup-2022-01-25/.

BIBLIOGRAPHY

Ministry of Foreign Affairs of the Russia Federation. "Video Message from the Minister of Foreign Affairs of the Russia Federation S.V. Lavrov to the Participants of the Second International Youth Forum 'Russia-Africa: What Next?' Moscow, October 24, 2022." October 24, 2022. https://www.mid.ru/ru/foreign_policy/news/1834826/?lang=en&ysclid=l9mze27pw8172677184.

Mo Ibrahim Foundation. *Africa and Europe: Facts and Figures on African Migrations*. London: Mo Ibrahim Foundation, February 2022. https://mo.ibrahim.foundation/our-research/data-stories/aef-african-migrations.

Mo Ibrahim Foundation. *2022 Ibrahim Index of African Governance—Index Report*. London: Mo Ibrahim Foundation, January 2023. https://assets.iiag.online/2022/2022-Index-Report.pdf.

Moncrieff, Richard and Onesphore Sematumba. "Massacre in Goma Clouds DR Congo's Elections and UN Mission's Future." International Crisis Group, September 15, 2023. https://www.crisisgroup.org/africa/great-lakes/democratic-republic-congo/massacre-goma-clouds-dr-congos-elections-and-un.

Moyo, Jeffrey. "Zimbabwean Regime Shifts Oppression to Social Media." *Anadolu Agency*, February 16, 2021. https://www.aa.com.tr/en/africa/zimbabwean-regime-shifts-oppression-to-social-media/2146273.

Mpako, Asafika, and Simangele Moyo-Nyede. "Zimbabweans Offer Bleak Outlook on the State of the Economy." *Afrobarometer*, June 24, 2023. https://www.afrobarometer.org/wp-content/uploads/2023/06/AD658-Zimbabweans-offer-bleak-assessments-on-the-economy-Afrobarometer-23jun23.pdf.

MPLA. "Press Release." Facebook, July 20, 2023. https://www.facebook.com/photo/?fbid=816907599804171&set=a.461826221978979.

Mueller, Lisa. *Political Protest in Contemporary Africa*. Cambridge: Cambridge University Press, 2018. https://doi.org/10.1017/9781108529143.

Mugerwa, Yasiin. "Has Museveni Delivered the Fundamental Change?" *Monitor*, last modified January 26, 2024. https://www.monitor.co.ug/uganda/special-reports/has-museveni-delivered-the-fundamental-change-1650042.

Mukunto, Kabale Ignatius. "Electoral Violence and Young Party Cadres in Zambia." *Journal of African Elections* 18, no. 1 (July 2019). https://www.eisa.org/storage/2023/05/2019-journal-of-african-elections-v18n1-electoral-violence-young-party-cadres-zambia-eisa.pdf.

Murwira, Zvamaida. "Our Work is Our Manifesto." *The Herald*, July 24, 2023. https://www.herald.co.zw/our-work-is-our-manifesto/.

Muwanga, Nansozi K., Paul I. Mukwaya, and Tom Goodfellow. "Carrot, Stick, and Statute: Elite Strategies and Contested Dominance in Kampala." In *Controlling the Capital: Political Dominance in the Urbanizing World*, edited by Tom Goodfellow and David Jackman. Oxford: Oxford University Press, 2023.

Mwai, Mercy. "Mungiki Gang on the Prowl, Claim Central Leaders." *People Daily Kenya*, November 23, 2023. https://www.pd.co.ke/news/mungiki-gang-on-the-prowl-claim-central-leaders-211431/.

Mwaura, Job. "Kenya Protests: Gen Z Shows the Power of Digital Activism—Driving Change from Screens to the Streets." *The Conversation*, June 22, 2024. https://theconversation.com/kenya-protests-gen-z-shows-the-power-of-digital-activism-driving-change-from-screens-to-the-streets-233065.

Mwesigwa, Daniel. "Uganda Abandons Social Media Tax but Slaps New Levy on Internet Data." CIPESA, July 1, 2021. https://cipesa.org/2021/07/uganda-abandons-social-media-tax-but-slaps-new-levy-on-internet-data/#:~:text=Introduced%20on%20July%201%2C%202018,Facebook%2C%20Twitter%2C%20and%20WhatsApp.

Naadi, Thomas. "Gabon Coup Leader Brice Nguema Vows Free Elections—but No Date." *BBC News*, September 4, 2023. https://www.bbc.com/news/world-africa-66705693.

Naadi, Thomas. "Gambia after Yahya Jammeh: 'I'll never get justice.'" *BBC News*, July 13, 2022. https://www.bbc.com/news/world-africa-61864383.

Naku, Dennis. "Military Vows to Go after Advocates of Coup." *The Punch*, February 22, 2024. https://punchng.com/military-vows-to-go-after-advocates-of-coup/.

Nantulya, Paul. "China's First Political School in Africa." Africa Center for Strategic Studies, November 7, 2023. https://africacenter.org/spotlight/china-first-political-school-africa/.

National Intelligence Council. *Sub-Saharan Africa Pitched Contests for Democratization through 2022: A Global Trends Paper*. Washington, DC: National Intelligence Council, February 2018. https://www.dni.gov/files/images/globalTrends/documents/GT-Africa_Democratization_ForPublishing-WithCovers.pdf.

National Unity Party. "National Unity Platform 2021–2026." December 23, 2020. https://issuu.com/kyagulanyi/docs/final_manifesto_2021-26.

Nendo Kenya. "The #Reject Revolution: When Tweets Take to the Streets. The Story of 25 Million Posts Powering Kenya's #RejectFinanceBill2024 protests." *Nendo*, July 8, 2024. https://www.nendo.co.ke/post/the-reject-revolution-kenyan-rejectfinancebill2024-protests.

The New Humanitarian. "Taylor still Looms Large as Election Countdown Begins." June 30, 2005. https://www.thenewhumanitarian.org/report/55205/liberia-taylor-still-looms-large-election-countdown-begins.

Newman, Nic, Richard Fletcher, Anne Schulz, et al., *Reuters Institute Digital News Report 2021: 10th Edition*. Oxford: Reuters Institute for the Study of Journalism, June 2021. https://reutersinstitute.politics.ox.ac.uk/sites/default/files/2021-06/Digital_News_Report_2021_FINAL.pdf.

New Vision. "Museveni Hails Katonga Heroes, Roots for Education and Wealth Creation." September 9, 2023. https://www.newvision.co.ug/category/news/museveni-hails-katonga-heroes-roots-for-educa-NV_169679.

Ngila, Faustine. "Protests against Government Policies are Roiling All Four Corners of Africa." *Quartz*, March 20, 2023. https://qz.com/protests-rock-south-africa-kenya-tunisia-and-nigeria-1850242880.

Nigeria Independent National Electoral Commission. "Presidential Election—2023-02-25—Presidential." Accessed April 8, 2023. https://www.inecelectionresults.ng/pres/elections/63f8f25b594e164f8146a213?type=pres.

Nigerians. "#Towards2023 Peter Obi's social media movement probably being pushed by small number of people inside one room." Facebook video post, August 4, 2022. https://www.facebook.com/watch/?v=1525721417861728.

Njeru, Lilys. "Why I Decided to Front Petition against Boda Boda Menace." *The Nation*, March 13, 2022. https://nation.africa/kenya/life-and-style/saturday-magazine/why-i-decided-to-front-petition-boda-boda-menace-3744774.

NOI Polls. "Summary of Results: Afrobarometer Round 9 Survey in Nigeria, 2022." *Afrobarometer*, August 26, 2022. https://www.afrobarometer.org/wp-content/uploads/2022/08/Nigeria-Afrobarometer-R9-Summary-of-Results-26august2022.pdf.

BIBLIOGRAPHY

Nordas, Ragnhild, and Christian Davenport. "Fight the Youth: Youth Bulges and State Repression." *American Journal of Political Science* 57, no. 4 (October 2013): 926–40. https://www.jstor.org/stable/23496665?seq=2.

Nothias, Toussaint. "The Rise and Fall . . . and Rise Again of Facebook's Free Basics: Civil Society and the Challenge of Resistance to Corporate Connectivity Projects." Global Media Technologies and Cultures Lab, April 21, 2020. http://globalmedia.mit.edu/2020/04/21/the-rise-and-fall-and-rise-again-of-facebooks-free-basics-civil-and-the-challenge-of-resistance-to-corporate-connectivity-projects/.

NP Admin. "Kagame Appoints Daughter 'presidential advisor.'" *NilePost*, August 2, 2023. https://nilepost.co.ug/news/166914/kagame-appoints-daughter-presidential-advisor.

NTV Uganda. "President Museveni's 2020 International Youth Day Address." YouTube video, 49:31, August 12, 2020. https://www.youtube.com/watch?v=B3Qohqjvz8M.

Nwonwu, Chiagozie, Fauziyya Tukur, and Yemisi Oyedepo. "Nigeria Elections 2023: How Influencers Are Secretly Paid by Political Parties." *BBC Global Disinformation Team*, January 17, 2023. https://www.bbc.com/news/world-africa-63719505.

Nyabola, Nanjala. *Digital Democracy, Analogue Politics: How the Internet Era Is Transforming Politics in Kenya*. London: Bloomsbury Publishing, 2018.

Nyabola, Nanjala. "Kenya: My Dress My Choice." *New African*, January 21, 2015. https://newafricanmagazine.com/9611/.

Nyerere, Julius K. *Democracy and the Party System*. Dar es Salaam: Tanganyika Standard Limited, 1963.

Obadare, Ebenezer. "Peter Obi and a Dream Deferred." *Africa in Transition*, Council on Foreign Relations, March 22, 2023. https://www.cfr.org/blog/peter-obi-and-dream-deferred.

Obadare, Ebenezer. "A Religious War." *Africa in Transition*, Council on Foreign Relations, April 11, 2023. https://www.cfr.org/blog/religious-war.

Obasanjo, Olusegun. "President Obasanjo's Inaugural Address to the Nation—May 29, 1999." Speech, Abuja, May 29, 1999. Accessed March 19, 2024. https://www.dawodu.com/obas1.htm.

Obulutsa, George, and Hereward Holland. "Kenya's Opposition Holds Vigils for Slain and Injured Protesters." *Reuters*, July 26, 2023. https://www.reuters.com/world/africa/kenyas-opposition-holds-vigils-slain-injured-protesters-2023-07-26/.

Ochi (@OchiJnr). "Nigeria's Tinubu has left the Zoom call," comment on X post, July 21, 2024. https://x.com/OchiJnr/status/1815151131053465955.

Odea, Jeje (@joshjeje2). "Road sign posts of the Zambian president reminding citizens that corruption is an enemy of development." X post, July 29, 2023. https://twitter.com/joshjeje2/status/1685265290295214080.

Oduor, Michael. "Africa's Covid-19 Corruption that Outweighs Pandemic." *Africanews*, last modified May 25, 2021. https://www.africanews.com/2021/05/25/africa-s-covid-19-corruption-that-outweighs-pandemic/.

OECD/UN ECA/AfDB. *Africa's Urbanisation Dynamics 2022: The Economic Power of Africa's Cities*. Paris: OECD Publishing 2022. https://doi.org/10.1787/3834ed5b-en.

Office of the Director of National Intelligence. "Emerging Dynamics—Societal: Disillusioned, Informed, and Divided." *Global Trends 2040: A More Contested World*, March 2021. https://www.dni.gov/index.php/gt2040-home/emerging-dynamics/societal-dynamics.

Ogundipe, Samuel. "Buhari Criticises Nigerian Youth as Lazy, Uneducated." *Premium Times*, April 19, 2018. https://www.premiumtimesng.com/news/headlines/265484-buhari-criticises-nigerian-youth-as-lazy-uneducated.html?tztc=1.

Okoye, John (@JOHNOKO68305804). "If Obi lose hope dash out. Nigeria youth are eager for a new Nigeria." X repost, December 30, 2022. https://twitter.com/JOHNOKO68305804/status/1608975662618120194.

Olind, Paul (@OlindPaul). "China ran a 3 year hacking campaign targeting Kenyan government agencies including a server exclusively used by NIS." X post, May 24, 2023. https://twitter.com/OlindPaul/status/1661253901981720576.

Olokor, Friday. "Elections: Imo, Rivers Results Manipulated, Says Yiaga Africa." *The Punch*, March 2, 2023. https://punchng.com/elections-imo-rivers-results-manipulated-says-yiaga-africa/.

Oosterom, Marjoke, and Simbarashe Gukurume. "The Risk of Authoritarian Renewal in Zimbabwe: Understanding ZANU-PF Youth," *CMI Brief* 2023, no.1. Christian Michelsen Institute for Science and Intellectual Freedom. https://www.cmi.no/publications/8797-the-risk-of-authoritarian-renewal-in-zimbabwe-understanding-zanu-pf-youth.

Osori, Ayisha. "Nigeria's Elections Have Bigger Problems than Vote Trading." *Al Jazeera*, February 17, 2023. https://www.aljazeera.com/opinions/2023/2/17/nigerias-elections-have-bigger-problems-than-vote-trading.

Owiny, Tobbias Jolly. "Go to the Farm and Dig, Museveni Tells Youth." *Daily Monitor*, August 28, 2022. https://www.monitor.co.ug/uganda/news/national/go-to-the-farm-and-dig-museveni-tells-youth-3928728.

Ownio, Winfrey, and William Ruto. "President William Ruto's Full Speech at the UN General Assembly." *The Standard*, September 22, 2022. https://www.standardmedia.co.ke/article/2001456275/rutos-full-speech-at-the-un-general-assembly#google_vignette.

Owoh, Ugonna-Ora. "The Word that Captures Nigerians' Feelings about the Future." *Foreign Policy*, August 12, 2023. https://foreignpolicy.com/2023/08/12/nigeria-japa-election-migration-tinubu-politics-economy/.

Oyero, Kayode. "FG Suspends Twitter 'operations' in Nigeria." *The Punch*, June 4, 2021. https://punchng.com/breaking-fg-suspends-twitter-operations-in-nigeria/?utm_medium=Social&utm_source=Twitter#Echobox=1622821655-1.

Oyero, Kayode. "'It's My Turn Actually!' Tinubu Says in Acceptance Speech." Channels Television, March 1, 2023. https://www.channelstv.com/2023/03/01/its-my-turn-actually-tinubu-says-in-acceptance-speech/.

Page, Matthew T. "A New Taxonomy for Corruption in Nigeria." Carnegie Endowment for International Peace, July 2018. https://carnegieendowment.org/files/CP_338_Page_Nigeria_Brief_FINAL.pdf.

Paice, Edward. *YouthQuake: Why Africa Demography Should Matter to the World*. London: Bloomsbury Publishing, 2023.

Paravicini, Giulia. "Congo's Outgoing President Kabila Doesn't Rule Out Running again in 2023." *Reuters*, last modified December 9, 2018. https://www.reuters.com/article/idUSKBN1O80DU/.

Peoples Dispatch. "'A slave who cannot assume his own revolt does not deserve to be pitied,' Says Ibrahim Traoré of Burkina Faso." August 2, 2023. https://peoplesdispatch.org/2023/08/02/a-slave-who-cannot-assume-his-own-revolt-does-not-deserve-to-be-pitied-says-ibrahim-traore-of-burkina-faso/.

Peralta, Eyder. "Uganda's Museveni Faces Tough Challenge in Presidential Election." *NPR*, January 12, 2021. https://www.npr.org/2021/01/12/955938674/ugandas-museveni-faces-tough-challenge-in-presidential-election.

Phiri, Sam, and Kiss Abraham. *Mapping the Supply of Surveillance Technologies to Africa Zambia Country Report*. Brighton: Institute of Development Studies, 2023, 121–35. https://opendocs.ids.ac.uk/opendocs/bitstream/handle/20.500.12413/18120/ADRN_Surveillance_Supply_Chain_Report_Zambia_Country_Report.pdf?sequence=7&isAllowed=y.

Rasmussen, Jacob. "Mungiki as Youth Movement: Revolution, Gender and Generational Politics in Nairobi, Kenya." *YOUNG* 18, no. 3 (2010), 301–19. https://journals.sagepub.com/doi/10.1177/110330881001800304.

Rédaction Africanews with AFP. "Burkina Faso: Former President Thomas Sankara Elevated to the Rank of 'national hero.'" *Africanews*, last modified October 5, 2023. https://www.africanews.com/2023/10/05/burkina-faso-former-president-thomas-sankara-elevated-to-the-rank-of-national-hero/.

Refworld. "Zimbabwe: The National Youth Service (NYS) Training Program: The Type of Training Involved; Age of Participants; Whether the Training Program is Mandatory; Whether There Are Exemptions; and the Penalty for Refusing to Serve or for Desertion (2001–2006)." Immigration and Refugee Board of Canada, June 22, 2006. https://webarchive.archive.unhcr.org/20230531011418/https://www.refworld.org/docid/45f147ce20.html.

Reid, Helen, and Chris Mfula. "Zambia's Chinese Debt Nearly Twice Official Estimate, Study Finds." *Reuters*, September 28, 2021. https://www.reuters.com/world/africa/zambias-chinese-debt-nearly-twice-official-estimate-study-finds-2021-09-28/.

Reno, William. "Fictional States and Atomized Public Spheres: A Non-Western Approach to Fragility." *Daedalus* 146, no. 4 (Fall 2017).

Republic of Cameroon—Presidency of the Republic. "Head of State's Message to the Youth on the 58th Edition of the National Youth Day." February 10, 2024. https://www.prc.cm/en/news/speeches-of-the-president/7047-head-of-state-s-message-to-the-youth-on-the-58th-edition-of-the-youth-day.

Republic of South Africa. "The Judicial Commission of Inquiry into Allegations of State Capture, Corruption and Fraud in the Public Sector Including Organs of State." June 22, 2022. https://www.statecapture.org.za/site/information/reports.

Resnick, Danielle. "How Zambia's Opposition Won." *Journal of Democracy* 33, no. 1 (January 2022). https://www.journalofdemocracy.org/articles/how-zambias-opposition-won/.

Resnick, Danielle. "Realizing the New Urban Agenda in Africa: The Centrality of Local Politics." *Brookings*, June 22, 2022. https://www.brookings.edu/blog/africa-in-focus/2022/06/22/realizing-the-new-urban-agenda-in-africa-the-centrality-of-local-politics/.

Reuters. "Ivory Coast President Ouattara's Party Pushes Him to Run Again," *Reuters*, October 1, 2024. https://www.reuters.com/world/africa/ivory-coast-president-ouattaras-party-pushes-him-run-again-2024-10-01/.

Rezvijs, Valerijs, Satyam Panday, and Tatiana Lyseno. *Sub-Saharan Africa's Demographic Transition: A Window of Opportunity for Growth*. New York: S&P Global Ratings, August 2021. https://www.spglobal.com/_assets/documents/ratings/research/100344423.pdf.

Ritchie, Hannah, Edouard Mathieu, Max Roser, and Esteban Ortiz-Ospina. "Internet." Our World in Data, April 13, 2023. https://ourworldindata.org/internet#internet-access.

Roberts, Tony. "Some African Governments Are Spending Millions to Spy on Their Citizens—Stifling Debate and Damaging Democracy." *The Conversation*, November 1, 2023. https://theconversation.com/some-african-governments-are-spending-millions-to-spy-on-their-citizens-stifling-debate-and-damaging-democracy-215554.

Ross, Aaron, James Pearson, and Christopher Bing. "Exclusive: Chinese Hackers Attacked Kenyan Government as Debt Strains Grew." *Reuters*, May 24, 2023. https://www.reuters.com/world/africa/chinese-hackers-attacked-kenyan-government-debt-strains-grew-2023-05-24/.

Rosson, Zach, Felicia Anthonio, Sage Cheng, et al., "Weapons of Control, Shields of Impunity: Internet Shutdowns in 2022." *AccessNow*, February 28, 2023. https://www.accessnow.org/wp-content/uploads/2023/03/2022-KIO-Report-Africa.pdf.

Ruto, William Samoei PhD (@WilliamsRuto). "Addressing youth on climate change and financing at the Champs de Mars, Paris, France." X post, June 23, 2023. https://twitter.com/WilliamsRuto/status/1672119927564644353.

Saddier, Marianne. "The Upright Citizens of Burkina Faso." *Africa Is a Country*, October 1, 2014. https://africasacountry.com/2014/10/the-citizens-of-burkina-faso/.

Sanny, Josephine Appiah-Nyamekye, Shannon van Wyk-khosa, and Joseph Asunka. "Africa's Youth: More Educated, Less Employed, Still Unheard in Policy and Development." *Afrobarometer Dispatch* no. 734, November 15, 2023 https://www.afrobarometer.org/wp-content/uploads/2023/11/AD734-PAP3-Africas-youth-More-educated-less-employed-still-unheard-Afrobarometer-18nov23.pdf.

Savage, Rachel, and Marc Jones. "Kenya's Double-Digit Debt Costs Sign of the Tough Times." *Reuters*, February 15, 2024. https://www.reuters.com/business/finance/kenyas-double-digit-debt-costs-sign-tough-times-2024-02-13/.

Schultz-Herzenberg, Collette, and Robert Britt Mattes. "It Takes Two to Toyi-Toyi: One Party Dominance and Opposition Party Failure in South Africa's 2019 National Election." *Democratization* 30, no. 7, July 11, 2023. https://doi.org/10.1080/13510347.2023.2228710.

Schwikowski, Martina. "Africa's Youth: A Ticking Time Bomb?" *DW*, December 4, 2017. https://www.dw.com/en/africas-youth-a-ticking-time-bomb/a-41605664.

Scott, Holly V. *Younger than That Now: The Politics of Age in the 1960s*. Amherst: University of Massachusetts Press, 2016.

Shahbaz, Adrian, Allie Funk, Jennifer Brody, et al., "Freedom on the Net 2023: The Repressive Power of Artificial Intelligence." Freedom House, 2023. https://freedomhouse.org/sites/default/files/2023-10/Freedom-on-the-net-2023-DigitalBooklet.pdf.

Shurkin, Michael. "Anti-French Sentiment in Africa: An American Perspective." *La Revue Internationale et Stratégique* 1, no. 133 (2024): 163–71. https://www.cairn.info/revue-internationale-et-strategique-2024-1-page-163.htm?contenu=article#pa23.

Siegle, Joseph. *Winning the Battle of Ideas: Exposing Global Authoritarian Narratives and Revitalizing Democratic Principles*. Washington, DC: National Endowment for Democracy, February 2024. https://www.ned.org/wp-content/uploads/2024/02/NED_FORUM-Authoritarianism-Narratives.pdf.

Silva, Marco. "Ugandan Internet Propaganda Network Exposed by the BBC." *BBC Verify*, January 20, 2024. https://www.bbc.com/news/world-africa-67803493.

BIBLIOGRAPHY

Smith, Stephen. *The Scramble for Europe: Young Africa on its Way to the Old Continent.* Cambridge: Polity Books, 2019.

Soares de Oliveira, Ricardo, and Susan Taponier. "'O Governo Está Aqui': Post-war State-Making in the Angolan Periphery." *Dans Politique Africaine* 130 (2012/13): 165–87, https://www.cairn.info/revue-politique-africaine-2013-2-page-165.htm.

Sommers, Marc. *The Outcast Majority: War, Development, and Youth in Africa.* Athens: University of Georgia Press, 2015.

Sommers, Marc. *Stuck: Rwandan Youth and the Struggle for Adulthood.* Athens: University of Georgia Press, 2012. http://www.jstor.org/stable/j.ctt46nngq.

Soraa, Thierno (@Ndiayetrust). "Même si Macron avait demandé a Macky Sall de ne pas se presenter." X post, March 20, 2023. https://twitter.com/Ndiayetrust/status/1637866959344656418?s=20.

Sousa, Liliana D. "Poverty & Equity Brief: Africa Eastern & Southern Angola." *World Bank Group* (April 2023): 1–2. https://databankfiles.worldbank.org/public/ddpext_download/poverty/987B9C90-CB9F-4D93-AE8C-750588BF00QA/current/Global_POVEQ_AGO.pdf.

Southern African Development Community. "SADC Electoral Observation Mission Preliminary Statement to the Harmonised Election to the Republic of Zimbabwe." August 25, 2023. https://www.sadc.int/document/sadc-electoral-observation-mission-preliminary-statement-harmonised-election-republic.

Sr_Comandante (@ManuchoComanda1). "População Senegalesa passa por cima da policia." X post, March 22, 2023. https://twitter.com/ManuchoComanda1/status/1638525548807827457.

Stark, Vicky. "Equatorial Guinea Vice President's Superyacht, Properties Seized in South Africa." *Voice of America*, February 16, 2023. https://www.voanews.com/a/equatorial-guinea-vice-president-s-superyacht-properties-seized-in-south-africa-/6966068.html.

Statistics South Africa. "South Africa's Youth Continues to Bear the Burden of Unemployment." June 1, 2022. https://www.statssa.gov.za/?p=15407.

Stearns, Jason. *Dancing in the Glory of Monsters.* New York: Hachette Book Group, 2012.

Steinhauser, Gabriele. "'Life Was Better under Mugabe:' Disappointment, Fear Cloud Zimbabwe Election." *Wall Street Journal*, August 23, 2023. https://www.wsj.com/world/africa/life-was-better-under-mugabe-disappointment-fear-cloud-zimbabwe-election-8ac63d5f.

Stockemer, Daniel, and Aksel Sundström. *Youth without Representation: The Absence of Young Adults in Parliaments, Cabinets, and Candidacies.* Ann Arbor: University of Michigan Press, 2022.

Tall, Borso. "Protests and Pressure Force Senegal's Sall to Back Down—for Now." *World Politics Review*, February 20, 2024. https://www.worldpoliticsreview.com/senegal-elections-democracy-sall/.

Taylor, Ian. "Chapter 6: The Role of Identity in African Politics." In *African Politics: A Very Short Introduction.* Oxford: Oxford University Press, 2018, https://doi.org/10.1093/actrade/9780198806578.003.0006.

Teyie, Selina. "Africa's Oldest President Forgets where He is while Addressing Global Summit." *The Star*, January 23, 2023. https://www.the-star.co.ke/news/africa/2023-01-23-africas-oldest-president-forgets-where-he-is-while-addressing-global-summit/.

Tharoor, Ishaan. "5 Crazy Things about the Gambian Dictator Who Just Survived a Coup Attempt." *Washington Post*, January 6, 2015. https://www.washingtonpost.com/news/worldviews/wp/2015/01/06/5-crazy-things-about-the-gambian-dictator-who-just-survived-a-coup-attempt/.

Thiago Costa//T.C (@ti_ticii). "For the people in the back." X post, January 19, 2023. https://twitter.com/ti_ticii/status/1615977631358545931.

TL Elder (@mwabilimwagodi). "President Ruto is going to go down as the most useless President of the Republic of Kenya." X post, November 5, 2023. https://twitter.com/mwabilimwagodi/status/1721094043973583038.

Tubiana, Jerome. "Europe Is Making Sudan's Refugee Crisis Worse." *Foreign Policy*, January 8, 2024. https://foreignpolicy.com/2024/01/08/sudan-darfur-refugee-crisis-eu-migration/#:~:text=The%20EU%20was%20then%20accused,as%20Hemeti%E2%80%94repeatedly%20bragged%20that.

Tuck, Angela. "After 20 Wasted Years, a Single Arrow Remains in the ANC's Quiver." *Vryeweekblad*, September 8, 2023. https://www.vryeweekblad.com/en/opinions-and-debate/2023-09-08-20-wasted-years-and-the-ghost-of-apartheid/?utm_source=substack&utm_medium=email.

Uganda Broadcasting Corporation. "Live: Museveni Addresses Nation on Matters of National Interest." YouTube video, July 20, 2024. https://www.youtube.com/watch?v=dYyNSruz4Mg.

Uganda Media Centre. "President Museveni Cautions the Youths against Wrong Ideology and Indiscipline." Ministry of ICT and National Guidance, August 18, 2023. https://www.mediacentre.go.ug/media/president-museveni-cautions-youths-against-wrong-ideology-and-indiscipline.

United Nations. "Global Issues—Population." Accessed March 29, 2024. https://www.un.org/en/global-issues/population#:~:text=More%20than%20half%20of%20global,projected%20to%20double%20by%202050.

United Nations. "Mali—Prime Minister Addresses General Debate, 77th Session." UN Web TV, 34:58, September 24, 2022. https://webtv.un.org/en/asset/k1y/k1ya9lo5mi.

United Nations. *A World of Debt: A Growing Burden to Global Prosperity*. Geneva: United Nations Global Crisis Response Group, July 2023. https://doi.org/10.18356/29589304-4.

United Nations. "World Urbanization Prospects 2018." Department of Economic and Social Affairs Population Dynamics, 2022. https://population.un.org/wup/.

United Nations Development Programme. *Journeys to Extremism in Africa: Pathways to Recruitment and Disengagement*. UNDP, February 7, 2023. https://www.undp.org/africa/publications/journey-extremism-africa-pathways-recruitment-and-disengagement#:~:text=February%207%2C%202023,and%20what%20makes%20them%20leave.

United Nations Development Programme. *Soldiers and Citizens: Military Coups and the Need for Democratic Renewal in Africa*. New York: UNDP, 2023. https://www.soldiersandcitizens.org/assets/UNDP_Soldiers_and_citizens_ENG.pdf.

United Nations Security Council. "Lusaka Protocol." December 22, 1994. https://peacemaker.un.org/sites/peacemaker.un.org/files/AO_941115_LusakaProtocol%28en%29.pdf.

US Department of State Global Engagement Center. *Yevgeniy Prigozhin's Africa-Wide Disinformation Campaign*. November 4, 2022. https://www.state.gov/disarming-disinformation/yevgeniy-prigozhins-africa-wide-disinformation-campaign/.

BIBLIOGRAPHY

Utas, Mats, and Henrik Vigh. "Radicalized Youth: Oppositional Poses and Positions." In *Africa's Insurgents: Navigating and Evolving Landscape*, edited by Morten Bøås and Kevin C. Dunn. Boulder, CO: Lynne Rienner Publishers, 2017, 25.

van de Walle, Nicolas. "The Path from Neopatrimonialism: Democracy and Clientelism in Africa Today." *Working Paper* 3, no. 7, Mario Einaudi Center for International Studies, June 2007. https://ecommons.cornell.edu/server/api/core/bitstreams/493ab0c8-9d08-42fc-816b-7b4ac1a23859/content.

van Staden, Cobus. "New Afrobarometer Poling Shows Both China and the U.S. Losing Popularity in Africa." China Global South Project, April 27, 2023. https://chinaglobalsouth.com/analysis/new-afrobarometer-polling-shows-both-china-and-the-u-s-losing-popularity-in-africa/.

Ver Angola. "Organizers of the November 11 March Reject Violence and Manipulation." November 6, 2020. https://www.verangola.net/va/en/112020/Society/22675/Organizers-of-the-November-11-march-reject-violence-and-manipulation.htm.

Vinay Lall, Somik, J. Vernon Henderson, and Anthony J. Venables. *Africa's Cities: Opening Doors to the World.* Washington, DC: World Bank Group, 2017. https://documents1.worldbank.org/curated/en/854221490781543956/pdf/113851-PUB-PUBLIC-PUBDATE-2-9-2017.pdf.

Vincent-Anene, Prince. "#EndSARS PROTEST: How Nonviolent Movement Became Violent." Nonviolence Project at the University of Wisconsin, July 26, 2022. https://thenonviolenceproject.wisc.edu/2022/07/26/endsars-protest-how-nonviolent-movement-became-violent/.

Vines, Alex. "Angola's Political Earthquake: The Aftermath of the August 2022 Elections." ISP online, September 7, 2022. https://www.ispionline.it/en/publication/angolas-political-earthquake-aftermath-august-2022-elections-36067.

Vines, Alex. "Angola's Transition to Technocracy Won't Be Victimless." *Foreign Policy*, August 25, 2017. https://foreignpolicy.com/2017/08/25/angolas-transition-to-technocracy-wont-be-victimless/.

Vines, Alex. "Why the Mali Coup Should Matter to the UK." Chatham House, August 20, 2020. https://www.chathamhouse.org/2020/08/why-mali-coup-should-matter-uk.

Voice of America. "Footage of Mali Soldiers Detaining President." YouTube Video, 0:56 sec, August 19, 2020. https://www.youtube.com/watch?v=TBwSUHQ10rE.

Wallace, Jeremy. "Cities, Redistribution, and Authoritarian Regime Survival." *Journal of Politics* 75, no. 3 (July 2013): 632–45. http://pscourses.ucsd.edu/ps200b/Wallace%20Cities,%20Redistribution,%20and%20Authoritarian%20Regime%20Survival.pdf.

Walsh, Declan. "Kenya Stares into 'Abyss' as Soaring Prices and Feuding Leaders Bring Chaos." *New York Times*, July 20, 2023. https://www.nytimes.com/2023/07/20/world/africa/kenya-protests-tax-hikes.html.

Walsh, Declan. "The World is Becoming More African." *New York Times*, October 28, 2023. https://www.nytimes.com/interactive/2023/10/28/world/africa/africa-youth-population.html.

Walter, Dzuya. "Boda Boda Riders Sue Gov't over Campaign Slogan, Say It Has Caused Them Psychological Trauma." *Citizen Digital*, January 4, 2024. https://www.citizen.digital/news/boda-boda-riders-sue-govt-over-campaign-slogan-say-it-has-caused-them-psychological-trauma-n334192.

Wandji, Paul Reinhard. "Cameroon: Government to Recruit 1,000 Social Media Experts to Combat Hate Speech." *Journal du Cameroun*, January 18, 2023. https://www.

en.journalducameroun.com/cameroon-government-to-recruit-1000-social-media-experts-to-combat-hate-speech/.

Wang, Tommy. "False Posts Misrepresent Tense Exchange between France's Macron and DR Congo's Tshisekedi." AFP Fact Check, March 27, 2023. https://factcheck.afp.com/doc.afp.com.33BQ7JJ.

Wilkins, Sam, and Richard Vokes. "Transition, Transformation, and the Politics of the Future in Uganda." *Journal of Eastern African Studies* 17, no. 1–2 (June 2023): 1–18. https://doi.org/10.1080/17531055.2023.2236848.

Wine, Bobi. "Freedom." June 26, 2018, track 6 on *Kyarenga*, Kamwokya Fire Base Studios, 2018, digital.

Women's TV—Liberia. "Full Speech by Col. Mamady Doumbouya, Coup Leader Conakry, Guinea." Facebook, September 6, 2021. https://www.facebook.com/womentvlib/posts/full-speech-by-col-mamady-doumbouya-coup-leader-conakry-guinea-dear-compatriots-/377706300694212/.

Woodhams, Samuel, and Simon Migliano. "Government Internet Shutdowns Have Cost $53 Billion since 2019." *TOP10VPN*, March 8, 2024. https://www.top10vpn.com/research/cost-of-internet-shutdowns/.

World Bank. "Angola: Overview." Last modified September 24, 2023. https://www.worldbank.org/en/country/angola/overview.

World Bank. "GDP Growth (annual %)—Zimbabwe." World Development Indicators, 2022. https://data.worldbank.org/indicator/NY.GDP.MKTP.KD.ZG?locations=ZW.

World Bank. "Government Expenditure on Education, Total (% of GDP)—Sub-Saharan Africa." World Bank open data, September 19, 2023. https://data.worldbank.org/indicator/SE.XPD.TOTL.GD.ZS?locations=ZG.

World Bank. "Unemployment, Youth Total (% of total labor force ages 15–24) (modeled ILO estimate)—Gabon." Accessed February 4, 2024. https://data.worldbank.org/indicator/SL.UEM.1524.ZS?locations=GA.

World Population Prospects, Department of Economic and Social Affairs Population Division. "Equatorial Guinea: Percentage of Population under 25 Years of Age." Geneva: United Nations, Last updated 2022, https://population.un.org/wpp/Graphs/Probabilistic/PopPerc/0-24/226.

X-Daily (@X_Dailly). "What's Nigerian politics maths?" X post, October 3, 2023. https://twitter.com/X_Dailly/status/1709221578309857473.

Xinhua. "Full Text: Keynote Address by Chinese President Xi Jinping at Opening Ceremony of 2024 FOCAC Summit." September 5, 2024. https://english.www.gov.cn/news/202409/05/content_WS66d964bdc6d0868f4e8eaa07.html.

Yahmed, Marwane Ben. "[Exclusive] Gabon's Brice Clotaire Oligui Nguema: 'This is not a coup d'état, but an act of liberation.'" *Africa Report*, September 22, 2023. https://www.theafricareport.com/322833/exclusive-gabons-brice-clotaire-oligui-nguema-this-is-not-a-coup-detat-but-an-act-of-liberation/.

Zeeman, Kyle. "'Whether we like it or not, this is the result of apartheid'—Lindiwe Zulu on Joburg CBD Fire." *The Citizen*, September 1, 2023. https://www.citizen.co.za/news/south-africa/results-of-apartheid-lindiwe-zulu-on-joburg-cbd-fire/.

Zimbabwe Daily (@ZimDaily). "Our Work is Our Manifesto." X post, July 25, 2023. https://twitter.com/ZimDaily/status/1683786736822788096.

Interviews

Linda Kasonde in conversation with author in Lusaka, conducted on August 9, 2022.
Joseph Kalimbwe in conversation with the author, Lusaka, August 2022.
Fumba Chama ("Pilato") in conversation with the author, Lusaka, August 2022.
Interview with Jacob Ouma in Nairobi in March 2022.
Irungu Houghton (Director of Amnesty International Kenya) in conversation with the author, Nairobi, 2022.

INDEX

Italic page numbers indicate figures.

Aalen, Lovise 109
Abiy Ahmed 19
Abubakar, Atiku 92
activism
    derogatory terms for youth activists 106
    Kenya 85–7
adulthood 105
Africa
    countries in *viii*
    perceptions of Africa/African-ness 38
African National Congress (ANC)
    dominance of in South Africa 14–15
    national events in the past, electoral success and 46–7
African Youth Charter 37
"Africa plus one" convenings, resentment of 131
Afwerki, Isaias 9
Ahmed Ali, Abiy 19
Alpha Conde challenge 64
Angola
    cross-country connections 96
    derogatory terms for youth activists 106
    income inequality 50
    national events in the past, electoral success and 49–51
    National Union for the Total Independence of Angola (UNITA) 49–50, 51
    People's Movement for the Liberation of Angola (MPLA) 15–16, 49–51
    permanent ruling party 15–16
Anku, Amaka 31
Armed Conflict Location and Event Data Project 31

artificial intelligence (AI) 115
Atiku Abubakar 17

Balai Citoyen (Citizens' Broom), Burkina Faso 18
al-Bashir, Omar 19
Benin, vote buying in 108
Biden, Joe 10
Biya, P. 1, 2
Bongo, Omar 12
Bongo Ondimba, Ali 12
Botswana
    sons of founding presidents 10
    vote buying 108
BRICS group 128
Buhari, Muhammadu 17, 34–5, 106
Burkina Faso
    Balai Citoyen (Citizens' Broom) 18
    churn without change 18
    cross-country connections 95
    democracy, support for 64
    military coups 63
    outside forces, blame placed on 72
    political consistency 64
    waning of optimism after coups 73

Cameroon
    Biya, President 1, 2
    cross-country connections 96
    disinformation and misinformation 116
    military coup, speculation about 74
    population growth 27
censorship, digital *114*, 114–15
Chad
    dynastic succession in 13
    military coup, reasons behind 65
    military coup of 2021 63

INDEX

political consistency 64
stability/volatility in Africa, US and 136
change agents
    hope invested in 91–5
    see also resistance to youth activism
China 123, 126, 127–8, 129, 133
Cincotta, Richard 27
cities, growth of 28–32, *29*
climate stress, urban areas and 30
collaboration/division, potential of online spaces for 35
collective action, urban areas and 31
colonial oppression, blame placed on by coup leaders 70–3
Compaoré, Blaise 18
connections, importance of for employment 109–10
connectivity, digital, reluctance to improve 114
co-option of young people 107–10
corruption
    cleaning up, US and 136–7
    Kenya 136
    military coups and 66–7
Cote d'Ivoire 10
coups d'etat
    external actors, blame placed on by coup leaders 70–3
    increased number of 63–4
    next, speculation about 73–4
    reasons behind support for 64–70
    "restoring the dignity of the people" references 71
    waning of optimism following 73
cross-country connections 95–7
    see also external powers
cross-country learning via social media 36
cultural norms, reinforcement of 105

debt restructuring in Zambia 134
Deby, Idriss 13
Deby, Mahamat 13
Democractic Republic of Congo
    access to information 35
    cross-country connections 95, 96
    dynastic succession in 11
    vote buying 108

democracy
    adaptive strategies used in Africa 7–8
    decreasing support for, military coups and 64–8
    deprivation and low trust in 66
    dissatisfaction with 4
    skepticism about 54–7
demographic dividend 27
demography, African
    entrepreneurism, youth population and 2
    latent threat, youth population as 2
    migration and 2
    politics and 3
    variations between countries 4
demonstrations, urban areas and 31
derogatory terms for youth activists 106
Desalegn, Hailemariam 19
diaspora communities, social media and 97
digital connectivity. political organizing and 3
    see also social media
disinformation 116
dividing lines between youth groups 110–11
division/collaboration, potential of online spaces for 35
do-it-yourself governance 85–6
dos Santos, Eduardo 15
Doumbouya, Mamadi 71, 72
dynastic succession 10–14

economic context for urban areas 30
education
    budgets for 36–7
    state investment in 30
elders, respect for, reinforcement of 105
elections
    defining national events and success in 45–54
    expanding electorates 3
    Kenya 17, 36, 83
    Nigeria 2023 92–4
    process of, lack of belief in 39
    Senegal 87, 96
    transactional relationship between youth and political candidates 107

Zambian election 2021, social media 88–9
employment
    connections, importance of 109–10
    disconnect with growth 30
    programs targeted to youth 108–9
    urban areas 29–30
#EndBadGovernance campaign, Nigeria 96
#EndSARS movement 91–2
Eni-Kalu, Tochi 31
entrepreneurism, youth population and 2
Equatorial Guinea
    dynastic succession in, likelihood of 13
    Teodoro Obiang Nguema Mbasogo 8–9
Eritrea
    dynastic succession in, possibility of 14
    Isaias Afwerki 9
Ethiopia
    censorship, digital 114
    churn without change 18–19
    collaboration/division, potential of online spaces for 35
    cross-country connections 96
    derogatory terms for youth activists 106
    Ethiopian People's Revolutionary Democratic Front (EPRDF) 18–19
    job opportunities offered to supporters 109
Ethiopian People's Revolutionary Democratic Front (EPRDF) 18–19
ethnicity as dividing line between youth groups 110–11
expectations, managing 87–90
external powers
    African governments' retention of power and 128–9
    "Africa plus one" convenings, resentment of 131
    authoritarian narratives of 126–7
    awareness of complexity and manipulation by 129
    blame placed on by coup leaders 70–3
    BRICS group 128
    as champions of alternative orders 127–9
    China 126, 127–8, 129
    competition for African favor, avoidance of 131–2
    complaints about 125
    coups d'etat, blame placed on for 70–3
    decline in popularity of 123
    disinformation campaigns by 128
    health programs, emphasis on 133–4
    messaging campaigns by 127, 128
    natural resources, African awareness of 123
    networks, need to broaden in African countries 131
    overinvestment in specific governments 132–3
    political use made of resentment of 125–6
    political volatility and 4–5
    popular satisfaction and 129
    priorities of, need for adjustment of 133–5
    responses to countries other than African 134–5
    Russia 126, 128–9
    surveillance and control, enhancement of 127–8
    suspicion and resentment of 123–5
    transactional relationships 131–2
extremist groups, youth involvement in 70

Facebook, ban on in Uganda 34
families, safeguarding of power within 10–14
favorable treatment for youth 107
Faye, Bassirou Diomaye 82–3
formal job opportunities offered to supporters 109
France, resentment of 124–5
FRELIMO (Mozambique Liberation Front) 15, 16

Gabon
    dynastic succession in 12
    military coup, reasons behind 65

INDEX

Gachagua, Rigathi 84
Gambia
    censorship, digital 114
    churn without change 19
    diaspora communities, social media and 97
generative AI 115
Ghana
    censorship, digital 114
    cross-country connections 96
Githongo, John 55
Gnassingbé, Eyadema 11
Gnassingbé, Faure 11–12
governing capacity, urban areas and 31
Guinea
    Alpha Conde challenge 64
    democracy, support for 64
    military coup, reasons behind 65
    military coup of 2021 63, 67
    outside forces, blame placed on 72–3
    political consistency 64
    waning of optimism after coups 73
Guriev, Sergei 116

Harding, Robin 31
health programs, emphasis on by external powers 133–4
Hichilema, Hakainde 87, 88, 89, 90
home ownership co-option strategies 108
Honwana, A. 3, 26

identity politics, urban areas and 31–2
income inequality in Angola 50
inferior status of youth 106
informal economy
    law and regulations, capricious enforcement of 108
    urban areas 29–30
infrastructure, state investment in 30
international relationships
    political volatility and 4–5
    see also external powers
Internet shutdowns 114, *114*
Isaias, Abraham 14

Jammeh, Yahya 19
Jett, Dennis 16
job opportunities offered to supporters 109

Kabila, Joseph 11
Kabila, Laurent Desiré 11
Kagame, Paul 10
Kainerugaba, Muhoozi 13–14
Kainja, Jimmy 114
Kaplan, Robert 2
Keita, Ibrahim Boubacar 63
Kenya
    activism 85–7
    censorship, digital 114
    China and 129, 133
    churn without change 16, 17
    connections, importance of for employment 109–10
    cross-country connections 95
    democracy, skepticism about 54–6
    diaspora communities, social media and 97
    disinformation and misinformation 116
    do-it-yourself governance 85–6
    Finance Bill 2024, protests against 86
    impatience for change 83–7
    protest movement 2024 31
    relationship with US 132–3
    Saba Saba Day 54
    social media, regulation of 113
    sons of founding presidents 10
    stability/volatility in Africa, US and 136
    state paramilitary youth movement 111
    vote buying 108
Kenyatta, Uhuru 83
Kyagulanyi, Robert (Bobi Wine) 53–4

land ownership co-option strategies 108
laws
    capricious enforcement of 108
    repression via 112–13
    social media 113
leaders
    criticism of, laws against 112
    hope invested in 91–5
    long-serving 8–10
    see also resistance to youth activism
legitimacy narratives from the past, electoral success and 45–54
Liberia
    cross-country connections 96

national events in the past, electoral success and 45
transactional relationship between youth and political candidates 107
loan programs targeted to youth 108–9
Lockwood, Peter 83
Lumumba, Patrice 70, 70n
Lungu, Edgar 87

Mafabi, David 52
Maiga, Abdoulaye 71–2
Malawi, cross-country connections of 95
Mali
   democracy, support for 64
   French government, blame placed on 71–2
   military coup of 2020 63, 67
   waning of optimism after coups 73
manipulation, digital 115–16
"math" discourse of 2023 66–7
migration
   discourse around 135
   from Nigeria 94–5
   youth population and 2
military coups
   external actors, blame placed on by coup leaders 70–3
   increased number of 63–4
   next country, speculation about 73–4
   reasons behind support for 64–70
   "restoring the dignity of the people" references 71
   waning of optimism following 73
misinformation 116
Mnangagwa, Emerson 48, 49
mobile Internet
   political connections and 32–6, 33
   see also social media
Moi, Daniel arap 54
Mozambique
   cross-country connections 96
   FRELIMO (Mozambique Liberation Front) 15, 16
   governing capacity, urban areas and 31
   job opportunities offered to supporters 109
   permanent ruling party 15, 16

Mozambique Liberation Front (FRELIMO) 15, 16
MPLA (People's Movement for the Liberation of Angola) 15–16, 49–51
Mueller, Lisa 31, 111
Mugabe, Robert 15
Museveni, Yoweri 9–10, 13–14, 34, 51–2, 105, 106

national events in the past, electoral success and 45–54
National Union for the Total Independence of Angola (UNITA) 49–50, 51
national youth strategies 37–8
natural resources, awareness of in Africa 123
Ncube, Owen "Mudha" 48–9
Ndiaye, Bamba 97
needs of youth, dissatisfaction with governments and 36–9
Nguema, Brice Oligui 12, 71
Nigeria
   access to information 35
   censorship, digital 114
   churn without change 16–17
   connections, importance of for employment 110
   cross-country connections 95–6
   cross-country learning via social media 36
   democracy, skepticism about 56–7
   diaspora communities, social media and 97
   disinformation and misinformation 116
   dividing lines between youth groups 110–11
   elections 2023 92–4
   #EndBadGovernance campaign 96
   #EndSARS movement 91–2
   leaders, hope invested in 91–5
   migration 94–5
   Not Too Young To Run movement 37
   social media bans 34–5
   Soro Soke generation 91–2
   Special Anti-Robbery Squad (SARS) 91–2
   vote buying 107–8

INDEX

Not Too Young To Run movement 37
Nyabola, N. 3, 35, 97
Nyerere, Julius 16

Obadare, Ebenezer 93
Obasanjo, Alusegun 56
Obi, Peter 92, 94–5, 110
Obiang Nguema Mbasogo, Teodoro 8–9, 13
Obi-dients movement 92–3, 94–5
Odinga, Raila 17
online organizing *see* social media
Oosterom, Marjoke 109
opposition movements, urban areas and 31
Ossa, Albert Ondo 12
outside powers
    African governments' retention of power and 128–9
    "Africa plus one" convenings, resentment of 131
    authoritarian narratives of 126–7
    awareness of complexity and manipulation by 129
    blame placed on by coup leaders 70–3
    BRICS group 128
    as champions of alternative orders 127–9
    China 126, 127–8, 129
    competition for African favor, avoidance of 131–2
    complaints about 125
    coups d'etat, blame placed on for 70–3
    decline in popularity of 123
    disinformation campaigns by 128
    health programs, emphasis on 133–4
    messaging campaigns by 127, 128
    natural resources, African awareness of 123
    networks, need to broaden in African countries 131
    overinvestment in specific governments 132–3
    political use made of resentment of 125–6
    political volatility and 4–5
    popular satisfaction and 129
    priorities of, need for adjustment of 133–5
    Russia 126, 128–9
    surveillance and control, enhancement of 127–8
    suspicion and resentment of 123–5
    transactional relationships 131–2
Outtara, Alassane 10

Paice, Edward 2–3, 123
Pan-African laboratory 95–7
People's Movement for the Liberation of Angola (MPLA) 15–16, 49–51
perceptions of Africa/African-ness 38
permanent ruling parties 14–16
police brutality 91
policy-free political parties 16–20
political connections, technology and 32–6, *33*
political participation by youth 37–8
    lack of enthusiasm for of youth 55
    skepticism about democracy 54–7
political parties
    permanent rule by one 14–16
    policy-free 16–20
politics, youth population and 3
population, youth
    Cameroon 27
    democracy, dissatisfaction with 4
    growth of 25–7, *26*
    as latent threat 2
    map showing *28*
    migration and 2
    politics and 3
    Uganda 27
    variations between countries 4, 27
property-related co-option strategies 108
protests, urban areas and 31

Ramaphosa, Cyril 46
Rawlings, Jerry 70, 70n
regulations
    capricious enforcement of 108
    see also laws
religion as dividing line between youth groups 110–11
Reno, Will 17

repression via laws 112–13
Republic of Congo, dynastic succession in, possibility of 14
resistance to youth activism
  censorship, digital *114*, 114–15
  co-option of young people 107–10
  derogatory terms for youth activists 106
  disinformation and misinformation 116
  dividing lines between youth groups 110–11
  inferior status of youth 106
  Internet shutdowns 114, *114*
  repression via laws 112–13
  respect for elders, reinforcement of 105
  surveillance of online activities 113
respect for elders, reinforcement of 105
ruling parties, permanent 14–16
Russia 71, 126, 128–9
Ruto, William 83–7, 132–3
Rwanda
  censorship, digital 114
  dynastic succession in, possibility of 14
  Kagame, Paul 10
  surveillance of online activities 113

Sall, Macky 81, 82, 96, 132
Sankara, Thomas 70, 70n
Sassou-Nguesso, Denis 14
Sata, Micheal 87
Scott, Holly V. 25
Senegal
  cross-country connections 95, 96
  derogatory terms for youth activists 106
  diaspora communities, social media and 97
  impatience for change 81–3
  repression via laws 112
  Russia and 129
Siegle, Joseph 126
Soares de Oliveira, Ricardo 49
social media
  access to information 35
  bans on by governments 34–5
  censorship, digital 114–15

cross-country connections 95–7
cross-country learning via 36
diaspora communities and 97
disdain for leadership shown on 64–5
disinformation and misinformation 116
manipulation by the state 115–16
"math" discourse of 2023 66–7
Nigeria, after 2023 election 93–5
Pan-African laboratory 95–7
political content on 32, *33*
political organizing and 3
popular platforms 34
potential for collaboration/division 35
regulation of 113
surveillance of online activities 113
Zambian election 2021 88–9
socioeconomic status as dividing line 111
Sommers, Marc 26, 105
Sonko, Ousmane 81–2
Soro Soke generation, Nigeria 91–2
South Africa
  African National Congress (ANC), dominance of 14–15
  national events in the past, electoral success and 46–7
Special Anti-Robbery Squad (SARS) (Nigeria) 91–2
stability/volatility in Africa, US and 135–7
stasis, political *see* political stasis in Africa
state investment in education and infrastructure 30
state paramilitary youth movements 111–12
state violence 113
stereotypes about the continent 38
Stockemer, Daniel 38–9
sub-Saharan Africa, variation between countries 4
Sudan
  censorship, digital 114
  churn without change 19–20
  derogatory terms for youth activists 106
  military coup 67, 69–70
Sundström, Aksel 38–9

INDEX

surveillance
  external powers, and enhancement of 127–8
  of online activities 113
symbolic commitments to youth priorities 37–8, 107

Tanzania
  Chama cha Mapinduzi (CCM) 16
  cross-country connections 96
  permanent ruling party 16
Taylor, Charles 45
technology
  access to information 35
  cross-country connections 95–7
  cross-country learning via 36
  diaspora communities and 97
  disdain for leadership shown on 64–5
  Pan-African laboratory 95–7
  political connections and 32–6, *33*
  potential for collaboration/division 35
  see also social media
The Continent (online newspaper) 36
threat, youth population as 2
Tinubu, Bola 92, 93
Togo
  dynastic succession in 11–12
  state paramilitary youth movement 111
transactional relationships
  external powers 131–2
  between youth and political candidates 107
Traoré, Ibrahim 71, 72
Treisman, Daniel 116
Tshisekedi, Felix 125–6

Uganda
  boda-boda drivers, state interference and 107
  censorship, digital 115
  cross-country connections 95, 96
  disinformation campaign by Russia 128
  dynastic succession in, likelihood of 13–14
  job opportunities offered to supporters 109

loan programs targeted to youth 108–9
Museveni, Yoweri 9–10, 13–14, 34, 51–2, 105, 106
national events in the past, electoral success and 51–4
population growth 27
social media bans and regulation 34, 113
state paramilitary youth movement 111
vote buying 107
unemployment in urban areas 29–30
UNITA (National Union for the Total Independence of Angola) 49–50, 51
United Party for National Development (UPND) (Zambia) 89
United States
  decline in popularity of 123
  as ill-equipped for era of volatility 130
  networks, need to broaden in African countries 131
  stability/volatility in Africa 135–7
  suspicion and resentment of 123–4
  Zambia and 134
urbanization 28–32, *29*
Utas, Mats 70

Vigh, Henrik 70
violence, state 113
volatility/stability in Africa, US and 135–7
vote buying 107–8

watermelon strategy 88
Wine, Bobi 7, 53–4

youth
  definition of 26
  as inferior status 106
youth politics
  population growth 25–6, *26*
  1960s 25
youth population
  democracy, dissatisfaction with 4
  entrepreneurism and 2
  migration and 2
  politics and 3

as threat 2
  variations between countries 4
youth priorities, dissatisfaction with governments and 36–9
Youthquake: Why African Demography Should Matter to the World (Paice) 2–3
youthscapes 3

Zambia
  China and 129
  cross-country connections 95, 96–7
  cross-country learning via social media 36
  debt restructuring 134
  election 2021 88–9
  expectations, managing 87–90
  Patriotic Front (PF) 87, 88–9, 129
  social media on political content 32
  state paramilitary youth movement 111
  surveillance of online activities 113
  United Party for National Development (UPND) 87, 88, 89
  US and 134
  watermelon strategy 88
  ZANU-PF (Zimbabwe African National Union–Patriotic Front) 15, 47–9, *48*
Zenawi, Meles 18–19
Zimbabwe
  access to information 35
  churn without change 17
  cross-country connections 95, 96
  derogatory terms for youth activists 106
  governing capacity, urban areas and 31
  job opportunities offered to supporters 109
  national events in the past, electoral success and 47–9, *48*
  permanent ruling party 15
  repression via laws 112
  state paramilitary youth movement 111
  vote buying 108
  ZANU-PF (Zimbabwe African National Union–Patriotic Front) 15

ABOUT THE AUTHOR

Michelle D. Gavin is the Ralph Bunche Senior Fellow for Africa Policy Studies at the Council on Foreign Relations. She is former US Ambassador to Botswana and Representative to the Southern African Development Community. She served as a Special Assistant to President Barack Obama and Senior Director for Africa at the National Security Council and spent several years working on foreign policy issues in the US Senate. She lives with her husband and two children in New York City.